The Story of An Amana Winemaker

Helen and George Kraus in the sales room of the Old Style Colony Winery.

Joan Liffring-Zug photo.

The Story of
An Amana Winemaker

by George Kraus
as told to E. Mae Fritz
with wine recipes
by Helen Kraus

Penfield Press
Iowa City, Iowa

Dedicated to our children
Donna, Kandyce and Dennis

Edited by John Zug
Cover painting by Judy Waterman
Graphic design by Esther Feske

For assisting with this book, special thanks go to my mother, Helene Kraus, my uncle, Fred Schinnerling, Carl Metz, Howard Durner, Rudolph Blechschmidt, Otto Geiger, Leonard Graf and Rudolph Pitz.

The Story of An Amana Winemaker

ISBN 0-941016-15-3 Softbound
ISBN 0-941016-19-6 Hardbound
Library of Congress Catalog Number 84-60091

Published and distributed by
Penfield Press, 215 Brown Street,
Iowa City, Iowa 52240

Type set by The Typesetting Connection, Ltd.
Printed by Julin Printing Co., Monticello, Iowa

Contents

Preface

It is time to tell of Kraus Wines from Amana. Over the years, visitors to the winery have repeatedly asked: Is the wine made here? How are the wines made? How did the winery start? How old is the building? What is Amana? Who is George Kraus?

The man, his wines, his winery, his home, his family and his community are an overlapping pattern of his German and American heritages. For him, life began within the confines of a communal religious society in eastern Iowa. To outsiders, the Amana Colonies appeared clannish and strange, almost mysterious. Inside, the code of the sparse, sheltered, austere existence taught young George diligence, promptness, honesty, orderliness, thrift and obedience. It taught him the good way, the right way, the Amana way as the only way for him to live his life. For life after the commune, however, it left him with what he saw as a formidable set of shortcomings—limited education, language barriers and scant social skills—shortcomings he discovered in himself near the end of his childhood when the communal lifestyle in Amana was abandoned. Once they were sprung from the protective custody of their cloistered Colonies, the villagers set out to make it on their own, to make it in and with the world "outside."

This is the story of how one young Amana man took the lessons he had learned in old Amana and made them work for him in a new and changed Amana. This is the story of a man who leapfrogged four generations of yesterdays to catch up with today.

I first met George and Helen Kraus when George's partnership sold its agricultural equipment manufacturing company. My husband, Wayne, is a representative in western states for the company that bought the business.

I am a native Nebraskan and former Iowan now living in Phoenix. "Amana"—their freezers were the competition when I was an Iowa District Home Economist for another appliance firm. "Amana"—that was where we ate dinner after Big Ten football games at Iowa City.

Wayne and I became friends of George and Helen. We visited their home and winery. I heard the story of George's family connection to the old-style German wines and to Amana.

Friends and customers had urged George to write a book. When George learned I was a writer, he asked me to help him tell his story. Krauses and I have joked about my last name. "Fritz" seems to be just the right name for a writer helping to tell the story of a German winemaker.

—E. Mae Fritz

Amana in the early 1900's.

Horses at the Middle barns, early 1930's. Rudolph Kellenberger photo.

1. Pinochle and Piestengel

It was one of those bitter cold, snow-white, January nights like we get smack in the middle of an Iowa winter. This one was in 1949. It was Saturday night, a night folks in Amana customarily spent with friends. Helen, my wife, and I were invited to our neighbors to play pinochle.

It was only a two-block walk to Willie and Dorothy Zuber's house, but temperatures had dipped close to zero, so we bundled up—but my head was bare. When I was younger I couldn't be bothered with hats or caps. I claimed my heavy head of hair—dark brown then instead of white—kept my head warm. Besides, I moved so fast, cold never caught up with me.

We stepped out the door into a bright, beautiful night. There was a full moon and no clouds. The moonlight sparkled on the snow and lit up the night. It was still. The only sound was the crunch and squeak of our rubber-soled boots. We watched our step. I didn't dare slip. In a sack I had a bottle of my newly-racked, year-and-a-half-old *Piestengel* wine—our contribution to the evening's refreshments.

By the 1940's, homemade wine and home brewed beer generally were no longer served to guests in Amana homes. Most people still made their own, but did not consider it good enough for company. By then, those who could afford it offered whiskey highballs to the men and Coca Cola to the women. But that year my rhubarb wine had turned out just extra special nice. Its flavor was excellent and the color was absolutely clear and perfect. It was *lieblich*, better than good. When wine turns out that good, you want to share it with friends.

At Zubers, we didn't lose any time getting to the game. Wine would come later. At one time, card playing and other adult games were *verboten*, forbidden, in Amana. But by this time, cards were accepted as a friendly pastime, as long as nobody got hurt by losing too much money. For us, it was a relaxing evening of inexpensive entertainment with the women playing as partners against the men.

Talk was light and easy. We kidded about missed tricks and bidding goofs. Between hands, there'd be a joke or a fetching story about a child, relative or friends, the usual talk among couples. Eventually, talk turned to money—how to spend it, save it, stretch it, but mostly, how to get more of it. None of us were looking for lots and lots of money. We only wanted "pin money," money above a regular paycheck. I was parts and service manager for an equipment and machinery dealer in Cedar Rapids. I had started with the firm as a clerk in 1943 when I was 21. My paycheck went for our regular living expenses. Helen had gone to beauty school and she had weekly customers. But at seventy-five cents for a shampoo and set, she didn't make much profit. When it came to buying any extras, we were always short of change. We thought if we could find a way to make a little more money each month, then we would be able to spend it as we pleased, to have a little fun, and still not cut into our everyday necessities. Spending "pin money" shouldn't hurt, it should make you feel good. Instead of "pin money," we should have called it "fun money," because we really wanted more money to put a little fun in our lives.

Working as I did in a city, and to anyone from Amana, Cedar Rapids was a big city, I met and talked with all kinds of people from many different walks of life—farmers, bankers, truckers, businessmen. I soon found out there were many ways to spend money, more ways than I would ever have dreamed of. Little by little, I saw that Amana folks dressed and lived more and more like the people of Cedar Rapids or Des Moines, but still there remained many differences. I was particularly struck with how people on the outside enjoyed themselves. Even more than enjoying themselves, they seemed to feel entitled to spend money just to have a good time. They worked hard at their jobs, just like I did, but when they weren't on the job, they knew how to take it easy, how to have fun. They talked about sights they'd seen, trips they'd taken, new cars, appliances and other conveniences they'd bought their wives and children. I wanted to do that, too, for my family.

Helen and I married in 1944. Donna was born in 1948. Already we could see it was going to take more than Helen's beauty work and my wages to give ourselves any extras. Later on, we had another daughter, Kandyce, then a son, Dennis.

When the subject of money came up in Amana, over the card table or anywhere else, I always knew how the conversation would go. We'd talk it to death, but that's all we'd get done. Underneath all the talk, I'd scold myself.

"Don't just talk, do something! This time, come up with something!"

No matter who we talked with or how long we talked or how often we talked about money, we always ended up with one big "BUT..."

"BUT we don't have an education."

"BUT we don't have any talent."

"BUT this, BUT that..."

We were all in the same boat. We told ourselves we were held back. We had all been raised in the same religious communal life style in which our parents, grandparents, great-grandparents and in some cases, great-great-grandparents had been raised in the Amana Colonies. In exchange for work, families were housed, fed and clothed. With this economic security came rules and regulations aimed at keeping them isolated and insulated from the outside world. They lived in multi-generation households where German, not English, was the spoken and written language. They went to schools where lessons were taught and recited almost exclusively in German. Schooling was grade school for everyone, high school for a few and college for only one or two students in any generation.

That's how it had been until the "Great Change" in 1932, when the communal system was voted out and The Amana Society was formed as a new corporation to run the 26,000 acres of agriculture endeavors and various other industries. I was in grade school at the time and, although I didn't understand the new words being tossed around, like "stock," "shares," and "stockholders," I did see the excitement the Great Change caused. My parents didn't let their limited knowledge of the outside world dampen their enthusiasm for a chance to be on their own. They looked forward to having the freedom to choose where and how they lived and worked and, yes, even how they played. It's a wonder they'd been able to make any headway in dealing with the modern world when you consider where they started, but they had. By 1949, those of us in the next generation wanted to make even more headway.

We couldn't change the past, but maybe we could change the future and the future of our children. We sure hoped so. We wanted to get a piece of the action, to be part of the action we saw going on all around us and we wanted to stay right here in Amana to do it. We didn't want to move away.

At first, many of us were too timid for our own good. By staying in Amana and talking only with Amana friends, we didn't overcome our timidness. If you are somewhat afraid and you then talk to someone else who is also afraid, the two of you tend to squelch each other's ideas for change until you both end up being too scared to try to make a change, to take a chance.

Still, a few around the Colonies were trying. In the late forties, small, private home workshops were springing up here and there. A good market was built up for hand-made, homemade crafts. All of those who were making a go of their little businesses seemed to have a couple of characteristics in common, characteristics that went beyond the fine quality of the goods they produced. They all had reputations for being hard workers and they were known for their friendliness. Not only did they get along well with folks they knew, they knew how to meet and talk easily with strangers, too. Furthermore, those two qualities didn't necessarily depend on their education, how well they spoke English or how much outside contact they had had before the Great Change. If a person was ambitious and pleasant, those two things gave him or her the confidence to beat the old bugaboos of language and lack of outside experience.

I suppose everyone likes to think he or she is friendly and hard-working. Helen and I wanted to believe we were. Friends said we were. If that was so and if that's what it took to make a go of a home business, then we thought we ought to give it a try. But what kind of business? That was a puzzle we had mulled over and over in our minds since before our first baby was born.

Midway through the card game that Saturday night, Stoney—that was Willie's nickname—poured the gift wine. Everyone sipped it, complimented its "truly excellent taste" and "beautiful color." I suppose I should have protested, said all of that wasn't so, just to be polite, but I knew that wine was exceptional, so I sat back and listened. Then I realized that other words were banging around in my head. I heard my own voice saying right out loud:

"Why not make wine to sell?"

It had come to me in a flash and in a flash I had blurted it out!

Well, that ended cards for that night. The game was over, stopped right in the middle of a hand. We never knew who won or lost the game that night. No more tricks were played. No more scores were tallied. We used the score pad and pencil to figure out finances needed to set up a winery and to estimate prospective sales. The four of us looked at winemaking from every side. We went over Amana's growing tourist traffic, the automobile count, the supplies needed for just one batch of wine, and so on.

From the time the Amana Colonies were established in 1854, this has been a community of wine drinkers and winemakers. Wine was used in church rituals, but more than that, it was an accepted part of life for every working man and woman. During the communal years, each village had its own vineyard, made its own yearly supply of wine, and oversaw allocation of that wine to all adult members of that particular village. Many families supplemented their wine allotments from the community stock by making a little extra family wine on the side. I grew up watching and helping my grandfather Schinnerling make Middle's community wine and also helped him and my father make wine for our family. Eventually I became the family winemaker. I made it as a hobby. It was something I did for my family and my friends. I made wine on weekends and in the evenings.

I had no intention of quitting my job if I started a winery. I would continue to make wine only in my spare time. I wasn't going to put everything into a winery, although the one winery that was already operating in the Colonies in 1949 had a good business, selling both to tourists and to local folks.

Both the old community and family wines were made by combining juice, sugar and water. Nowadays, this old method of winemaking is called "formula wine." It's the same way our ancestors made their wines for many generations in Germany, long before they came to the United States. It's the same way I still make wine.

Sugar was one of the major items I had to plan on buying if I went into winemaking in a big way, plus more barrels and jugs for bottling the finished wine. All in all, estimated start-up expenses came to about $500. Helen and I had managed to put aside a little savings in the few years we had been married. We had agreed that we would dig into those savings when and if we thought we were onto a good thing, a sure thing. As the winery idea was tossed around, I kept an eye on Helen and I listened to her reaction, too. As near as I could tell, she was for it.

"George," she said at one point, "you make the wine and I'll sell it!"

Boy, that sounded good to me!

When she said that, I knew she was with me on the deal and that wiped out any flickering doubts. What could be better than the two of us working together in our own, brand new, little business!

There are stipulations to becoming a bona fide, licensed, bonded winemaker, one who makes and sells wine to the public. I didn't know all the specifics involved in getting state and federal permission to operate a winery, but I did know formulas and processing procedures had to be approved by a federal agency. That meant I had to submit all of that information in writing. There was one small catch to that. Nothing had ever been put down on paper, not here in Amana or in Europe, by anyone in my family as to how the old-style wines were made. None of the recipes or directions had been recorded. Winemaking had been handed down by word-of-mouth. It was taught by on-the-job training. A winemaker learned to make wine by working with an experienced winemaker. That's how I had learned. Now I had to start from scratch and write out the whole process. With that job facing me, I was sure wishing that, as a kid, I had paid closer attention to every single little thing I had seen papa and *Opa*, grandfather, do when they made wine down in our cellar. If I had ever dreamed that one day I would be making wine to sell...

Well, with the Zubers we had talked half the night away. Warmed by the last round of *Piestengel*, Helen and I headed back into the deep-freeze night. It was after midnight and ten below, but we were so fired up about selling wine, we didn't even shiver.

2. The First Batch

All day Sunday, the winery was all I could think about. Helen and I talked about the weather or the baby and right in the middle of a sentence, wine came up. We didn't say anything new, we said the same words that had been said the night before.

"It's not too big a job."

"I know perfectly well how to make wine, good wine."

"You'll just be making bigger batches of it, that's all," Helen said.

"It's no big deal," we'd both end up saying.

We knew, if after I had made the wine and if by some crazy chance it didn't sell, it wouldn't be a problem. It would just mean we would have a supply, a BIG supply of wine on hand, wine which we would pass out to our families and to our friends. In Amana, wine would never go to waste.

We had made the decision, we were going to start a winery and I couldn't wait to get going on it. Once I decide something, I do it!

We had had some experience with state laws regulating home businesses. After Helen finished beauty school in Des Moines, she worked in a Cedar Rapids shop before she opened a shop in our home after we were married. That was when we found out there had to be a separate, outside entry for her shop and that all work related to her business had to take place in an area completely separate from family living areas.

By fixing up the basement, walling up one corner of it and opening a new ground level door through the north basement wall, we could meet all of those requirements for a winery. Later, federal law called for security bars to be installed over all the winery windows but the bars weren't part of our first costs. I planned to get by with the equipment I had on hand, the small, family-size crusher, press and vats. Until I saw how business went, I wasn't going to make any radical changes.

On Monday, as soon as I got off work, I stopped by the lumber mill for prices on boards, nails and necessary materials for the basement partition and door. If I was going to make wine, I wasn't about to miss out on making rhubarb wine that same spring, so I had to get going right away. I phoned suppliers for the other things I needed—barrels, bottles and a stock of sugar. My deadline was Memorial Day. That was the day new batches of *Piestengel* were always started. It was a holiday and I'd have the day off from work.

Memorial Day 1949 dawned bright and sunny, a perfect day to pull rhubarb. It's a day I'll never forget. I was up early. I couldn't wait to get to the garden and start yanking rhubarb stalks. My plan was to make four hundred gallons of wine. That was eight times the amount I generally made each spring. Four hundred gallons of wine, that's all I could think of while I pulled—and did I pull!—I pulled just about every stalk in our little patch.

By the time I'd snapped off the leaves, hosed the stalks and had them piled up on the lawn, it finally began to sink in what a really big batch of wine I was about to tackle. Now, I can't say I was honestly worried about what I was about to do; rather, I was just real, real excited about it. The prospect of having that much wine all at one time down in my cellar really had me charged up.

Stoney, my pinochle playing friend, couldn't stay away. He came over and helped me set up the crusher out in the back yard under the shade of a big elm tree. It was too nice a day to be stuck down in the cellar. Besides, by working outdoors, we figured to save ourselves hours and hours of work scrubbing rhubarb juice off the basement floor and walls.

Rhubarb, when it's ripe, when it's full of juice, spurts juice everywhere. With the old crusher, it was even worse. If my press was old, my crusher was primitive. It was worse than old. It was made entirely of wood. Anything and everything that came in contact with the juice or the wine, back then, was wooden. Metal, except stainless steel, can't be used in winemaking because metals trigger chemical reactions with the acids in the juice and that in turn causes off-flavors in the finished wine. That old crusher even had wooden bearings under its two ten-inch wooden rollers. It stood at table height, on a wobbly, four-legged stand. Each roller had its own crank but the two cranks were on opposite ends of the crusher, so it took two men to run it. You could say it was a two-manpower machine. Stoney cranked on one end and I cranked on the other. With one arm we cranked and with the other we fed rhubarb stalks through the narrow, half-inch space between the rollers.

When we reached down to pick up stalks, our faces were right in line with the spittin', spatterin' juice. It hit us right in the face, got all over our arms. We got the full dose and did it sting! That rhubarb juice smarts, especially when it gets you in the eyes. I wish we had a movie of that so I could laugh about it now, although it sure wasn't funny when we were doing it. It was tiresome and it was messy. Every so often, we had to stop to rest and wipe off our hands and faces.

I now wish I had never gotten rid of that old crusher. I should've kept it, set it out on the deck as a conversation piece. I don't mind talking about that old crusher, just as long as I never have to use it again. I would have quit making rhubarb wine a long time ago if I still had to use that old machine.

The mangled rhubarb stalks fell into a trough under the rollers and then into a small, wooden collecting vat. As the vat filled up, the pulp was moved pail by pail, heavy wooden pails, inside the basement where it was poured into larger vats where it soaked in its own juice for three or four days. The soaking tubs were, I suspect, leftovers from the days when *Opa* made village wine. They were twenty inches deep, forty inches across, made of narrow oak slats fitted together in grooves and held by four bands of wide steel rings. They sat flat on the floor. When they were full, they couldn't be moved. They were too heavy. That's why they couldn't be used to catch the pulp when it came out of the crusher. Not even two men could have moved those vats once they were full. They were varnished inside and out to make them easy to clean and also to prevent them from giving the wine a woody flavor. One vat didn't hold quite a hundred gallons. To mix four hundred gallons of formula, I had to repeat the recipe five times. Standing empty all winter, the vats dried out and leaked like sieves. Four or five days before I needed to use them, I lugged buckets of water to fill them up. They soaked up the moisture, swelling their cracks shut. That was a chore I always dreaded, but I had to do it so as not to lose any of the precious juice.

When the pulp was ready to press, it was dipped, again with buckets, out of the vat and dumped into the press. The press was old but it was solid and sturdy. It had a 100-pound capacity. That was the extent of the pressure that could be brought to bear on it with the hand-operated screw ratchet. The ratchet was mounted on an "H" frame and it forced an inch-thick, round, wooden disc down onto the pulp inside the press basket or drum. The tiny basket of an inch-and-a-quarter oak slatting was only sixteen inches across. Juice oozed out the bottom of the press into yet another old, flat-bottomed, wooden vat.

It took a lot of time—slow, tedious time—and effort to load, clean and then reload that dinky press, but that same little old press saw me through the first several years in the wine business. It wasn't fast and it sure wasn't easy when I was processing large quantities, but it did do a very thorough job of pressing as long as I was careful not to overload it.

Thinking back to that day, and it was a long one, somehow we did manage to stick with the job and we got all the crushing done and had the juice carried into the basement before the sun went down. Today, with motorized and electrified equipment, I process that same amount of rhubarb in only a couple of hours. There is one thing to be said for old, hand-run machinery, though. It's not likely to have a breakdown. Simple machines have fewer moving parts—the manpower may get tired and give out, but all it takes to fix that is a little rest.

Four days from the time I pulled the rhubarb, I had the first big batch of wine mixed and set to ferment in eight fifty-gallon barrels. The barrels were lined up in a row against the basement wall. I had never set more than one barrel of wine at one time. Looking at all of those barrels, eight of them, was something! Instead of wondering if I could actually sell all that wine, I was thinking ahead to fall, thinking about finding a supply of grapes so I could set more wine. All the rhubarb wine needed was time. I wouldn't have to spend any time on it until next spring. And in October, six barrels of Concord grape wine joined the rhubarb wine in quiet fermentation.

Sometime after the rhubarb wine was set, the thought occurred to me that I'd better get my license and find out what kind of papers I had to have in order to run a winery. So I wrote a letter to the Bureau of Alcohol and Tobacco Tax Unit under the United States Internal Revenue Service requesting an inspection. In a few weeks, an inspector knocked on our front door. I ushered him in, down the stairs and over to the winery's little corner of the basement. I proudly presented my eight barrels of rhubarb wine.

The inspector walked over to the barrels. He tapped first one barrel, then another and another, until he had tapped all eight barrels. He turned to me with a puzzled look on his face.

"They're full!" he said. He said the words as though he thought the barrels would be empty. He was surprised that they weren't.

"Sure," I said, real casual-like, "if we want to go with wine big, we have to have lots of wine."

He was standing right square in front of me, looking me straight in the eye. I could tell this thing was getting serious.

"How come you made the wine already?" he asked.

Before I could even answer, he said, sternly, "You can't make wine until we come out and inspect and say you can make wine." Then he proceeded to give me a lesson in how it was supposed to be done.

"First, before you ever make wine, we have to come. You have to be inspected first, to see that you are properly set up. Like, you have to have an outside entrance, and that you have. And you have to have the winery set up away from living quarters, and that you have. But you are supposed to have written out the formula for the wine, gotten it approved, have a license number for the winery. When you have done all of those things, then we come to see your winery. When we see that everything is set up and everything is in order, then you can make wine, but not before!"

Well, I sure didn't know it worked that way. I thought to have a winery, I had to have wine. I didn't want to show my ignorance to the inspector. I shrugged my shoulders, probably looked a little sheepish, just waited for him to finish his spiel.

"But the rhubarb was ready," I told him, "I couldn't wait, I had to start the wine."

Now, it's a funny story and I laugh about it, but I sure wasn't laughing at the time. While I didn't want the inspector to think that I didn't know better, I wasn't worried about what would happen to the wine. If the inspector said I couldn't sell that wine, I knew I wouldn't have to dump it. Plenty of Amana folks would be tickled to get the wine as a gift.

So through the old federal boy's whole lecture, I just stood there, kept my mouth shut, listened and let him review the laws.

After he had had his say, he was more than helpful. I didn't have to trouble myself figuring out how to handle the problem; he figured it out for me. To the inspector's way of thinking, being one step out of order wasn't all that ruinous. He merely labeled the fermenting wine "family wine," and went on to explain to me that after I had all the paperwork done and a license had been issued recognizing the winery as a legal, bonded facility, then he would label the wine as "commercial stock."

Many inspectors who come to check Amana wineries have never been to a winery that makes other than grape wines. It's an educational experience for them and gives them a chance to get acquainted with many new wines. Over the years, the inspectors have become good customers. I stress the word "customer" because, obviously, we don't dare make a gift of wine to them when they come here to do their job. They are here on duty and aren't allowed to accept anything and we must not offer them anything. That would be a bribe. So when they try the wine and they like it, they have to buy it.

Wines are traditionally named after the place of their origin and after the name of the dominant product or variety used to make them. Our ancestry is full German. We have a German name. We speak German. It made sense to use Kraus as the brand name of our wines and put it on the labels, too, along with the name of the individual wine and the name and address of the winery.

Naming the winery was easy. "Old Style Colony Winery" describes exactly what our wines are and how they are made. It was and is my choice to make wine the old-style way by getting the juice directly from the whole, fresh produce. That's how my ancestors did it when they made wine in Europe and Germany and here in Amana during the old colony days.

Some months passed after that first inspection before the mail finally brought papers certifying "George Kraus as owner-operator of Old Style Colony Winery in Middle Amana, Iowa."

The date on my very first approved formula for *Piestengel* is January 18, 1950.

It had taken a whole year from the time the idea first hit me for it to be made official. The winery was legal and I had been declared a winemaker. In another few months, the wine would go on sale.

3. The Werkzeuge

The founders of Amana were men and women who had formed a religious sect, an offshoot of Lutheranism, in Europe in the early 1700's. They called themselves Inspirationists and they believed their *Werkzeuge*, or leaders, could receive divine guidance in the same manner as the inspired prophets of old. Their beliefs led to their persecution and they felt compelled to leave their homelands for America.

My mother's ancestors were part of the first settlement at Ebenezer, near Buffalo in upper New York State in 1843. So were all of Helen's ancestors. As more and more of the followers came over from Europe, they needed more land. A search committee located the top-notch farm land that became Amana, with timber for buildings, and a river that could provide water power for the mills they intended to operate. They wanted a climate conducive to producing abundant grain crops and gardens.

The committee also found large deposits of sandstone, limestone and clay. All were well-suited to masonry construction. They bought about 26,000 acres of fertile land, including groves of oak, walnut and cherry trees along the banks of the Iowa River.

In 1855, the first of a thousand colonists headed west over the Great Lakes waterways to Chicago. There they took the train as far west as the Mississippi River and made the last leg of their journey to their new community in wagons. The Schinnerlings, my mother's family, and the Millers, Helen's mother's family, and the Bergers, her father's family, were all part of that first group.

The name "Amana" came from the Old Testament Book of Solomon and means "remain faithful." To the new settlers, it was more than a name. It was a practicing philosophy. Here in Amana, they restored and relived their Old World ways in undisturbed obscurity within a self-contained, self-sufficient, communal church society. They practiced communism to the extent that each member donated his wealth, his earnings and his labor for the good of all. But it wasn't communism with a capital "C" as we know it today. It was a religious commune, based on monogamous marriages and with a firm belief in the wedding vows and a commitment to fidelity. The members of the colony were not aggressive. They did not seek converts to their church or their commune.

We are often reminded of the need to explain the Amana communal life because, in the last ten years or so, we have had people in the wine shop who were, or would have been what was commonly referred to at one time as "hippies."

"Oh, ho, a commune, huh?" they'll say. "Well, we've been looking for a place like this ever since we left the coast." From the way they talked and the way they acted, they seemed to have the idea they could move right in and settle down right here in Amana.

I've heard Helen, in her quiet but emphatic way, explaining to them that Amana is not and never was that kind of a place.

"I don't think Amana is what you are looking for," Helen tells them. "Amana isn't a place where men and women all live together without being married and it was never like that. It was never a nest of people living all free and easy in a swinging life style. Many people did live in one house, that was true, but they were all people who belonged to just one family. They were families who were related by marriage and by blood. Even though they all lived in one house, they all had separate rooms."

Copying the European pattern, people and animals alike were clustered within the seven Amana villages—Amana, Middle Amana, High Amana, West Amana, East Amana and South Amana, plus Homestead, a settlement the Amana Colonies purchased in 1861. Homestead had been established as a railroad stop when the Rock Island Railroad tracks reached that spot. Ownership of Homestead provided the Colonies with a railroad link to the outside. Shipments from the Amana calico and woolen mills were loaded at Homestead, as were boxcars full of grain. Locally, the name "Amana" is used only for the main village of Amana. The other villages simply go by "Middle," "West," "High," "East" and "South."

The seven villages were no farther apart than the distance that could be traveled by ox cart in one hour, about one or two miles. It made sense. It gave them easy access to the plots of farm land between the villages and they were never more than a one-day round trip by wagon from the other villages. Today, by car, you can get from one village to the next in a few minutes.

Middle, home to four generations of my family, was laid out in 1862. It is the second largest village in population. Amana is the largest. Middle had a pharmacy and a physician, but more importantly, it had the number two woolen mill and the Colony's print shop. All printed forms used for record-keeping at the general store, the wine cellar and the mills along with all school textbooks and church hymnals were printed and bound there. The Colonies had no newspaper or magazine. Official messages and pronouncements were delivered in speeches by the elders either at church or at community meetings.

Each village had its own store, church, school, bakery, dairy, livestock barns, sawmill, butcher shop, vineyard and winery. Some of the bigger operations, like the flour mill or woolen mill, were single operations, or at the most, in two different villages. In the manner of a German *dorf*, little town, the shops and multiple-family dwellings were on one long main street with several shorter, irregular streets branching away from the main thoroughfare.

The streets are now asphalt-covered but I remember when they were dirt roads. In rainy times or after a winter thaw, the heavily loaded wagons with their steel rimmed wheels sank several inches deep in the soft roads. In the winter, that mud would freeze up and be in such jagged sharp peaks that they cut and skinned your face if you were unlucky enough to fall down when you crossed the street. In the spring, after the mud dried out, the streets were smoothed with horse-drawn grader blades to fill in the ruts. Horses were used on the farm equipment and some on wagons but mostly the heavy wagons were pulled by oxen teams. Since Middle had the woolen mill, a cabinet shop, wagon shop and a millwright shop, it had lots of traffic. Wagons rattled and lumbered up and down the streets the year round.

When lots of people needed to go from one village to another for a special church service, a wedding or a funeral, they were ferried back and forth in horse-drawn spring wagons that had several wooden seats hung between their high box sides. It was like an open-air bus. Sleighs were used in the winter when the snow was deep enough. In Iowa, that was January, February and perhaps in December and March. A few members built their own bobsleds, small enough to be pulled by a single horse. A ride in a bobsled was a big occasion. So seldom did we do anything just for fun when we were kids, that even a bobsled ride was a real fun time. We huddled down under heavy blankets and all but sailed over the snowy pastures and meadows.

All property, land, buildings, equipment and livestock were owned by the Amana Society, which paid taxes under Iowa law as a corporation. Two or three generations were assigned living quarters in one home. There were, for example, a man, his wife and their children and one set of parents, either the man's parents or his wife's parents, and one set of grandparents. The village elders decided who lived where, but of course the older generation in a household used their influence to help the elders decide who lived where.

Each home had a common dining-sitting room and several small bedrooms. There was no need for a kitchen in the home. All food was prepared in large community kitchens. Every man and woman over school age was assigned a job in the village. For many of the men in Middle, including my father, that meant taking a shift at the woolen mill. Other men were farmers. They might be on the field crew and tend the crops or they might be herdsmen for the beef and dairy cattle. Some were swine men or butchers or millers or blacksmiths. Still others were harness makers, wagon builders, coopers, shoemakers, broom makers, tinsmiths or handymen.

The tinsmith in Homestead was my great-uncle, Peter Fels. He made pails, buckets, tubs, cups, plates, cooking and baking utensils and tableware such as knives, forks and spoons. There was a job for everybody. You name it and somebody in Old Amana did it. There were painters who made the yearly rounds of the houses and buildings, painting only the insides of the structures. They didn't paint the outside wood on any buildings in the old days. If a window got broken, or a door hinge came loose, the elders were notified and a handyman was sent right over to fix it.

The work duty for most women was the kitchen. That also meant they tended the vegetable and herb gardens. They managed flocks of laying hens kept for a fresh egg supply, and the fat hens which were baked and stewed, and the younger chickens, the broiler size as they are known today. The vegetable gardens were scattered around the backyards throughout a village and herbs grew at the kitchen doorway. The cooks just stepped out and snipped a few herbs to toss into the soup kettle or stewpot. The only women who did not have a regular work assignment were mothers who had at least one child under two or three years old. Those mothers stayed home to care for their little ones.

The three- to seven-year-olds went to *Kinderschule*, kindergarten or preschool, and were cared for by one or two of the older women. School was considered "over" when a youngster reached fourteen years of age or had progressed through eighth-grade level work. The eleven church services each week were required attendance for every man, woman and child.

Middle was just as picturesque in the early days as it is now, sheltered under century-old and older oaks, elms and maples. The segment of the seven-mile canal that flows through Middle looks pretty, although it wasn't dug to add beauty. It was dug to carry water for powering turbines that ran the looms and other machinery in the mills and factories. Digging was started in the 1860's and went on for several years. Every yard of dirt was hauled up and out of that ditch by dirt scrapers pulled by horses and oxen.

In order to build up the fall of the water so it created power, the canal or millrace was extended five miles west from the mill in Middle, to take water from the Iowa River between South and West. The canal continued two miles on east to serve the woolen mill at Amana. As other mills and factories were added and power needs increased, the canal was deepened to increase the water flow. A dredging boat was rigged up to gouge the canal another eight to ten feet deeper, right down the center of the channel. That boat was kept in constant service from then on, weather permitting, cleaning out the mud and sludge that built up on the bottom of the canal.

Years later, electric motors replaced the water-powered turbines in the plants, but the canal remains, edged here and there with graceful, swaying willow trees and spanned by several wooden bridges and two highway bridges. It is an attractive part of the Amana scene and the water power is still used to generate electricity. Along the way, the millrace flows through the lake which is along the east side of Middle. Middle extends to the edge of the lake.

Some call it "Amana Lake," but to me, it's always just been the lily pond. The lily pond is the home of the American lotus, yellow nelumbo. Late in June, tens of thousands of huge, round, green leaf pads rise up through four feet of water and unfurl under the summer sun's warmth to cover large sections of the two-hundred-acre lake. Four weeks later, there's another uprising. Pointed, egg-shaped buds shoot through the dense, floating leaves and burst into huge, satiny, yellow blossoms. The flowers close each evening and unfold again when the sun comes up the next day. The flowering display lasts from the middle of July well into August. When that pond is a mass of color, it is a beautiful sight. If a breeze picks up the lilies' fragrance and floats it across the pond, it fills this whole village. The pond is a summertime showplace for us every bit as much as it is for tourists.

Behind the Middle Amana woolen mill was a good fishing hole. Rudolph Kellenberger photo.

4. The Krauses Come to Amana

The Kraus family was among the few latecomers to Amana. They were not members of the Inspiration movement.

Fredaricka and Paul Kraus, my father's parents, married in Germany when both were twenty-one years old. My *grosselterns,* grandparents, saved Paul's wages and sold household possessions to buy passage on a ship for Boston for themselves and two children. When my Aunt Mina Hergert was ninety-four years of age and still living in Middle, she did not remember the trip from Germany to Boston in 1894, but she did remember that her family settled first in Middleborough, Massachusetts, where my father, Charles, was born. In 1899, they moved to the Amana Colonies. By then, they were homesick, and a chance to live with people who spoke their language sounded very good to them.

I try to picture my grandparents stepping off the train over at the little depot with four youngsters. No one was there to meet them. I imagine them standing there with everything in the world that they owned on their backs and tied up in a few parcels. Then, in one big whoosh of steam, the wheels of the train turned slowly and the train pulled away, shaking the ground under their feet and leaving them behind, huddled there on the platform.

I'll bet their knees were shaking. Intercontinental and transcontinental travel is taken for granted today and we forget what courage it took for our ancestors to strike out and go from one country to another, one life-style to another, one language to another. They had to be, as they would have said, "stout."

The first thing they did was to join the Inspiration church. They subscribed to the Laws of Faith, twenty-four Rules for True Godliness and twenty-one Rules for the Examination of our Daily Sins in addition to a Creed and the traditional

Protestant Lord's Prayer and the Ten Commandments. Committing themselves to those beliefs was also a commitment to the communal way of life. They lived first in South, but after *Opa* was assigned to Middle's woolen mill, they settled here.

When my father reached working age, his duty was in the woolen mills also. He was a dyer. He dyed yarns that were later woven into blankets and yard goods. He married Helena and they were assigned to live with her parents, Carl and Lina Schinnerling. Carl was the village winemaker. Lina was the village head gardener. Their home was in the church building because the winemaker had to live near his wines, and they were stored in the basement of the church.

My brother, sister and I were all born in the church building. Children were born at home in Old Amana with either the village doctor or midwife in attendance. I am the oldest in my family. I was born in 1921.

Papa helped *Opa* some when the village grape wine was made and he also helped out with the small batches of family wines—wild blackberry, elderberry, dandelion, currant and, of course, rhubarb. Rhubarb grew in the garden behind our house. Mama and *Oma*, grandmother, hunted the woods just outside of the village for berries and currants. When I was old enough, I helped make family wines, too.

My first winemaking job was pulling rhubarb stalks. If a child could lighten the load for an adult, the child pitched in and helped. Whoever the child hung around, that was the adult who got the child's help. Since Papa worked long hours at the mill and was away from the house all day every day but Sunday, I hung around *Opa*. *Opa's* work, a great deal of it, was right at home, down in the wine cellar. And where *Opa* was, that's where I was when I wasn't in school.

Now that I am a winemaker, you might think that, as a kid, I was particularly attracted to making wine. I can't honestly say I was. But I can say, I sure liked to be with *Opa*. I liked helping him out with his work and I liked being useful to him. *Opa* taught me plenty. I didn't realize just how much I had learned from him until after I was married and we started making our own wines.

As I look back, I see all the connections, big and little, that led me to become a winemaker. My ancestors learned the old methods of making fruit and vegetable wines while they still lived in Germany where those methods were commonly practiced. They next had to come to this country—and not to just any spot in the United States, but to this very spot in this very state to this one small, communal colony where the old-style wines were still being made. Next would come the upheaval in the commune followed by reorganization. My families would go out on their own, out into the middle of a depression where they would scramble to make ends meet. After all of that took place, then the repeal of prohibition came, making it legal to make and sell alcoholic beverages again.

There are two vital family connections that come into the picture, too. My father was the only son and one of only two children out of a family of nine who stayed in Amana after reorganization. He not only stayed—and this is the last and most important connection—he married the village winemaker's daughter.

Germans are well-known for their winemaking skills and their wine drinking. Fredaricka and Paul were not surprised to find wine was just as much a part of the life in Amana as it had been in Germany. But they were surprised to find wine provided to them right along with housing, food, clothing and other basic necessities. It wasn't troublesome to them. It was a change they got used to quickly. In fact, they had no difficulty adapting to the Amana life. Their years of hard work and frugal living in Germany and Boston had prepared them well for their new life. It was actually easy for *Oma* and *Opa* to fit in their new community.

Fitting in, everything and everybody alike, the same, as nearly identical as possible, was the way the founders wanted life to be in Old Amana. Even the buildings looked pretty much alike. Homes, schools, stores and shops looked so much alike on the outside, some barns could have been mistaken for houses. Not even the village church bore any distinguishing marks. It had no steeple, no cross.

For my birthday in 1967, Helen gave me an oil painting of Middle's church, my birthplace. The painting was done by Ruth Schmieder, a well-known Amana artist. She was a classmate of mine all through school and she took up painting as a hobby. Her work became so well-known, she soon was selling her pictures. She lives in Middle, enters art shows, puts on exhibits and still wins her share of awards. Her painting shows the church in a snowy winter scene. She chose to do it at that time of the year because that's when the trees are bare and that's the only time the building with its many tiny-paned windows can be seen in its entirety.

Amana architecture has remained essentially unchanged since the first buildings were erected. Most buildings are box-like, either square or rectangular in outline, with simple, straight lines and a high, steep roof often broken by several gables. Windows were double sashed and typically were made of 15 or 18 tiny glass panes. No land was or is wasted in front yards. Buildings hug the street and sidewalks. Back yards were and are filled with vegetable gardens. Logs from the community-owned timbers were cut, sawed and planed to make siding, studs, rafters, doors, shingles and flooring. Exterior wood was left unpainted, to weather to a dull patina. Wood was so plentiful, they figured it was cheaper to rebuild than it was to buy paint and spend man-hours repainting the buildings every few years. Stone and brick buildings have been left, for the most part, untouched, except where a little trim has been painted. The light brown limestone was quarried nearby and they also made their own bricks here, too. They had rock crushers, grinders, and big kilns for baking the bricks.

Compared to all the bright colors seen on houses nowadays, Amana buildings might seem monotonous, but it should be pointed out that rules in the old days didn't permit any decorations on the buildings and that applied to painting as well as any fancy millwork or trims. To the founders' ways of thinking, buildings were strictly utilitarian and shouldn't be fancied up in any way.

The boardwalks, now seen as quaint, charming, rustic, even artistic, were laid down on pathways between homes, churches, school, the mill, kitchen and general

The Kraus family, 1915. At right is Charles Kraus, father of George. The woman and man at left front are his parents, Fredaricka and Paul Kraus.

George and Helen Kraus are with their children, Kandyce (left), Donna and Dennis, 1964. All the children helped in the winery with bottling and selling.

store not for looks, but for very practical reasons—to keep pedestrians out of the snow and mud so walking was made safer, easier and faster. Another consideration was equally as important—boardwalks spared wear and tear on shoes and clothing. Repairing or replacing shoes and clothes cost money—not the individual's money, the community's money—but money all the same and they avoided spending money if they possibly could.

Walking was the only way people got around within a village. For longer trips between villages, people rode in wagons but even those trips were strictly business. No one was supposed to hitch up a horse and take a buggy ride just for the pleasure of taking a ride.

Everything had to have a reason, a purpose, even nature. Landscaping was functional. The many beautiful trees shaded buildings in summer and shielded them from winter's harsh winds. Nothing was planted for looks alone. Grape vines clinging to trellis supports on the east, west and south sides of the homes were attractive, but they were more than merely ornamental. They acted as protective insulation from summer heat while producing a few baskets of grapes for jam, jelly or wine.

Today, Amana villages look like one big flower garden. From May to October, tulips, daffodils, peonies, irises, geraniums, pansies, marigolds, cannas and chrysanthemums border and edge the walks and yards. It was not always this way. Such flowery displays were considered purely decorative, frivolous, and were discouraged. Occasionally that rule was flouted when bright red, yellow and orange zinnias streaked unexpectedly through a backyard vegetable plot in between rows of potatoes, beans, radishes, carrots and beets.

We never thought of our homes or yards as drab. They may have been plain, but they were neat, clean and orderly. Yards were mowed and trimmed as neatly as they could possibly be without power mowers and edgers. Littering was never a problem, not like it is now. There was absolutely no trash, no grunginess in Old Amana and everyone took great pride in taking care of the buildings, inside and out. Amana still has that well-cared-for look and it is beautiful. Amana may be old, the buildings may be old, but none of them are rundown and dilapidated.

The old rule against paint was relaxed a little when it came to the inside walls of the homes, although the catch to that was, there was only one color they could use—a light sky blue. It was called "Amana Blue." It was the only paint the general store stocked. Actually it wasn't really a paint, it was more of a wash, like white wash. It came as a powder and had to be mixed with water just before it was applied. It was brushed on. Painters used long-handled brushes to reach the high ceilings and walls so they didn't have to pack ladders with them from house to house.

Getting the walls of your house done was a messy sloppy job. The wash didn't have a painty smell. To me, it was a very pleasant smell, all fresh and clean. I liked it.

It was a smell I associated with spring because painters came to paint only after the wood-burning heaters were no longer in use. That meant summer was almost here.

The main room of most houses got a fresh coat of "Amana Blue" almost every spring. The heaters were generally fairly clean burning, but now and then they belched out a little puff of smoke if the back draft, the damper, wasn't fully opened up before opening the firebox door to put more wood on the fire. Only the main room, the living-dining room, was heated. That room also got the most use and it needed freshening up more often than the bedrooms. Bedrooms were never heated unless a little heat filtered in from the main room. Getting up in a cold bedroom in the winter sure got your day off to one fast start, I can tell you! When you are coming out of a nice, warm bed and your feet hit the cold, bare floor, boy, you move!

The blue walls of the rooms were bare except for church-related hangings, either needlework samplers or prints which had been made from an original religious painting. Usually those pieces were hung in the bedroom over the head of the bed. If they could, they made some of the wall hangings for a purpose, too. We have an old print titled "Tranquility" which was framed in such a way that when the picture itself is dropped forward from the wall in a "V," it makes a small storage space for personal papers. We still have some needlework samplers that were done by Helen's great and great-great-grandmothers. Samplers were always in German. The words were taken from religious quotations, Bible verses, prayers and other meditations and were lovingly stitched with fancy embroidery and simple cross-stitches in coarse canvas.

Nothing in the homes or in the dress of the people was to be an adornment. Nothing was to be for looks alone. Picture-taking fell in that category, so naturally, there were rules forbidding the use of cameras in Old Amana. That accounts for the lack of pictures to record the early days.

Only a few select people, those considered to be the "V. I. P.s" of the time, owned a camera or had access to one. The only old family pictures we have are a few from Helen's family. A friend of her grandfather owned a camera and he liked to take pictures of machinery, horses hitched to buggies and wagons, nothing very personal. Who knows how the man got the camera or film for the camera or how he got away with taking pictures? We do know that somehow, even in the days of the rules, they did have their ways of getting around the rules.

It seems that if anything was a pleasure, it was probably forbidden in Amana. If it was enjoyed, it was forbidden. It was considered wrong to like anything too much. With that kind of thinking, it is easy to see how they came up with the long list of things they were against and they sure had a lot of "no-no's"—no games, no parties, no cards, no music outside of church, no dancing, not for grown-ups, anyway. Life in the old country, in Germany, hadn't been that strict for my grandparents, Fredaricka and Paul, but they took life in the Colonies with the new rules to heart and did their best to live up to them.

Talk was their main recreation. The women talked in the kitchens. They knew the recipes by heart so they didn't have to keep an eye on any cookbook and while their hands were busy, they passed the time visiting. Men talked on the job, too, but not the men working in the mills and factories. It was too noisy to talk when the mill machinery was running. Factory workers and mill hands did their talking after hours over a glass of wine. Most men worked an eight-hour shift, six days a week. At times a crew might have to put in a ten- or twelve-hour day. None of the men worked harder or longer than the women. As soon as she was fourteen years old, an Amana girl was assigned kitchen duty.

I remember the long hours the women spent in the kitchen and in the garden. They left the house at five o'clock in the morning, every morning, even Sundays. They might fix a breakfast of fried potatoes, bread and jam for six o'clock pickup and at the same time they began preparation for the noon meal and supper. Supper was served at six o'clock in the evening but that wasn't the end of their day. They usually didn't come home until seven or eight o'clock, after the pots and pans were washed and the kitchen cleaned, ready for them to begin all over again the next morning.

Kitchen work called for strong hands, arms and shoulders. Any labor-saving equipment they were lucky enough to have was all hand-operated. It was a big job just to hold the big bowls they used to stir up huge batches of dumpling dough, biscuits, noodles or cake batters. Mixing up one big cake took twenty to thirty minutes. Helen whizzes up a cake now with an electric mixer in a few minutes.

They did have ice-boxes, though. That surprises many who tour Middle's old community kitchen. The ice-box is gigantic! It's three or four times larger than an ordinary, family-size ice-box. Some who see it mistake it for a big oak cupboard. It almost touches the ceiling. Only the over-sized, chrome, snap latches on its doors give it away as an ice box.

Ice was delivered twice a week to all village kitchens and butcher shops from the Colonies' own ice house, which was right here in Middle. It wasn't an ice plant where ice was manufactured. The ice used in Old Amana was made by the cold weather. It came out of Middle's lily pond.

A friend, Carl Metz, worked the ice harvest when he was a young man. He was one of four or five of the strongest young men in Middle assigned to help the ice house boss a couple of weeks in the dead of winter. To hear Carl tell it, harvesting ice was one cold job; it was "pinching cold," so cold you felt as though somebody was pinching your nose shut real hard.

Some winters, the ice went down thirty to thirty-six inches. Using long, one-handled saws, the young men cut the ice into strips six to eight feet long. Those strips were then cut into blocks, blocks that were about twelve inches square and twenty inches long. Once the blocks were cut, they were fished out of the water with a pair of monster ice tongs and heaved onto a sled to be hauled up to the ice house by a

Making ice was an annual wintertime activity. Rudolph Kellenberger photos.

team of horses. The ice house was just beyond the end of our street. As a boy, I remember seeing the horses pulling the sleds of ice past our house and I also remember how, on hot summer days, I liked hanging out at the ice house just hoping I would find a sliver or a chip of ice to suck to cool off. That ice was so clear, it was as clear and clean as commercial crystal ice.

The ice house looked like a granary but it was built differently. Each of its four walls was really three walls. The outer wall was of solid wood siding. Next to it was a narrow air space and then two more thin board walls. The space between those two thin walls was filled with sawdust. The sawdust acted as insulation. It worked. Ice in the ice house never seemed to thaw. I never saw any puddles of water inside the ice house and they never ran out of ice from one year to the next. The dirt floor was covered with ten inches of sawdust and sawdust was packed between and around the layers of ice blocks.

Middle's old ice house was, in a way, the forerunner of the refrigeration plant at which the first Amana freezers and refrigerators were built. That plant put Amana on the map as far as the rest of the nation and the world was concerned. Hardly a day goes by that customers in our shop don't remark that they know all about Amana from the Amana freezer, refrigerator or Radarange microwave oven they own.

"Is that big plant we saw as we drove to your winery the place where they make the Radaranges and the freezers?" they ask.

"Does the Amana Society own that plant?"

We tell them the name's the same but the Amana Society no longer has any business connections to the plant or to the products made there. The plant is now a division of the Raytheon Company.

It was not always so. In 1934, shortly after the Colonies were reorganized, George Foerstner, a young member of the Amana Society, knew of an Iowa City business in need of a beverage cooler. To Foerstner, making such a cooler sounded like a job the skilled craftsmen of Amana could handle. They could and did. After the first, small job, they went on to make portable ice-boxes, ice chests, coolers and eventually got into full-scale commercial production of locker plants, freezers, refrigerators and air-conditioners. As the business grew, it turned to the Amana Society for necessary capital and factory space. It just so happened, the woolen mill in Middle was empty. It had been idle since early in the 1930 Depression.

The only use the old mill got was when a couple of my buddies and I sneaked in there during the winter to practice pitching baseballs. We got the idea from Bill Zuber. Bill was also a Middle resident. He is not to be confused with Willie "Stoney" Zuber, my pinochle-playing neighbor and friend, although "Stoney" and Bill were related by marriage.

Bill Zuber was winning baseball games for Middle when I was about eight or nine years old. Later, he went on to pitch for the Cleveland Indians and the New

York Yankees. During the time he was with the Indians, he always came back to Middle during the off-season. Two or three weeks before spring training, he began to work out in the old vacant woolen mill. After Bill retired from baseball, he operated a restaurant, "The Dugout," in Homestead until 1982 when he died.

When the old mill became a factory, that was the end of our indoor baseball practice field.

The refrigeration business grew until it reached a point where it was too big for the Amana Society to handle. Foerstner and several Iowa businessmen formed a syndicate to purchase the company from the Society. They operated it until 1965 when it merged with the Raytheon Company. Throughout the changes, the founder remained at the helm and the plant has continued to employ many Amana residents. Many at the management level are from Amana. Other small Iowa towns have seen their young people move away over the last twenty years in order to find work in larger midwestern cities but the refrigeration plant has helped keep Amana's young people at home.

Guided tours are scheduled regularly during the tourist season and we suggest visitors take time to see the plant and its facilities. And they should ask their guide to point out that part of the plant which once was the old woolen mill, the building from which the entire Amana manufacturing operation sprang.

By the time Helen and I were growing up, even before the community kitchens were closed, families were permitted to have small iceboxes in their houses to keep perishables from their own gardens or leftovers from the community-furnished meals. Ice wasn't delivered to the homes, however, and going for ice was my twice-a-week chore in the summer. After I had hauled the block of ice home in my wooden coaster wagon, I washed the sawdust off and lugged the block in to the ice-box.

When visitors in our wine shop remark about seeing the old community kitchen down the street, we remind them to watch for the little wooden platform along the street and near the walk leading to the kitchen. It's the platform where dairymen left cans of fresh milk early every morning. They picked up the empties from the day before and left the full ones. When there was a good snow cover in the winter, milk was delivered with horses and sleds. We kids were tickled when the snow got that deep. It meant that if we got up a little early, we could hitch a free ride on the milk sled before it was time for us to go to school. Seven or eight of us boys hooked our small sleds onto the runners of the milk sleds. The biggest boys hooked on first, then two or three more hooked on behind them, making a sled train. And was it fun, especially if the horses got up a trot, took a corner too fast, causing the end sled to skid and dump its rider head-first into a snowbank.

My old sled hangs in our garage. Papa had it made at the wagon shop. It has a top of three-quarter-inch wooden slats which is bolted to steel runners and braces. It was so well made, it's still in good shape. I'll have to remember to get it down for our grandchildren to play with the next time they are here when it's snowy.

Wintertime reminds me of the good times I had sledding. Ice skating was Helen's favorite winter fun.

"Ice skating," she said, "was only for older children, those twelve to fourteen years old and old enough to be out without their parents at night. That's when we skated, at night, after school was out, after our chores at home were done and after supper. We carried kerosene lanterns to see our way a mile and a half through the fields to a little pond which lay between the hills near West. Once at the pond, we built a big bonfire. The fire warmed us and also gave us light so we could see to fasten clamp-on skates to our high-topped, laced shoes.

"By the time I was old enough to go skating, the Great Change had taken place and many girls wore ready-made, store-bought snow suits. They were a heavy blanketing, rather bulky and not all that pretty but they were very warm and because they weren't made by our mothers or grandmothers at home, they were special to us."

It must have been a welcome relief to the women of Amana when they no longer had to make the clothing they and their children wore. I remember how *Oma* and Mama sat for hours sewing by lamplight after they had already done a full day in the kitchen, a day that often began on the handle of the old, iron water pump a few steps down from the kitchen porch. Every drop of water used in the kitchen had to be pumped from the spout of that pump into a long, low, wooden trough and then it was dipped up and carried inside in heavy, wooden buckets. The trough and buckets are all dried out and weathered now, just like the long backless benches on the porch where the cooks beat the heat in the summer. Any kitchen job that could be picked up was carried out to the porch and there they sat down to do it—stringing beans, shelling peas, peeling potatoes or seeding or pitting fruits. Churning butter was another good sitting down, porch job.

The old churn looks like a small wooden barrel. It would hold at least five gallons of cream, sat sideways on the floor and was cranked by a handle at one end of the drum. Inside the drum, wide, flat wooden paddles flip-flapped, beating the cream, separating butterfat from buttermilk. When they had the butter, they didn't throw the buttermilk away. It went into pies, cakes, cookies and nut breads. The kitchen crew didn't bake breads and coffee cakes. Those were made fresh every day at the village bakery just down the street and were delivered to the kitchen. The bakers put their goodies, still fresh and warm from the hearth oven, into a bread box that was as large as a small steamer trunk. Even though the breads were never wrapped, the bread box kept them fresh until they were sliced and served.

Behind the kitchen door, there's a hat rack. A few time-worn bonnets hang there now, giving the feeling someone's Mama or *Oma* might just have come in, hung up her bonnet and put on a floor-length apron before she tackled her share of that day's meals.

Women in Amana always wore bonnets. They even kept right on wearing them after they were no longer required to. They would never have dreamed of being out and about without a bonnet on their heads in Old Amana. Those bonnets had wide, stiff brims that all but hid their faces. The bonnets were washable, with bows that tied under the chin and a little capelet that extended out over the shoulders.

The big pots, pans, skillets and roasters on the stove and work table draw their share of comments. They needed over-sized, institution-type utensils. Cooking for a village in Old Amana was very much like cooking in one of today's busy restaurants. Spoons, spatulas and forks were not only larger than normal, they also had extra long handles enabling the cooks to stand back away from the hot stove and yet still be able to turn meats, stir soups or stews or gravy—always there was gravy!

If it were judged on looks alone, the old cookstove could pass for one of the built-in cooktops seen in kitchens now. It's mounted atop a long, low bricked firebox and fills one corner of the first room of the two-room kitchen. A front opening in the firebox facilitates building the fire or adding a stick of firewood to maintain steady cooking. A ready supply of firewood is piled outside the door, under the shelter of the porch roof. The stove's cooking surface is thick, sheet iron with a few removable lids cut in it so the cook could add a stick of firewood directly beneath a pot or skillet if she needed to turn up the heat, so to speak. Heat was turned down simply by moving a pot to the back of the stove, farther away from the fire.

Directly across from the stove in another corner of the room and looking every bit like a big, sheet metal cupboard, is the baking oven. It has four wide shelves, wide enough to hold lots and lots of cake or pie pans or cookie sheets all at one time. Heat was carried to and dispersed around the oven by a long pipe from the wood-burning heater standing in the center of the room.

Just a few feet from the oven is another built-in, the old, wooden sink complete with two huge wooden tubs once used for washing dishes. The sink has a drainpipe but no faucets. Remember the water was bucketed in. Wood was used a great deal in Old Amana—it was cheap, they had lots of it in the timbers they owned. They didn't have to buy it, not like they did tin. They made do with wood, wherever and however they possibly could.

A big baking cupboard takes most of one wall in the room. It has screened sides, doors of punched tin and its empty shelves once were filled with the juiciest pies and the best cakes in the world.

When Helen has time to show the kitchen, she likes to play a quiz game with her guests.

"What's this?" she'll ask as she shows a leggy, tin gadget that barely looks sturdy enough to support its crank.

"It's a string bean cutter," she answers. "Beans went in here, the crank was turned and beans came out here—all neatly frenched."

Then she points to a tall, skinny, prickly tin tube standing in the middle of a flat, round tin pan.

"Know what that is used for?" She goes on to explain the potato ricer. "Boiled potatoes were put in the top, then pressed with the wooden stomper, forcing the potatoes through the little holes and making them look just like fine noodles."

The cooks had many ways to fix potatoes—potatoes, meat, bread and gravy—those were the mainstays of the noon and night meals that came out of the old kitchen.

Seldom does Helen find anyone who can guess what the large, screen cage in one corner of the kitchen is. Inside the cage are small, wooden boxes in various sizes and shapes. The boxes all have small holes drilled in their sides.

"The cage is a cheese keeper," Helen says. "Cheese was formed in the boxes. The holes in the boxes let out the liquid, the whey, so it drained out as the cheese was pressed. Cheese was taken out of the boxes every so often to be kneaded with the hands. That worked out even more of the whey and also gave the cooks a chance to help form and shape the cheese into nice, firm rounds."

Kneading the cheese was hard work; all of the kitchen work was hard work. Although they had some hand-cranked tools which made some kitchen tasks go faster, the cranks still had to be turned. From the hours I've spent on the end of a crank in the winery, I know how tiresome cranking can be.

Two walls of the kitchen's second room are lined with dish cupboards and the giant icebox is in one corner. Three long tables form a "U" around the heating stove in the center of the room. Single men and women of the village ate their meals in this room. Kitchen diners were mostly men, bachelors, who were extra hands at the mills, hired to do the special jobs which required skills not found among the village laborers. Most of the men were brought in for short-term employment and they bunked together in a dormitory near the mill.

The village church bell was rung at mealtime. An adult or an older child from a household would be sent to the kitchen to pick up the food for the whole family. The food was carried home in baskets or tin boxes. Our family used a tin box. Its two lids were hinged at the middle to make it easy to slip family-sized pots in and out of the carrier. The carrier kept the food hot on the short walk back home where it would be served family-style at our own table and with our own dishes and tableware.

Just the mention of tableware can still cause Helen to cringe.

"The word 'tableware' always reminds me," she says, "of the two Saturday morning chores I had to do every single week. They were two jobs I despised. One was polishing the tableware—the knives, forks and spoons. It wasn't silverware or stainless steel. It was tin. They had wooden handles but the knife blades, fork tines and spoon bowls were tin. They were punched out by the tinsmith at the local shop. By dipping a wet rag in soft, sandstone powder, the tin part of the tableware could be polished to a surprisingly shiny luster."

Just talking about it makes Helen shudder.

"Ohhhhh!" she'll moan, "it was such a gritty mess! Rubbing sandstone on tin sent shivers up and down my backbone. It sounded like scraping chalk on a blackboard or dragging a shovel on concrete. Oh, how I did hate the awful, screechy sound of that messy job! But I polished the tableware every Saturday even if I didn't like it. It was my job. I was told to do it and I did. I just gritted my teeth and I did it!" She was very obedient.

Her other Saturday job was cleaning glass chimneys from the half dozen kerosene lamps used to light her family's home. A cotton webbing wick draws kerosene from a lamp's bottom bowl. If the wick should burn jagged, flames whip up one side of the chimney, smoke up the glass and cut down on the amount of light the lamp puts out. For the best light from a kerosene lamp, the chimney must be kept clean. At the Miller house, Helen cleaned them. She worried through each chimney.

"I was so careful," she said, "to get each one sparkling clean without leaving any towel lint on the glass. I was afraid I would break a chimney and that made me nervous and jittery. I hated that job, too."

Once she'd done her two dreaded jobs, the family ate their noon meal and it was bath time. Then came the best part of Saturdays for Helen.

"In fresh, clean clothes," she says, "at last I could relax, knowing the rest of the day was mine to spend in a quiet, thoughtful way, preparing for Sunday worship. I always read. All week long, I looked forward to those few hours with my books. How I loved having every Saturday afternoon all to myself."

Many other old pieces of cooking equipment are displayed at the kitchen—meat grinder, vegetable slicer, cherry pitter, coffee bean grinder, scales. Coffee beans were bought by the sack and coffee was ground fresh for every pot made. It was faster to weigh rather than measure large quantities of ingredients, so scales were an essential item for weighing out flour, sugar, butter—butter, for sure, and lots of it, the richer the better was how they cooked in Old Amana.

Even though the small, metal, single-burner portable stoves were primarily used in the homes, there is one of those in the old kitchen. They look somewhat like a lantern and burn kerosene like a lantern. They were suitable for reheating soup, warming milk or making tea if someone in the family was ill. Or, if there was a birthday in the family or a relative came to visit from outside, then some special dish or dessert could be prepared at home on one of the little stoves.

I have to wonder how the women who did all the kitchen work could manage to find time to help with the gardening, too. Garden work actually began in early March when they planted seeds for tomatoes, cabbage and other vegetables in hot frames on the south side of the kitchen building. After the soil in the garden warmed up and frost was no longer a threat, the seedlings were transplanted outdoors in the garden plots.

They grew everything from asparagus to squash to watermelon, even leeks, and celeric—that's celery root—which went into soups. They managed to keep endive and celery alive and thriving long into the winter months by digging trenches right in the dirt floor of the kitchen's basement. That basement was a sight to see after they had harvested all the vegetables and stored them for winter. There were a hundred or more families living in Middle and the entire village was fed out of the gardens all summer and still there was always plenty to keep over through the winter. The basement walls were lined with long, wooden shelves. Some shelves were slotted to allow air to circulate and keep the cabbage heads and potatoes dry and fresh. Carrots and parsnips were buried, just as though they had been planted, in big beds of sand which were piled on the floor. Onions were tied together in bunches by their long, dry stalks and hung from the basement rafters.

Only tomatoes and a few apples were ever canned. Apples were sorted as soon as they were picked and hauled to the kitchen. Blemish-free apples went into wooden barrels in the basement and they stayed fresh enough to eat most of the winter. Some apples along with the summer fruits—peaches, pears and apricots—were dried in a small drying oven or they were spread out to dry on long sheets of screening in the attic of the kitchen.

With cabbage, they made sauerkraut, of course—they liked their kraut. Kraut and sour green beans were put down in five- and ten-gallon stone crocks. Those two vegetables were delicious and very popular. In a good year, when they had more cabbage and more green beans than they could use, they sold the surplus kraut and sour beans to outsiders. Such sales were arranged by the elders who made sure the money went into the Colonies' coffers and not into the pockets of any kitchen workers. In Old Amana, no one was ever supposed to accept any money.

Another one of my favorites from the old kitchen was creamed new peas and new potatoes. We had peas only in the summer. There were never enough peas to can or dry. It took several bushels of fresh peas in the pod to shell out enough to feed a village. In a good year, the kitchen would serve fresh peas only two or three times.

Menus were predictable. If you knew the day of the week and the month of the year, you could come pretty close to guessing what you would be eating for supper that night. I was always one of those who looked forward to mealtime. I had a little trouble from time to time remembering mealtimes were for eating, not for talking, especially not for children's talking. If I forgot and talked or laughed when I shouldn't have, Mama would give me a quick warning look. It was kind of a squinty frown. It doesn't sound very threatening but it was all the reminder I needed not to be too naughty. For any kid who liked to eat as much as I did, being sent to bed without my supper would have been tough punishment. I made sure that never happened to me.

The food of Old Amana was like life itself in Old Amana—simple, hearty and basic. And was it good! In our family, we still prefer many dishes fixed the old Colony way—spinach, red cabbage, cucumbers, tomato salad, potato salad, liver dumplings, spaetzle, potato dumplings, dandelion greens—why, I get hungry just mentioning the names of those wonderful dishes!

"*Du warst ein guder bub.*" "You were a good boy." Now that's a phrase I heard a lot as I was growing up. Mama and *Oma* said those words to me every time I cleaned up my plate. I would eat everything on my plate, then with a thick slice of bread, I would mop the plate clean. Then I ate the bread. That was the best part of the meal.

We were taught it was a sin not to clean up our plates. Leaving food on your plate was wasteful. Waste, carelessness, tardiness, shoddy work—they were against all those things and more in Old Amana. By today's standards, some of their rules about personal behavior and public conduct would have seemed pretty severe. But I must say, rules aren't all bad. In fact, many of the rules that were right for Old Amana are just as right today. They had some practical applications for their rules.

Take thriftiness as an example. Being thrifty in Old Amana didn't mean saving a penny here and there until you had a dollar. Thriftiness had nothing at all to do with cash money as far as the individual was concerned. Thriftiness in Old Amana meant not being wasteful, getting the most and the best out of everything. It applied to all things, large and small. By taking proper care of their livestock and crops, they had the fewest losses and got the highest production. By using all tools and machinery correctly, they eliminated many costly break-downs and reduced careless damage to expensive equipment. They tried to avoid unnecessary wear and tear on furniture and carpet in the homes. Even as a child, I remember being cautioned repeatedly not to tear my clothes or scuff my shoes.

The old lessons have stayed with me. Not a day goes by without one or two of the old lessons cropping up. They affect the decisions I make and they affect the way in which I do whatever job is at hand.

Spraying the apple orchard, early 1900's.

5. Remembering When

The Colonies did not have any rules requiring residents to dress alike or so nearly alike they appeared to be wearing a uniform. All clothing, however, was made from fabrics that were woven at the local mills and then were cut and sewn into garments either by the village tailor or by the women of a family. It was understandable that the finished garments would all bear a striking resemblance.

Everyone, regardless of sex or age, was admonished "to dress not to be conspicuous," which was interpreted to mean no decorations, no adornments, no trimmings. For the sake of a little variety and to provide a faint touch of individuality, a very young girl's dress might be closed with contrasting ribbon ties or a button. A fine lace collar might dress up a young woman's dress. Chances are, the lace would have been tatted or crocheted by the woman's great-grandmother. Of course, in Amana, there were no jewels to be handed down or passed on to daughters and granddaughters. Whatever valuables a family might once have possessed would have been willingly donated to the True Inspirationists' cause before the family had left Europe.

Similarities in the clothes worn in Old Amana may have contributed some to the confusion that still exists in the minds of many people who come to Amana for the first time expecting to see the Amish.

"Where will we see the horses pulling black buggies?"

"Don't men wear beards any more?"

"Don't men dress in black suits and wear stiff, broad-brimmed hats any more?"

It's surprising how often we still hear those questions. I believe much of it stems from the similarity in the spelling and the sound of the names—Amana and Amish. Not only are those two names alike, but the Amish are referred to as "Mennonites," which sounds a lot like "Amananites," the name used to identify people who live in Amana.

The Amish and Amana are two different groups. They are not related in origin, in dress, in what they believe or how they practice their beliefs. Both groups, it is true, did originate in Europe, both have religious foundations and both are found in Iowa. However, Amana is located *only* in Iowa. The Amish have settlements in other states and other countries. Horses were once used extensively in Amana but they pulled enclosed buggies only for special occasions. Buggies are part of the Amish lifestyle. As far as I know, Amana never had any rules on shaving. In the early days, a few men did have beards.

I remember very clearly the sameness and the plainness of the clothing, particularly the clothes men and boys wore. Our clothes were so plain, I mean p-l-a-i-n! There was no forgetting them. Until boys were ten years old, we wore knee-length pants, nothing as stylish and fashionable as knickers, but just regular, straight legged pants cut off at the knee and hemmed, and we wore long stockings which were hand-knitted by the women and girls in the family. In the summer the stockings were cotton, in winter, wool. We wore suspenders, not store-bought ones, nothing that fancy. Our suspenders were wide strips cut from the same heavy, wool twill that our pants were made of. Generally boys' pants were black. Once in a while we had blue ones, navy blue, so dark it was almost black. I may have had one or two pairs of pants that were dark brown. I had no say in what color pants I wore. The color of the pants depended entirely on what color the Amana mills happened to be turning out to stock the general store at the time I outgrew my clothes.

The thought never entered my head as a youngster, but my clothes were not only homemade, they were home-grown; they were really and truly home-spun. The wool in my pants was actually sheared from the backs of Amana-raised sheep. The clipped wool went to the mill to be washed, cleaned, carded, spun and dyed. More than likely my own father even dyed the wool, since that was his job at the mill.

My shirts were made of a material that would be comparable to muslin. They were bulky and coarse. Once in a while, the mill put out a light blue cotton; then all the children wore shirts and dresses made from that material. There was no getting away from it. We all ended up looking alike because we all wore clothes made from the same fabric that was woven by the same mill. In the early years, all the sewing in Amana was done by hand. Later Mama and *Oma* had a sewing machine, a Singer treadle machine.

Helen never wore the little, dark blue-black and gray calico prints the Amana mills were famous for. That item was dropped out of production during World War I. Southern textile mills weren't able to furnish the fine grade of cotton needed for imprinting the dainty patterns and the special cotton dyes they had been getting from Germany were no longer being exported.

Like the boys, little girls, too, wore heavy, long, handknitted stockings. Some even knitted their own stockings along with knitting mittens and scarfs for other members of their family. Before a girl was old enough to start school, she was taught to knit. It might appear little girls were sitting around, doing nothing, but more than likely, they were knitting. In any idle moment, they pulled knitting needles and yarn out of an apron pocket and you could hear their needles clicking away as they added a few rows of stitches to whatever sock or mitten they were knitting on at the time. By the time Helen was knitting, girls weren't being pushed so much to knit.

"I had a little more leeway," Helen said, "with what I made, and I once knitted red and white striped socks for my doll. I was eight years old by then and while I did have to learn to knit, I certainly never had to knit as much as little girls in Amana used to.

"By then I was doing simple embroidery. As I grew older, the stitches grew finer, the design more difficult. By the time I was a teenager, I was decorating sheets, pillow cases and towels, the things girls put in their bridal hope chest. Needlework wasn't thought of as a talent or an art then, not like it is today. It was just another one of the things young Amana girls were 'supposed' to learn to do."

Like they were "supposed" to wear bonnets just like the grown-up women did. All little girls in Amana looked like the little sunbonnet girls pictured on notepaper, quilts, and aprons today. Amana girls didn't wear bonnets to look cute or pretty; they wore them because they were to keep their heads covered at all times when they were outdoors.

At high school, Helen first began to notice the differences in clothes and hair. She and other girls studied fashions and hair-dos in magazines and they tried to copy the pictures. Who knows, maybe that was the start of her interest in wanting to study hairdressing after she finished high school. Quite honestly, it was a whole new experience for any young woman or man from Amana to make that kind of a decision. Helen says herself just the fact she got to make the decision to go to Des Moines to beauty school was just as important to her as actually going.

As children, we had been told what to do. Children never made any decisions. And we weren't just told, we were directed. It was like a command. At home or at school, there was never any consideration given to what interested the child or suited the child's abilities or talents, let alone what the child liked, cared about or wanted. When your life is completely directed in that kind of upbringing, it is really quite amazing that any of us were able to later make up our minds about anything. The constant demands and stern discipline at home, school and church did, however, instill many good habits in us. We are now able to see how well some of the habits regarding hard work, promptness and following the rules have paid off in our adult lives.

"Behave dich, behave dich, behave dich." "Be good, be good, be good." I must have heard those words a million times while I was growing up. They played over

and over like a broken record. I heard them anywhere and anytime, no matter where I was, what I was doing, who I was with or where I was going. *"Behave dich."* Those two words fit and were applied to E-V-E-R-Y little thing in a child's life.

Like all Amana children, Helen and I grew up respecting our elders, doing our best at school and doing our home chores promptly and thoroughly. As children, we couldn't possibly have known how well those demanding practices would serve us later in our lives. Those same ingrained habits helped us to be hard-working students—Amana youngsters have a reputation for being good students—and to become hard-working adults.

When I first started school, classes were held six days a week the year 'round. The school year was divided into "winter school" and "summer school," with only a short vacation break between the two sessions. Our teachers were members of the Colonies and were selected by the village elders to be the schoolteachers. Grades were not designated as first, second, third and so on. Instead, students covered basic reading, writing, spelling, and arithmetic at the pace that best suited each individual student. History and geography were added to the studies of those who were about to finish their schooling—those who were thirteen or fourteen years old.

Most children were all through with school and ready for their first grown-up work assignment at fourteen if not earlier. That's pretty young to be told what job you are to do, and probably do for the rest of your life. Neither Helen nor I had to go through that process. The Great Change put a stop to that. From what I have heard from some folks who experienced that as a teenager, they thought it was quite an ordeal at the time. Now they laugh about it.

I get a kick out of hearing Carl Metz tell about what he went through when he turned fourteen. No other boys or girls in Middle turned fourteen years old the same time he did, so he had to stand up in front of the *Brudderath* all by himself when it was time for him to get his work assignment. All of the village elders were seated at one long table in the church room and there stood Carl. He says he was as scared as any kid could be, but tried hard not to let on just how really scared he was.

"For a year or so," Carl said, "I'd been going by the shoemaker's shop every day after school let out, thinking maybe when classes were over for me, I'd like to work with him and learn the shoemaking trade. The elders sometimes asked new workers if they had a preference where they would like to work. I was all set to give the shoe shop as my first choice.

"Well, right at the time, the First World War was on and the local mills had a big order, a contract with the government to furnish wool blankets to the United States Army. The mills were pushing hard to meet the contract date; they couldn't collect their money until they filled the order. All new workers were being sent to the mills and that's where I went.

"I never said a word—it was unheard of for anyone to protest or refuse to go where he was assigned. I was too young to work in a factory but once I was at the mill, I found out there were others working there who were also underage. Whenever a government inspector came on the premises, all of us young guys had to hide. We ducked quick down behind looms or yarn carts or whatever was handy."

Carl's initiation into the working ranks of the community turned out okay, though. When the contract was met, he got his chance to work with the shoemaker.

When I was in the third and fourth grades, summer school lasted only half a day. We went in the morning. After 1932, there was no more summer school and that meant no more English lessons at least for a while. That may sound unusual, but in Amana, it wasn't. School was the only place the children heard or used any English words. German was the only language spoken at home, church or on the job in any of the villages.

Even after reorganization in 1932 when more and more of our classes were taught in English, the continual switching back and forth between German and English became more noticeable and more difficult, at least for me.

When I was on the job in Cedar Rapids, I spoke nothing but English, but in our home, Helen and I spoke nothing but German. More and more English-speaking people were coming to Amana and to our home in the late 1940's and early 1950's and it became very apparent that we needed to know and to use more English. But the one thing that made the biggest impression on us was having our first child, Donna, start school. She had a very limited English vocabulary—"Please," "Thank you," and "Good morning," was the extent of it. As parents, we realized we had to make some changes for the sake of our children—we had Kandyce by then. Like many others in Amana, we had had a radio in our home for years but radio had never made the impact on the language in Amana that television did. Television brought in English-speaking voices like radio did, but right along with the voices, it brought pictures right into our living rooms. Television made English lessons quick and painless for children and adults alike.

We still converse in German with friends and relatives because it is still their way of speaking.

The mix of the English and German languages has left most Amana people who are over forty years old with a slight accent or dialect. The German which was and is spoken here is not pure, academic German, but it is a mix of conversational German that was used in various provinces of Germany. Over the years it has come to be called "Colony Deutsche" (Colony German).

When your children are in school, it is natural to make comparisons between their schooling and your own. The one thing in particular that I noticed was how much our children liked school. They really seemed excited about going to school.

Well, back when I was in school, I wasn't all that happy to be there, where I had to "sit still" and "be quiet." I felt tied to my desk. I wasn't the only one. Many of the other boys felt that way, too. The only thing we really liked about school was recess—playtime.

In some ways, our school was an extension of church. Both places drummed it into our heads to always be polite, courteous, neat, clean, honest, cheerful, truthful, hard-working and so on. All of those things and more were, as I understand it, taken from a set of church rules.

Recess gave us a break during the school days, and Christmas and Easter gave us two big breaks in the school year. A kid's life was pretty much school-church-chores so the holidays were special to us because they changed our daily routines and gave us other things to enjoy, like the foods which were and are such an important part of celebrating anything in Amana. The days and weeks before Christmas all we could smell was the sweet, spicy cookies, Yule breads and fruitcakes being baked.

At school, classrooms were decked with crepe paper streamers which swagged in from the sides and corners of a room to converge at the center above a huge, expandable, red paper bell. For us kids, Christmas wasn't Christmas until that fragile, old, tissue paper bell was carefully unfolded and hung in its place.

Homemade fresh green wreaths on the front doors of the homes were the only outside signs of Christmas, but inside, every family had some kind of Christmas tree. It might have been a small pine, spruce or cedar cut in the woods or it might have been a scraggly, wispy, artificial tree. Other trees were contrived by sticking fresh evergreen branches into holes drilled in an upright post which was fastened to a wooden base. Ropes of tinsel and popcorn were draped around the tree, dodging candles and hand-cut paper snowflakes. The little, finger-size multi-colored candles were burned a few minutes each evening for several days starting with Christmas Eve. And though I never heard of any fires having been caused by the candles, I'll bet the grownups all held their breath the whole time the candles burned for fear the whole tree and the whole house would go up in flames.

Christmas services at church were important, too, but probably not as important to the children as Santa Claus. We hung our stockings on Christmas Eve and then rushed downstairs the next morning to see what Santa had left us. There'd be candy, bright colored *Kandel-zucker,* rock candy, nuts and maybe an orange or a banana. Oranges and bananas were popular stocking stuffers because they were such rare treats in Amana. They came from such far, far away places where it was hot and sunny. Anything that wasn't home-grown or homemade was a treat.

If we got a package, a real, wrapped-up gift, it was sure to be something useful, something we needed—a new coat, a dress or a shirt. Helen says she received a new blanket for her bed one Christmas and that was considered a suitable gift for a child. And once I got a bike, but then, most boys got a bike for Christmas after 1932. After our parents were able to get out and away from Amana more, they saw what other children had and they got the idea that children in Amana should have some of the same things. Having a new bike was great, but it wasn't as much of a thrill to me as getting a radio a few years later.

I don't think there was anyone in Amana, young and old alike, who didn't think Christmas was the best day of the whole year. I could see that my parents and grandparents looked forward to it just as much as the children did. They were a little more relaxed. It wasn't a change that lasted. The next day, the day after Christmas, everything was back to rigid and strict again. Once the day itself was over, the Christmas spirit evaporated pretty fast.

Easter didn't quite match the happy anticipation and excitement that went with Christmas, but it came close. Easter gave the children something to look forward to during the long winter months. Easter week was ram-jam crammed with extra church services every noon and every evening. Very little meat was served with any meals in observance of the six weeks of Lent, and Good Friday was a day of fasting. Come Easter Sunday dinner, the kitchen staff cooked up a big splurge. There'd be ham, roast beef, pies, cakes—the works.

Amana children thought sure as the world there was an Easter Bunny. They believed in the Easter Bunny at Easter just as surely as they believed in Santa Claus at Christmas. Kitchen staffs nurtured those fantasies by staying up until all hours of the night for days ahead of Easter dying and hand decorating hard-boiled eggs by the crate and baking and decorating *Oster Hasse,* Easter Bunny, cookies by the dozens. Three different sizes of cooky cutters were made by the tinsmith from "baker's tin," a heavy metal which was polished to look like chrome. The cutters were shaped to look like running, leaping and sitting rabbits and they ranged from four to eight inches across. After the cookies were baked, they were lightly coated with a powdered sugar frosting and then sprinkled with shredded coconut. Raisins were stuck on to mark the bunnies' eyes.

Easter Sunday was strictly a religious day. An egg hunt for the children was not considered appropriate for that holy day. But mid-morning of the day before, on Easter Saturday, women from the kitchen played the Easter Bunny and hid the fancy eggs and cookies down around the barns in nests of clean hay and straw. If it happened to be a spring where Easter came late in April and clumps of new, green grass already dotted the yards, then the bright colorful eggs and white fluffy cookies were nested down in the grass around the houses. Those nests were particularly easy for the children to spot.

Every child had his or her own Easter basket. With basket shops right here in the Colonies, baskets were always plentiful. But our Easter baskets were not toys, they were not to be used when playing. Easter baskets came out of the closet on the evening of Good Friday, ready for the egg hunt the next morning. When the hard-boiled eggs and cookies had all been eaten up, then the empty baskets were put away. Easter baskets were for Easter and Easter only.

Amana Easter eggs are so beautiful, they are almost unreal. They are in the brightest colors—yellow, red, blue, green and purple—all with a rich, marbled effect. Helen showed a box of the dyed eggs to visitors in our shop one Easter and, at first, she had a hard time convincing them the eggs were eggs.

"Those can't be real chicken eggs," one woman said, "I've never seen such gorgeous colors, not even on Easter eggs."

As Helen described how the egg coloring process is done, the woman finally began to believe Helen knew what she was talking about. Helen should know how the eggs were colored; she did it for our children for many years, and did it the old Amana way.

"Dyeing Easter eggs is one long, tedious job the way it is done here," Helen said. "It's not quick and easy, dip the egg in, dip it out and suddenly the egg is all nicely colored. The job is a pain, a real honest-to-goodness pain. I mean it hurts! The eggs have to be dyed when they are hot, HOT!!

"While the eggs boiled, the dye was mixed up, using the powered dyes from woolen mills, the same dyes that were used to dye wool fibers. The dye was mixed with lime to make a sticky paste. I doubt very much if the Food and Drug Administration would approve of the process.

"A hot, hard-boiled egg is taken in the hand and swished quickly through a bowl of the colored paste and then the hot egg is flipped back and forth between the hands. You keep that up until all of the egg shell is thoroughly coated with color. The palm prints of the hands give the eggs their distinctive marbled effect.

"We started with the yellow color first—it is the lightest color—and then worked up through all the other colors to purple, which is the darkest. The dye from the lighter colors might still be on your hands but it would easily be obscured by the darker colors. Your hands were stained for days. The dye just had to wear off."

Just imagine how many dozen eggs the women had to dye if they were to be sure they would have enough so all the children in the village could hunt eggs on Easter Saturday morning and find enough eggs to fill their baskets? Whatever pain it caused the women, I'm sure they thought the eggs were worth it when they saw what a bright spot they were in the children's lives.

Christmas and Easter were happy, pleasant interludes in childhoods that were otherwise day in and day out, dull and generally pretty quiet and routine. We had few pets to play with or to take care of. There were cats galore but cats didn't need taking care of. They took care of themselves by taking care of mice.

A friend of Helen's grandmother came to visit from Kansas City once and brought a little, yellow canary in a cage.

"It was a gift," Helen said, "but it was a gift that wasn't around very long, I'm sorry to say. A cat got the bird."

As kids, we sometimes had to look hard to find ways to keep busy and yet stay out of mischief especially after there was no more summer school. By then, I was too young to have regular work duties but I was too old to play with the younger children. The summer I was nine, two other boys and I hung around the village herdsman, the man in charge of the dairy herd. He "let" us milk a few cows for him every morning and every evening. I think that shows how desperate we were just to have something to do.

Talking about long days, our Sundays were the longest days of any week. On Sunday, no one was allowed to do anything but read. No work of any kind was done other than, of course, kitchen and livestock chores. Even on Sunday, people and animals still had to be fed. Children were not even supposed to play until after the afternoon church service. All we did on Sunday was go to church and eat, and go for walks on nice days.

The watchtower is at the lower left in this view of Middle Amana in the early 1900's. *From* The Amanas Yesterday, *© 1975, The Amana Society.*

6. Old Wine Ways

Wine drinking was a custom Amana settlers brought from Germany, where winemaking and wine drinking had always been part of their everyday lives. The elders viewed excessive use of wine just as they viewed overindulgence in anything. Too much food, too much free time, too much of anything, as far as they were concerned, was bad. Well, except work. That could never be overdone.

I'm told that while some in Amana liked their wine more than others, drunks were not a problem. Wine drinking for refreshment and relaxation was condoned, drunkenness was not. If someone made a habit of drinking too much wine and then couldn't show up for work, that would have been totally unacceptable in Old Amana!

People had ways of using a little wine to turn ordinary duty into a small party. There are still some fellows around who served duty on night watch. They have a lot of stories to tell.

Each village had a watchtower, or designated the roof of the church or another high building as the watchtower. Middle had a tower built just for that purpose. It was a small, square room on stilts that made it more than two stories high. You could get to the room only by climbing a ladder. The watchtower was manned from 9 p.m. to 4 a.m. Men in a village took turns on watch duty. A duty period lasted one full week, seven straight nights out of every month. Most watchmen were from the farm details. Factory workers were exempt from watch duty so as not to disrupt the mill shifts.

A watch team was usually made up of two, three or four guys. They were to overlook the village from their perch and they were also supposed to climb down the ladder and walk every street in the entire village at set intervals throughout the night. Primarily, they were on the look-out for fires, but they were also to take notice of any strangers who might wander inside the Colony perimeters, and that happened every so often. They were also authorized to signal the approach of any potentially dangerous storms, and alert the people to head for the nearest basement or cellar for shelter.

Fires were a serious threat in Amana, especially during winter months when hundreds of wood-burning stoves and heaters were fired up to heat homes, shops, schools and mills. There were "chimney fires," fires that erupted in an attic or on the roof from sparks from the smoke stacks. If they got to the fires soon enough and with enough water, they could usually save the building. In 1924, I think it was, they lost a grain elevator. It burned clear to the ground. Another time, a couple of years earlier, an entire woolen mill was lost. Sometimes they did lose a complete house or barn. Fire was a big scare in the old days, so night watch was, after all, pretty serious business, or it was supposed to be serious business.

Before a man served his first watch duty, he would be schooled in how to sound the appropriate alarms on the town bell, the same bell that called worshipers to church services and called the people to pick up their meals three times a day at the village kitchen. Breakfast call rang at six o'clock in the morning, dinner calls—dinner was at noon—were rung twice, once at half-past eleven and once at half-past twelve. Supper call was at six o'clock in the evening. Those calls were all "regular rings," meaning, the bell clapper beat a steady, back and forth, side to side, "Clang-Clang-Clang-Clang-Clang!" A bell can be rung to give a variety of sounds, depending on the dexterity and rhythm of the tugs on the bell's rope.

The fire alarm ring was called *Sturm*, but it doesn't mean what it sounds like. It means sirens, like "Help!" or "Come fast!" For that ring, the rope was pulled short and fast so the clapper beat against only one side of the bell. What was heard was first a loud "DING!" followed quickly by a soft "ding," and the two sounds ran close together so they came out sounding like one continual ringing, "DING-ding-DING-ding-DING-ding-DING."

When the fire bell rang, every man in the village was to drop whatever he was doing and run to the fire. The towns were all so small, it was easy to see where the fire was. The men followed the crowd and they followed the smoke. It was tough to fight fires without a main water system, but from the first, they did have a small, horse-drawn fire engine with its own manual water pump.

By the time of my childhood, they had a real fire truck, an old International Harvester truck with a fire engine chassis and its own pump, hoses and ladders. That truck served all seven villages.

It was the intention of the elders that watchtower duty be divided among the older men. What actually happened, though, was that when the man in a family, say the father, drew watch duty, he sent one of his sons, usually a teenager, to take the father's turn on night watch. And that's when night watch turned into a party.

Boys that age can somehow always manage to turn any kind of work into some fun and excitement. They didn't mind losing a little sleep, they liked being out at night and they were willing to take a few chances and pull a few pranks on each other. At the same time they were cutting up, they felt perfectly safe. They were performing a vital service to the community, doing an honorable duty by being on night watch. They were confident no one would get after them for any of their stunts.

Night watch meant plenty of eats. That was another reason teenagers didn't mind filling in for their fathers on night watch. Kids that age are always hungry. The kitchen sent the watch team an extra meal, a late supper. It was a full meal, not just sandwiches or a snack. Steak and fried potatoes were a big favorite, topped off with a slice of pie or a piece of cake. Along with supper came a little extra wine.

Food and wine, that will draw a crowd every time. At least it did in Old Amana. The way the young guys saw it, if a friend had watch duty, it was your duty to make his job less of a burden by keeping him company on the job. That was the excuse used by other teenage boys to get out of the house at night, but what they really wanted was to get to the watchtower and get in on some food and wine and stir up a little bit of fun or trouble. Watch crews even played cards while they were on duty and card playing in Old Amana was definitely, most definitely, out. There weren't even supposed to be any cards in Amana, but they had them. They played a few hands while they ate the food and drank the wine. They really thought they were living it up.

One of the best stories I have heard about night watch happened on a cool November night, cool enough so a fire had to be built in the tiny, little heater in the tower. Unbeknown to the watch duty crew, a couple of their buddies had climbed the tower ladder carrying another ladder so they could get on top of the tower roof. They covered the top of the chimney with a piece of metal, and then left. Smoke filled the watchtower room and drove out the workers, coughing and sputtering. Their eyes were watering. They were sick, and they were mad! Their friends, the pranksters, hid behind a building to watch all the commotion they had caused. To them, it was one hilarious night.

7. Geimeindschaftlicher Wein

Talking about Old Amana winemaking is really talking about two kinds of wine—community wine and family wine. Both were made the old country way, the German way, by mixing juice with water and sugar and letting them ferment together. One was community approved and one was not. Not only was community wine approved by community elders, they made the *weinmeister*, vineyard overseer, responsible for growing the grapes, making the wine each year, and also for seeing to it that all adults in the village received their fair share of the wine.

Making wine at home for the family's own use was not in accordance with the rules of the community. It may not have been approved, but family wine was very much present in Old Amana.

Geimeindschaftlicher wein, community wine, was nearly all made from the grapes from the village vineyard. Only a few grapes from the vines that grew on home trellises went into wine. Like all projects in Amana, community wine was from start to finish a community-wide endeavor. The Colonies bought the vines, and the vines were raised on land owned by the Colonies. The elders of each Colony assigned workers to tend the vines, to harvest and process the grapes into wine and to oversee the distribution of finished wine to the members.

Community is the literal English translation for the German word *geimeindschaftlich*, but it is one of the German words that means much more than the English word for it. *Geimeindschaftlich* means that each person in a group of people has exactly the same rights. It means that what is here is for all. The English word "community" doesn't cover all of that in its meaning.

Verteilt, divide, was another word used a lot in Amana. All goods and materials were to be divided equally among all members. *Verteilt* applied to the jobs that individuals performed, where they lived, what they wore, what they ate, right down to the wine they drank. Every adult man—boys as young as fourteen and who were no longer in school but held an assigned work detail were considered adults—and every adult woman over eighteen received a wine allotment. It was called a wine ration. A wine ration was one of the assumed privileges of the Colonies. Everyone worked for the good of the community, for the good of everyone else in that community. Therefore, everyone was entitled to his or her share of the results of the work and that included community wine.

Wine drinking was seen as neither a virtue nor a vice but rather as an accepted part of life. The Bible has many references to wine. Wine is part of the rituals and ceremonies in most religions. The Amana church used wine only for its annual *Liebesmahl*, love feast, a communion service. Before the turn of the century, it became an every-other-year celebration.

The pageant of the Lord's Supper, *Liebesmahl*, is the holiest of the Amana church services. It is a lengthy observance. It took more than one Sunday to conduct the services for all adult members of each village church. Members were served communion according to their place in the community, elders were first and they were followed by adult men and women who were seated in an order that reflected age, marital status, number of children and other considerations. On *Liebesmahl* Sunday, church services lasted all day, broken only by a brief recess for lunch.

The service varied slightly from village to village. In West, where Helen's grandfather was an elder, they passed plates of bread up and down the benches. The bread was followed by a goblet of wine, wine from the community stock, and everyone drank from that one goblet. When her grandparents died, Helen was given one of the communion goblets used at West. It's only six inches tall, and while it is crystal, it isn't delicate. In fact, it's fairly sturdy and has a bowl the size of a large apple. The bowl is decorated with a pressed design of grape clusters and grape leaves. It doesn't hold much wine so it had to be refilled quite often as it went from person to person, up and down the benches. And, no doubt, some patrons, those who were fond of wine, were inclined to swallow rather than taking the customary sip.

For Middle's *Liebesmahl*, everyone sat at long tables. The men were on one side of the church room and women on the other, just as they always were for regular church services. Everyone in a group shared one wine goblet. Usually there were four people in a group, but those who were higher up in the village, elders or crew bosses, sat at tables of only two people.

When the officiating elder gave the signal, everyone was to take a turn having a drink from the goblet. The signal to drink was given several times throughout the service, so, naturally, the little goblets had to be refilled quite often.

The community tried to be as emphatic about the wine dispensation as they were about all other social behavior. The attitude was simply this: if a man worked, he got wine. Even a fourteen-year-old who was doing a man's job as helper to the millwright or blacksmith was entitled to a man's portion of wine. In practice, the kid would sip wine from the communion goblet at church, but it was just understood that he would not drink his wine ration. Rather, he would pass it on to his father or his grandfather, whichever of the two older men liked wine the best.

Now, that's not to say fourteen-year-old boys weren't getting their chances to drink some wine on the sly now and then with other teenagers like themselves. Most of them were, but they weren't drinking a lot and they weren't doing it very often. It was very important, however, that they not be seen drinking wine openly at home. It was important to the adults and to the young men alike. Girls at fourteen also had work duty but wine wasn't issued to them until they were eighteen. Even then, they passed their rations on to the men in the family. Girls didn't sneak around to try their hand at drinking wine like the boys did.

Women more or less accepted the fact wine was not for them. In most families, the men drank the women's share of the wine right along with their own. As Helen was growing up, she never saw a woman drink wine socially.

There are differing accounts as to what constituted a wine ration and how often it was issued. I rely on what *Opa* Schinnerling told me. He was Middle's winemaker. He gave out the wine, so he had to know what was official in Middle. *Opa* said each man was allotted twenty gallons of wine a year and each woman, twelve gallons. That's not to say that's how much wine they drank, that's just saying how much they were entitled to have from the community stock of wine, down in the church cellar. I would say it was fairly certain that anyone who really liked his wine and wanted, say, twice that much, would have had his ways to get it. He might drink his wife's ration, or a son's ration, or he might barter for it in trades with others who didn't care that much for their share of the wine.

The amount of community wine available to be doled out each year was affected by the grape harvest and the rate of spoiling in the fermenting wine. Rations were lowered if there were shortages and increased if there was a bumper grape crop. Those variances may have contributed to the discrepancies heard today regarding the old wine rations.

Opa said he was instructed to set more wine than Middle actually needed in order to allow for any losses due to formulating and fermenting accidents. In a lean year, to make the juice go farther, he stretched it, mixing the formulas weaker in order to come out with an adequate volume of wine. Wine made "light," using only one-third juice to two-thirds water, for instance, wouldn't generate enough alcohol to make a good quality wine. *Opa* would have some barrels in every batch that would turn out better wine than other barrels and he was supposed to draw the wine for the elders from the good barrels. Leaders somehow seem to get preferential treatment over the rest of the people, even in Old Amana.

Opa often felt apologetic about the quality of the "gift wine," another term they used for the wine ration. He would feel sorry if it had a *Stich*, a touch of sour, and was on the verge of turning completely sour and being spoiled. But if that was all he had to give out, he gave it out, and his customers never turned it down.

On the day wine was issued, each household sent an adult member of the family to collect the rations for all adults in that family. In Middle, they trekked to the church basement on wine day carrying pails, jugs, pitchers or flasks. Community wine was never bottled. It ran directly from the barrels into the receptacles each household provided. The person collecting the wine presented the proper number of cards, each one made out in the name of the person due to get wine. When the elders gave out work assignments, they also gave work cards. It was *Opa's* job to punch out the cards and, on his books, to check off the name and the date wine was issued before he turned on the spigot on the wine barrel and filled the jugs. He at least did his part of going through the motions of keeping track of where the wine went and tried to prevent anyone from getting more than his share.

Depending on who you talk to in what village, you hear various claims—that wine day was twice a month, on the first and third Tuesday or that it was twice a month but on the first and third Friday. According to what *Opa* told me, he gave out wine weekly and it was usually on a Friday.

The confusion as to how often and when wine was issued might have stemmed from the fact that workers who did heavy, outdoor labor, were served extra wine. Much like the coffee breaks of today, they had their wine breaks. The boss or manager of a crew picked up the daily wine rations from the wine cellar. The amount of wine he drew was based on the number of men he was to have working for him on that particular day. That meant bosses were coming to the wine cellar six days a week. That little extra wine every day on the job might have been one of the fringe benefits for the workers of Old Amana. It wasn't as though they were sitting around, drinking wine by the glassful. They weren't. Each man dipped his little tin cup only once at each break and that only amounted to an ounce or two of wine.

Workers who ate their noon meals at the community kitchen also got a cup of wine with their meal. Wine the kitchen served was not charged to individual wine rations but came out of the community wine stock.

Factory workers and mill hands did not have wine breaks and they were not allowed to drink wine with their noon meals. Working in the plants wasn't considered as strenuous as working the fields, working with the livestock or on other outdoor assignments. They didn't want plant men to be relaxed or sleepy from a little wine, not when they had to handle fast-moving shuttles, spinning bobbins and other mill machinery.

Supper at home with the family meant, at least for the men, another glass of wine. That serving came from the household's wine allotment.

Opa had another rule and that was: "No one is to be issued more than two gallons of wine at any one time." But like some of the other community rules, it depended on who wanted the rule bent and who had the "say" about breaking rules.

Those with the "say" got what they wanted and that applied to wine rations, too. There were no provisions for enforcing that rule either and I don't know that *Opa* was ever challenged on it. If he was, he kept the incident to himself.

While wine drinking was almost exclusively for men, some women did try to hold back their portion of the household wine ration by putting it in a bottle separate from the rest of the gift wine. They didn't keep it back for themselves. They wanted to have wine on hand so they could offer it to the men guests that might stop in for a visit, such as company from another village or from outside. Women might sip a glass of wine on wash day, particularly in the winter months.

Washing clothes and bed linens was done every Monday. Families with a baby washed as often as two or three times a week. Laundry was done in wash houses, small buildings separated from the main house by just a few feet. The wash house had a small stove, just big enough to hold the boiler used to heat wash water. It didn't put out enough heat to warm even that small building on cold days.

Washing went on all morning. It meant standing on a concrete floor, hands and arms plunged deep in strong, homemade lye soap suds in both hot and cold water, handling wet clothes and getting their own clothes, the clothes the women were wearing, as soaked as the clothes they were washing.

Clothes were hung out to dry, to blow dry, on lines strung on poles beside the wash house. In the winter, the wet clothes froze. They were stiff as boards. They were brought into the main house and were hung near the heaters to finish drying. Freezing got rid of a lot of the wetness in the clothes, so by the time they had thawed out in the house, they were barely damp.

It didn't take them long to finish drying, ready for the next big chore, ironing. It was work to hang the clothes out to freeze, but it was worth it, not just because they then dried faster indoors but because it made them smell so fresh and clean.

There were only two conditions that ever stopped the women from hanging clothes outside—a downpour and a blinding snowstorm. Otherwise, they lugged the big baskets of wet clothes outdoors and clipped them to the lines with wooden clothespins and hoped for a nice breeze to whip them dry.

"In really cold weather, when temperatures were below freezing, the fingers and hands got so cold, they were numb and had no feeling below the elbow," Helen says. "And the wet clothes, they turned to icicles right in your hands, your bare hands!"

Winter wash day was enough to drive the stoutest teetotaler to have a touch of wine to stave off the chills. In fact, it was on a wash day when Helen was about ten years old that she had her first sip of wine. She was helping *Oma* Miller do the laundry during Christmas vacation.

"*Oma* had a little wine," Helen said, "and she gave me just a sip, too. *Oma* said the wine was purely medicinal, that it would make me feel warmer and I wouldn't catch a cold."

8. Making Community Wine

By the 1860's each of the seven villages had established a vineyard. Community-wide winemaking operations took place from about 1860 until Prohibition. Middle's five-acre plot was an oblong patch of land, bounded by fields of corn, alfalfa, wheat, oats or barley. It contained mostly Concord grape vines and a few Sedonia and Clinton varieties.

Bare-root grape seedlings were planted early in the spring in rows 300 to 500 feet long and six feet apart. Posts were sunk along each row and double strands of smooth wire were strung from post to post. When the new vines grew long enough, they were tied to the wire with willow twigs. That was all the care the vineyard needed its first year, other than a few cultivations done with a single horse hitch and a small, walk-behind pronged cultivator. A new patch of grape vines doesn't bear fruit its first year. It takes two years to get the first harvest and more than that before the vines are up to their peak production.

The winemaker was in charge of the vineyard. *Opa* didn't have to do all the work himself. He could call for extra hands in the spring for pruning and tying, in the fall for picking and then again later in the fall for clean-up. Every man who held a wine card was responsible for tending at least thirty grape vines each season in exchange for the wine he received from the community stock.

Grape harvest came late in August or the first week in September. That seems early compared to the late September and early October grape harvests now, but the Iowa climate and soil made grapes ripen faster and earlier.

Grape harvest in an Amana village was an all-out event. It was work but it was a social event, too. When the village winemaker said the grapes were ready, he put out the call: "*Morge wehre die Traube abgeschnitte*!" "Tomorrow we pick the grapes!"

Word spread quickly through the village. School was dismissed. Mills shut down. Shops were closed. By the next morning, picking and hauling crews were lined up and ready to go. All activity was stopped for one day to pick grapes. To get the grapes picked and headed toward the wine barrel in one day took everyone's help.

It was a fun day. The kitchen workers packed lunches and took them right out to the vineyard in big baskets. Everyone sat on the grass at the edge of the field to eat—it was one big picnic. Eating a meal outdoors was unheard of in Old Amana. It only happened on grape-picking day.

In the vineyard, it was a day-long battle with the bees and wasps. The insects love nice, juicy, ripe grapes. They swarmed in, punctured the grape skins, sucked out the juice and stung any picker who got in the way. Pickers fought with their hats and bonnets and a few choice German cusswords. They didn't want to be stung, but just as importantly, they didn't want the bees and wasps to steal the precious grape juice. The next day, pickers nursed a few backaches brought on by stooping over and craning their necks to find the grape clusters which were hidden up under the thick leaves.

Men and women worked together, one on each side of a row, snipping the clusters with clippers and then gently piling them in wicker baskets. Low, flat-bed wagons waited at the ends of the rows to haul the filled baskets to the press house.

Middle's press house was a one-story, clapboard building on a concrete floor. It had 2,500 square feet of room. It was adjacent to the church building where the wine would eventually be formulated and fermented in the basement. Extra help was needed to work at the press house on grape-picking day. It took strong arms and backs to unload the grapes and crank them through the crusher while they were still fresh and then get the lightly crushed pulp immediately into the press to extract the first-run juice.

From first-run juice, they made first-run wine. About sixty percent of all the community wine was made from first-run juice. First-run wine had a fairly low alcoholic content. It might have gone as low as eight or nine percent alcohol. An alcoholic content that low placed first-run wine at a somewhat greater spoilage risk. But it had a lighter, clearer color and was much sweeter than the second- and third-run wines and many people preferred it.

After the first-run juice was drawn, the crushed and pressed grape pulp pre-fermented. It stood four to five days to draw out all the juice and to put all the naturally-occurring sugars and yeasts into solution. They became part of the pre-fermenting action. During the standing time, the dark blue skins of the grapes released color pigments into the pulp, lending much more color to the second- and third-run juices which in turn added to the color of second- and third-run wine. Second-run wine had noticeably more substance, texture and body than first-run wine. Its alcoholic content was higher and would be approximately twelve percent, considerably higher than that of first-run wine.

From the third, last and hardest pressing came the very last drops of juice they could get out of the pulp. Third-run juice was rich and thick. From it, they made

Drester wine. *Drester* wine was the driest, least sweet, of the community wines. It had the darkest color and the thickest body, and its alcoholic content was the highest of the three wines. Sometimes it went as high as fourteen percent. The real wine drinkers, those who wanted all they could get from a wine, went for the *Drester* wine. They considered it to be the very best of the old Colony wines.

The grapes were crushed with an old crusher that was very much like my first old crusher except that it was much larger. It, too, was made entirely of wood. It stood three feet tall. It had fatter, longer and heavier rollers than my little crusher. It was big enough to handle the grapes just as fast as they were dumped into the hopper. Two men turned the cranks on opposite ends of the crusher. The rollers were kept spinning constantly, sending the grapes through the fat, grooved and notched rollers in one fast and easy whirl. The mangled grapes fell into a sloping trough that fed them down into a huge wooden vat. In later years, a small gasoline engine was used to crank the crusher.

The next part of the process—moving the crushed grapes into the press without losing any of the juice—sounds like a pretty tricky and pretty messy maneuver. Middle's first old press was, of course, wooden, and it was square. Can you beat that? A square press! Carl Metz says it was about four feet square and was made by the village cooper. Narrow oak slats were fitted and grooved so they fit snugly together and the bottom of the press was like a shallow drawer. It slid in and out.

One side of the press was swung aside, the tray was slid out, a gunny sack was laid over the tray's slatted bottom and grape pulp was dipped out of the vats with wooden buckets and very carefully spread out in an eight-inch layer over the sack. They put another sack on top of the pulp and piled on more pulp until they had a stack four feet high on half of the tray. The tray was eight feet long, but the press was only four feet wide, so they did only half of the tray at one time.

They slipped the full half of the tray into the press very easily, being careful not to topple the whole stack over, although the gunny sacks did help stabilize it. Then they closed the side of the press and slowly lowered the top of the press. It was made of two thicknesses of heavy plank. It was fairly heavy all by itself. Even without screwing down the jack, juice started running out the bottom of the press right away. That was the first-run juice, the juice the grapes gave up easily with hardly any pressure from the press. They wanted first-run juice to barely drip and ooze out naturally.

While the first half of the tray dripped, they loaded the other half, the side that extended beyond the press. When the first side quit dripping, the sides of the press were opened, the press top was released and the first side of the tray was shoved on through, on out the other side of the press. The second side of the tray was then in position to be pressed after the sides of the press were locked back in place and the top lowered so dripping could resume.

To unload the trays and get the pulp into a vat to pre-ferment, two men, each one taking hold of the gunny sacks at the corners, gave one quick flip and flipped the pulp off the sack and into a vat. Carl said it wasn't as messy as it sounds and it was a fast and efficient way to unload the tray. And they had to work fast. They went through that whole business of the trays, the grape pulp and the sacks for an entire crop of grapes, all just to get that first-run juice.

The vats of lightly pressed grape pulp then sat and pre-fermented four or five days before the pulp was bucketed back into the press for the second and third runs of juice. In the meantime, the winemaker formulated the first-run juice and got that set to fermenting. Each run of juice was kept separate from the others from start to finish. From juice to wine, each juice was mixed, fermented and racked separately. I often wondered how they kept it all straight.

I also wondered how they got the juice from the press house over to the church basement where it fermented and was stored until it was dispensed. Moving the juice was a cinch. Juice was poured down a drain in the press house, went into an underground tile, free-flowed through the tile and was caught by vats in the church basement. It was all very neat and simple.

I've heard it said that some community wine was made by the standard winemaking method by using grape juice alone, with no sugar and water added. Without written records, there's no way of knowing for sure. *Opa* only made wine the old way, with sugar and water, the same way I make wine. His sugar stock was stored in the church basement in small, wooden barrels.

Once *Opa* had formulated the juice, sugar and water, the mixture was ready to go into the big barrels. It was moved with the aid of a small hand pump. That pump was the only labor-saving device *Opa* had, but it did make the last step of his processing the easiest. Pressing was the hardest part. It was physically demanding because of the large amounts of grapes being pressed and also because of the size of the press. The press was hand-operated. Pressure was exerted by a dual ratchet-type pair of jacks set on top of the planked press board. A long, steel lever which stuck out from the ratchet was used to turn the jack screws, forcing the press board down on the grapes. Two of the biggest, strongest men in the village manned that lever. One man alone could never have screwed the jack down to the last notch. Even with two men, they had to put everything they had into it until they were red in the face, getting every last drop of thick, heavy, dark purple juice out of the grapes.

That press had a five-ton capacity, so it took lots of manpower and lots of muscle to take the pressure to a peak. My first little old press wasn't nearly that big, and couldn't handle nearly that much pressure. It was a one-man press and it left me weak by the time I had it screwed down tight. Whew! It tires me just to think about it.

In a good year, Middle's five-acre plot yielded more than 40,000 pounds of grapes. They got, on the average, eight gallons of juice for every hundred pounds of grapes, a total of around 3,200 gallons of grape juice from all three juice runs.

Some may talk about how many gallons of juice there are in a bushel of grapes but that doesn't take into consideration the size of the baskets they used in Amana. They picked grapes in Amana-made willow baskets. They were larger and they held more than a standard bushel. I feel it's more accurate to express the amount in pounds rather than by the bushel basket.

From 3,200 gallons of juice, they made more than 6,000 gallons, probably closer to 6,500 gallons of wine. That sounds like a lot of wine for one village but let me use some round figures to show how that comes out pretty close to what was needed each year just for Middle.

I'll use the figure 200 for Middle's adult population back then. Half were men who got twenty gallons of wine each year. Half were women who got twelve gallons of wine each year. That meant they needed 2,000 gallons of wine for the men, 1,200 gallons for the women and that made a total of 3,200 gallons of wine just for regular yearly wine rations.

I'll add in the two daily wine breaks for each farm worker, cattleman, dairyman, outside worker, hand worker, butcher, baker and the other shop crews. Middle had a small number of workers in these categories because most of the men here worked at the woolen mill. I'll make that figure on the low side and say only forty of Middle's workers were entitled to a wine break. That wine was picked up daily at the community wine cellar by the crew bosses and was taken in gallon pails directly to the men on the job. They counted on getting forty two-ounce mug dips out of each pail of wine and that amounts to another 700 gallons of wine each year.

I mustn't forget communion wine for church and wine served at the community kitchen. That was another three or four hundred gallons a year. Allowing for some population fluctuations and personal changes in wine drinking, the men and women of Middle had to have been drinking around 4,000 gallons of wine each year. *Opa* aimed to set 6,000 gallons of new wine each fall but he said he felt more comfortable when he had 6,500 gallons of new wine working. He liked to have that much of a margin to allow for any losses.

He had more than that amount of wine in the church basement at any one time, of course, depending on the time of the year. By fall, there was the new batch, 6,000 to 6,500 gallons. In addition, the wine set the year before—the wine currently being issued—would be down to half, say 3,000 gallons. I wish *Opa* had written this all down. It seems to me that he had to have close to 10,000 gallons of wine on hand most of the time just to take care of this one village.

In a bumper year, *Opa* set all the wine he had barrels for, trying to get ahead in case the next year's crop of grapes ran short.

From my own experience with wine formulas, I know both the sweetness of the juice and the acidity of the juice affect what liberties can be taken in formulating and still produce good wine. I have the ranges written down. They have been accepted and approved, and by sticking to those figures, I know my wines will turn out great. *Opa* and the other village winemakers had nothing in writing. They went by what they could remember. They used trial and error and hoped for the best. Community winemaking was trusted to those who seemed to have a knack for tasting, sniffing and evaluating the juice. Eventually those few gained enough experience and judgment to turn out reasonably good wine batch after batch and year after year.

Since the wine they made was only for private consumption, they did not have to have their formulas approved by any governmental agencies, have a license or be inspected. They didn't bother keeping records, not even for their own information. As far as I am concerned, records are a key to making good wine. Keeping track of what is done, how much is put in, when it is put in, how long it ferments, all of those things and more, leads to standardization and uniformity in wine. But in the old days, they couldn't be bothered. They didn't have to take the time to write it down, so they didn't.

Winemaking amounts and directions were passed along word of mouth and with very little scientific understanding regarding the effect of fermentation temperatures and the length of fermentation. At times their results were somewhat uncertain. Then there were those "lucky accidents" when the wine would be noticeably improved. Then the winemaker would be scratching his head, trying to remember what he'd done to that particular barrel. When he thought he had it figured out, he guarded his information like it was a big trade secret instead of sharing what he had learned so other winemakers could benefit, too.

And, of course, rather than a lucky accident, there were unexplained disasters where a whole barrel of wine was lost. If wine goes bad, the whole barrel goes bad. There's no such thing as part of a barrel being good and the rest, well, questionable. If it is bad, it is all bad. If they lost one of the 2,000-gallon barrels, that was a big loss.

Middle had six or eight of the 2,000-gallon barrels. They also had several 400-and 200-gallon barrels. The smaller barrels were necessary in order to make the three different wines from the three juice runs. All of the barrels were used over and over. Keeping them in use was the best way to keep them tight so they didn't leak. They had to be cleaned between uses. Sometime during the late summer, well ahead of grape-picking day, a barrel cleaning crew was called up. The winemaker was authorized to recruit help for the job. Part of the crew handled the water hoses and brushes on the outside of the barrels and part of them, the skinny ones, wiggled their way through the big bung hole and got inside the barrels. They put on hip-high, rubber boots and with stiff push brooms and buckets of warm water, they gave the insides a good scrubbing. Water for barrel cleaning was heated on a little stove in the basement. After the barrels were brushed with the warm water to loosen the old wine settlings, they were rinsed out by sloshing buckets of cold water around inside the barrels. They aimed to get rid of every fleck of old yeast and pulp so there would be none of it to contaminate the fresh, new wine.

Who'd think barrel cleaning would have been a popular job? From what I've heard, it was. There were even volunteers for the job, volunteers hoping to collect a few dividends on the side. The work was done in the wine cellar, right beside the year-old, finished wine. Of couse, that new wine needed to be sampled, right? If there was any wine, any drinkable wine, left in the barrels being cleaned, that couldn't be wasted. That had to be polished off, too, right?

The skinny guy, the one inside the barrel, was on his honor not to drink all the leftover wine. He was to bail it out by the cupful to the rest of the crew. By the end of the job, the barrels were being cleaned by a happy and relaxed crew.

One woman in the village complained to her women friends because her husband's name was always called for barrel cleaning. Well, her husband was one of the volunteers. He wanted the duty. He was small enough to get inside the barrel and that was the best part of the job. He wasn't one to pass up a little extra wine for a little extra work—he wouldn't shirk his duty. By the time he went home at the end of the day, he was feeling pretty good, but his wife was very understanding. She blamed his tipsy condition on all the wine fumes he inhaled while he was inside the barrel.

Every other year, a barrel was supposed to be completely dismantled, each stave removed and scrubbed in every groove and ridge. Then the cooper came to the basement and reassembled the cleaned barrels. New barrels were carried down into the basement in pieces. If they'd been put together, they would have been much too large to carry through the cellar door. The 2,000-gallon barrels had to be laid on their sides and even laying down, they were eight and a half to ten feet tall.

After Prohibition when they no longer made community wine here, those old barrels stood empty, and of course they dried out. The staves shrank and pulled out of place. Eventually the barrels collapsed, fell apart, crumpled down on themselves and lay in heaps. The boards were hauled out and junked. It was a crime to let the barrels, press and other wooden equipment go. It is too bad it couldn't have been preserved and made into a complete winery museum along with the other old-time displays in Amana.

The same day the vineyard was plucked clean of its grapes, wagons passed up and down village streets collecting baskets of grapes women and children had picked from vines on the sides of the homes. A few baskets went to the press house and the rest were dropped off at the community kitchen and went into jam and jelly.

In the fall, after a killing frost and after the grape leaves had dropped, the vines were released from the trellis wires and bundled together so they lay flat on the ground. They were "put to bed" for the winter under thick, deep blankets of blue grass cuttings. The cuttings weren't packed down but were lightly pitched over the vines to provide a deep insulation with little weight.

In the early spring, when patches of snow still dappled the nooks and crannies of the north side of the hills, the vines were uncovered and pruned to leave only a few main canes on each trunk. Pruning scraps were piled in a corner of the vineyard and burned. The remaining canes, the second-year canes, were retied to the support wire. That job had to be done at the start of each growing season and it took hundreds and thousands of six-inch willow twigs. Cutting the twigs was a job for children old enough to safely handle a pair of blunt-nosed clippers. They gathered the thinnest, littlest twigs, stripped them of any tiny, new leaf sprouts that may have emerged and soaked the twigs in pails of water. The twigs needed to soak at least overnight, but they could soak longer without any harm. The pails of twigs were taken to the vineyard when it was time to use them, so they stayed moist, soft and pliable right up to the second they were tied. Willow cuttings were surprisingly strong yet they were supple and gentle. Once they were knotted firmly around the vines, holding them to the wire, they stayed in place for an entire season without skinning the bark or breaking the vine.

Youngsters who cut twigs in the spring or picked grapes in the fall didn't know about wine yet, but they sure knew about the sweet, delicious grape juice. They found excuses to stop by the press house and have a few cups of that refreshing juice fresh out of the press.

The men of the village kept a close watch on the press house, too. They weren't after any grape juice. They were there to get *Opa's* predictions on next year's wine—how much there would be, and whether it was likely to be a great year, a good year, an ordinary year or a less than ordinary year. They liked to keep abreast of the wine supply and its quality. The press house was a popular place for a few days each fall. It did double duty later in the fall. After the grapes were processed and the wine set, the crop from Middle's two apple orchards was picked. One orchard was at the northeast corner of the village. The other, just to the west, was between the large kitchen garden and the vineyard. *Opa* was in charge of the orchards as well as the vineyard.

The two orchards produced ten different kinds of apples from 100 to 125 trees. Most of the apples were picked and delivered to the kitchen to be sorted and stored in barrels in the basement or to be dried or to be made into preserves or canned. Dried apple slices were reconstituted with water and cooked with sugar to make applesauce, a favorite winter dessert. Late ripening apples went to the press house and were put through the same crusher and press that was used with the grapes. Some of the apple juice was used fresh and some was made into cider.

Mama remembers making *ladwerg*, apple butter.

"It was the hottest and most tiring kitchen job," she said. "The fruit sauce had to cook down and thicken very slowly. That took a long time over very low heat. All the time it cooked, it had to be stirred with a wooden spoon. The spoon had to keep moving so the apple butter wouldn't stick and scorch on the bottom of the pot."

Knowing how good the *ladwerg* would taste on warm, buttered bread, the cooks kept stirring.

9. Hinterlistiger Wein

Hinterlistiger wein, behind-the-back or on-the-sly wine, was the other side of winemaking in Old Amana. *Geimeindschaftlicher wein*, community wine, was always made from grapes but *hinterlistiger wein* was not.

If the Colony's rules had been strictly interpreted and enforced, *hinterlistiger wein* would never have existed. It could not have been made. But it was. Jars, crocks and even small barrels of it fermented in the cellars of many Amana homes. Those old family wines were as much a part of wine in Old Amana as was the community wine.

Family wines and community wine were made by the same method, by adding sugar and water to fresh juice. And though it was winemaking on a much smaller scale (they made only a gallon or two of some of the wines), it produced what was considered good to excellent quality wine. Many claimed they preferred it to the community grape wine. *Piestengel* was by far the most popular and the most common of the homemade wines.

The official attitude of the village elders was that only the "gift wine" was allowed but they did "forgive" the making of black currant, elderberry or wild grape wines for "medicinal purposes." Eventually they had to "overlook" the uncounted barrels of rhubarb wine that village basements harbored.

Yet every spring the elders went through the same old rigmarole that "rhubarb plants must be dug out and destroyed." They pretended to go through the motion of trying to stamp out the rhubarb wine by stamping out the rhubarb plants. But it wasn't all that easy to shut off that wine. It had become a village standby.

It had long been a habit in Amana homes to have a little bit of *Piestengel* on hand. Sure they got the "gift wine," the wine rations. But for some of them the "gift wine" wasn't enough, and for others it wasn't as good as their own *Piestengel.* It wasn't like it is today, where if you don't like one kind of wine, you just go to the liquor store and buy another kind or another brand. They had no money to buy wine, and wine wasn't one of the items they could sign for at the general store as they would sign for a new pair of shoes. If they wanted to give a gift to someone or wanted to pay back a friend for doing them a favor, they did it with a bottle of homemade wine. Back in the old days, wine was a "Thank You." It was a reward, a gratuity, and it served a purpose. Besides, they just plain liked it. No way were they about to give up making a little extra wine on the sly.

"On the sly" was an expression used for a lot of things in Old Amana, things which were done, as they said, "openly in secret." They would appear to comply with the elders when the "no rhubarb" directive was put out. They dug out a few plants all right, but they made sure they left two or three rhubarb plants, just enough so they could still make twenty gallons of *Piestengel.*

The story is told about one Middle resident who kept saving back more and more of his rhubarb plants each year until it got to the point that the elders simply could not ignore his patch any longer. He was called before the elders, the *Brudderrath.* If the *Brudderrath* felt a point could be made to the whole village by making an example of one offender, that's what they did. They had decided to get their message across to every rhubarb fancier in Middle by coming down hard on that one man. Going before the *Brudderrath* wasn't anything at all like being in court. It just meant he had to go stand up before the elders in their regular meeting room at the church.

"Do you have rhubarb in your yard?" they asked.

"Yes," he said.

"Chop it out!" they ordered.

A little later one of the elders noticed that the man still had a yardful of rhubarb, so he was called back before the elders.

"Do you have rhubarb?" they asked him again.

And again, he said he did.

"Even after we told you to hoe it out?" they asked.

And the man answered, "I hoed it and hoed it but the more I hoe, the better the rhubarb grows."

The elders saw they had a problem. They put their heads together and came up with another idea.

"If hoeing doesn't get rid of it," they said, "we'll put some kerosene on it."

The man stood up and said "NO! No kerosene in my garden!" He was really bristling. He meant every word he said.

And that ended it. That was the end of the discussion. That would have been going too far. It would have been stepping on too many toes and the elders took some pains not to step on too many toes. Pouring kerosene on *anybody's* rhubarb plants would have polluted the soil and would have had the whole village in an uproar. The people of the village, after all, elected the elders, so naturally, the elders recognized they had gone as far as they could on the problem. They "solved" it by avoiding any drastic action.

Then there was another man who had lots of rhubarb. He was reported to the elders and they told him to dig out his rhubarb plants. He agreed and he went home and dug them up. He dug them up, all right. He dug them up from one spot in his garden and replanted them in another spot.

When he was questioned by the elders, he said, "You told me to dig them up and I did." Nothing had been said about transplanting, so he hadn't done anything wrong, not in his mind. When it came to protecting the rhubarb, they had all the answers.

The druggist claimed he had to keep at least one rhubarb plant so he could make certain medicines. One fellow commented, "He likes his medicine fermented."

Despite the elders' annual anti-rhubarb campaign, rhubarb wine remained a fixture in the villages. Since they needed sugar to make on-the-sly family wines, they had to be a little devious in getting the sugar. All cooking and baking was done either at the village kitchen or bakery. Very little sugar was allotted for home use, to sweeten coffee or tea. I have never been able to get anyone to be very specific about how they managed to get the sugar. Maybe they said they wanted extra sugar to bake a cake or cookies or to make jelly or jam for a gift or to make Christmas candy. Some may have gone so far as to "borrow" sugar from the community kitchen.

On-the-sly wines were made by those who wanted them badly enough that they were willing to take the risk involved in making them. They weren't selfish with their wines. They shared them with family and friends, but the sharing stopped short of giving away any personal secrets on how the wines were made. They were made mostly by men, down in the cellar, although the few women who did get into winemaking at home were often the expert winemakers. Women may have been more particular about cleaning the crocks and barrels. They may have paid closer attention to measuring and to watching the calendar, so they knew what to do when, and knew how well fermentation was progressing.

It wasn't easy to make wine on the sly. In a way, it was kind of tough. If they were good at it, it was a skill and a talent they didn't care to advertise. They couldn't go around bragging about their wonderful wines, the wines they weren't supposed to be making in the first place. By hiding the fact that they made wine at home, they also had to hide whatever success they had with the wine—it was a double whammy! Of course, their family and close friends knew what they were up to. And, if the wine should flop, no one had to know.

Like community wine, secret family wine was not made from a recipe. No records were kept on how much juice, water and sugar went into a wine or how long the wine fermented. All spring and summer, fruits and vegetables were gathered from the garden and the timber. When enough juice and sugar had been saved up, a small batch of wine could be started. It was stirred up and set down in a dark corner of the cellar. Then the winemaker just hoped for the best. Winemakers with the best memories, those who remembered from one year to the next the proportions of juice, water and sugar they had combined and how long they let it ferment, were the ones most likely to have good results with their wines. There's an old saying, "A winemaker's memory is his greatest asset." It's true.

Making on-the-sly wine tested their memory and their ingenuity. Wine had to be made without benefit of regular winemaking equipment or kitchen utensils. None of the homes had fully equipped kitchens then. They had no money to order utensils and the village store didn't stock such items. They used table knives and forks or they "borrowed" wooden mallets and potato mashers from the community kitchen—anything to get the juice oozing out so fermentation could be started. Lack of equipment, no doubt, explains why almost all of the homemade wines were usually fermented in the pulp.

Once the outer skins were ruptured so juice could ooze out, fermentation could be started. They seldom pressed the pulp, but set the pulp in the same kind of heavy crocks and stone jars used to make pickles and sauerkraut. A few families had the cooper make ten- and twenty-gallon barrels for them so they could make larger batches of *Piestengel.* That put the cooper in on making the secret wines, too. Once they took the chance to have a small barrel made, they kept it busy, and often didn't take the time to give the barrel a good cleaning between uses. After a while, the barrels actually caused spoilage in the wine and with a few disappointments like that, they improved their sanitation habits.

If someone in a household was into winemaking, really into it, that household had several batches of wine going at a time. Rhubarb was set in May and others were started through the summer and fall. Staggering the starts that way, they were less likely to ever run out of wine.

After the lilac bushes were blooming in mid-May, they checked the rhubarb patch just about every day. In a typical spring, with plenty of rain and plenty of warm sunshine, the stalks were ready by the end of the month. Memorial Day was a holiday, and with the mills and factories shut down, the men had a day off. On their day off, they made *Piestengel*, just like I did when I still worked at my regular job.

I should mention that the correct German word for rhubarb is *rabarber. Piestengel* is really a German slang word for rhubarb. It's funny how the slang word has become the accepted word for that wine, not only here in Amana, but for those from around the country who have gotten acquainted with the wine and keep coming back for more.

One woman was tasting the wine in our shop. It was the first time she had ever tried rhubarb wine, only she called it "pie plant."

"You mean you make this wine from the pie plant?" she asked me, and when I said I did, she shook her head as though she still doubted me. But she bought a bottle to take with her because she liked it.

Piestengel had another name in Old Amana. If last year's wine was already gone and they were over-anxious, they drank the new wine too soon—way too soon. On the 4th of July, only a month after it had started fermenting, they gave it a try. There was no way it could have been finished. It would be very evident from the way the wine was still so active, churning up bubbles and all, that it was far from being thoroughly fermented. In that stage, it is cloudy, whitish colored and rather thick. It looked like milk to them, more like skim milk, I would say. But they couldn't wait.

"Let's try a milky way," they'd say. That's what they called the wine at that stage.

Drinking the premature wine was likely to make them very sick to their stomachs and it happened very fast, within an hour. Still they drank it.

Only a few families made wine from wild fruits. The fruits grew in the woods and timbers, often in inaccessible spots. Only a hardy soul would ever go gathering fruits in the wild. Wild grapes climbed the tallest trees and followed their branches out over creek and river banks, always just barely out of reach above the water. Wild blackberries snarled deep in the heart of thick, spiky undergrowth that often was thick with poison ivy and poison oak. Helen tells of the tortures she suffered picking blackberries "one berry at a time." It was slow and tedious and her arms and hands were streaked with scratches.

Large bushes of wild grapes grew next to Middle's toolshed. Each fall, the doctor sent his assistant to pick those grapes. No one else ever touched them. The doctor claimed he had to have the grapes so his assistant could make wild grape wine for the doctor's patients. But the doctor's assistant was puzzled.

"Every year I make the wild grape wine," he said. "Now, I don't drink wine, the doctor says he doesn't drink the wild grape wine, sick people tell me the doctor didn't prescribe wild grape wine for them. Still, the wine is gone. Next year, the doctor tells me again, 'Make more wild grape wine.'"

The doctor's assistant told his story in all seriousness, as though it was a real mystery to him. Then he'd wink.

Wine for a party was a "no-no," except after a wedding. Then it was okay to serve wine. *Hochzeit wein*, wedding wine, was always homemade. It was never community wine. The bridegroom's family furnished it along with homemade beer. Wine took longer to make than beer so families had an eye and an ear open to catch a clue, so they would know if a son was thinking of marriage. They had to plan ahead so they would be sure to have plenty of *hochzeit wein* on hand. If they caught the clue in time, they held back wine for a year or two ahead of the wedding. Two-year-old wine was considered the cream of the home wines, the very best wine they could serve to celebrate a wedding. If the bride and the bridegroom were from different villages, the number of people invited to the post-wedding party doubled. In that case, the bride's family furnished wine and beer, too.

Of course, homemade wedding wine had to be sampled as it fermented to make sure it was on schedule and would be ready in time. At the rate some of them sampled, they were lucky if they had wine left for the wedding. If they did run short, they could always count on their winemaking friends to donate wine from their family stock.

Weddings were held in the church in the bride's village, usually early on a

Saturday afternoon. Saturday was the one day of the week no other regular church services were held. A wedding ceremony was barely distinguishable from any other church service. There were no flowers. The bride did not wear a white bridal gown and veil. She wore a dark print dress, just like the Amana women always wore to church, only the bride's dress would have been brand new. All the women, including the bride, wore a *halztuch*, shoulder cape, a short black *schurze*, apron, and a *versammlung kap*, church cap. The small black, head-hugging caps tied under the chin and were homemade in all sizes and in various styles. A small girl might wear a cap crocheted with fine black cotton thread. Older girls and women wore caps of black silk netting or some other sheer black fabric with tatted or crocheted edgings.

The bridegroom dressed in a dark suit and white shirt, like all the other men in the wedding congregation except that his suit would have been brand new. No rings were exchanged. Amana churches did not have a piano or an organ. The only music was the singing of the bride's favorite hymn.

In the marriage pronouncement, an elder dealt with the couple's individual and joint duties to the union, the church, the community and their families. The couple then received hasty greetings from family and friends at the back of the church before everyone hurried to the community kitchen of the bride's village for lunch. After lunch, the party moved to the home of the bride's parents. That's when the homemade beer and wine were brought forth.

Toasts were not commonly offered in Old Amana, not even after weddings. They had no time for such formality. They got right to the wine. If they bothered to say anything at all, it was "*Prosit*," "Proceed." If they wanted a drink or a refill, they called for "*Schwaps*," which meant a splash or a sip. *Schwaps* is a German slang term for taking a drink.

Wedding parties were well-attended and enjoyed not only for the beer and wine, but for the good food prepared in the kitchen of the bride's village. There were rich butter and sugar cakes, the kind German cooks are famous for, and always there was the one special cake, the couple's cake. It wasn't a traditional tiered cake associated with today's wedding receptions but it was a special cake, one that was baked especially for weddings. Wedding cakes were baked in a special pan. Helen has one of the old pans. It is of "baker's tin" and was made at Homestead's tin shop. It has eight sides—four are pointed, like a star, and four are rounded. It's a deep, fluted pan with a center tube much like a bundt cake pan.

Helen says *rother marmor kuchen*, red marble cake, was a favorite wedding cake. It is made with sour cream and has two different flavors in two different colored batters which are marbled together in the pan, symbolizing the bride and the bridegroom becoming one in marriage. All of the cakes at a wedding party were frosted and decorated but that one special cake was trimmed more elaborately than the rest, so it would stand out among all the other cakes.

Young girls, girls eleven and twelve years old, served at wedding parties.

"Never beer or wine!" Helen is quick to say. "Only food!"

Even though the teenage girls were at the party to serve, they didn't consider it work. To them it was a lark and they were proud to be there, proud that they were old enough to be present if only to serve. It was a sign they were almost grown-up. They passed trays of cake, sandwiches, pretzels and soda crackers, yes, soda crackers, those tiny, round ones that are the size of a nickel. They are called "oyster crackers" by many people because they are usually served with oyster stew. And were those salty little bites gobbled up fast! They were a welcome contrast to the sweet cakes and the sweet wine. The crackers were store-bought and that qualified them as a treat in Old Amana, too.

Summer weddings were the most fun. If the weather was nice, the party spilled outdoors on the lawn, under the trees. Singing, eating and drinking went on for as long as the refreshments lasted.

The Middle Amana vineyard and apple orchard, 1915.

10. Samplers

With that much homemade wine in the villages, a group of local wine experts quite naturally evolved. Their serious sampling was done on Sunday during the interlude between morning church services and the noonday meal. Naturally they were called the Sunday samplers. It was an unofficial title for an unofficial position. Yet it was a position each one saw as a duty and a responsibility. They used the excuse that it was necessary for somebody to know which wines were good and which wines were bad. It was a self-imposed obligation. Each man appointed himself to the job.

Like on-the-sly winemaking, on-the-sly sampling was tolerated and overlooked. It was all but accepted.

If after church on Sunday seems like an odd time to sample wine, remember, it was the only day of the week they had off. Even the farm workers could get in on wine sampling then, because the few Sunday chores required their services for only an hour early in the morning and again late in the afternoon. If they could sneak it in for an hour or so on weekdays, they might also sample about 4:30 to 5:00 in the afternoon, the same time as today's happy hour or cocktail time.

The samplers worked hard at their wine tasting, you bet they did. They took their work very seriously and they were fair, without bias or prejudice. They never met a winemaker they didn't like and they sampled each and every wine they were offered.

To qualify as a sampler, a man had to make several batches of wine each year and he had to have a reputation for turning out at least drinkable wines. They didn't have to be great wines, not even good wines, just drinkable.

Samplers never worked alone. They sampled with three, four or five comrades. They were a "panel of experts." For those experts, the wine did not have to be bottled and placed before them on a table covered with a white linen cloth, to be poured into crystal clear wine glasses. They were mobile. They went where the wine was, right to the wine cellar, and they took the wine straight from the barrel's spigot.

Each little clique was composed of very close friends, next door neighbors or fellow workers. Wine, to them, was homemade for home consumption. Its quality or its scarcity didn't affect its price on the market or its success in the market place, because there was no market. The only thing that mattered was the pleasure the wine gave the drinker. The methods used to make the wine in the first place were so basic, so rudimentary, they felt fortunate when and if one of them produced a barrel of wine worth bragging about. And when a fellow bragged, he had better be prepared to pass out samples to prove his brag. Even among friends, they didn't take his word for it. The proof was in the sample.

When wine was ready to be sampled, word was quietly, discreetly passed in a roundabout manner to the winemaker's sampling cohorts while the congregation meandered around outside the church after the services. The men signaled with a slight nod of the head, a wink or a casual hand gesture to let each other know where they were to meet that day. They did not use the word "wine."

By not saying "wine," they thought no one would know what they were up to. They weren't any better with that disguise than they were in hiding their winemaking. It was all a game. The samplers pretended they were fooling everyone else and everyone else pretended they didn't know what the samplers were doing. All dressed up in their Sunday best, black suits and hats, the samplers mingled nonchalantly with the crowd, slipping the word.

"Jetzt is es zeit." "Well, it's time," they'd say.

"Heute versuche ma meiner." "Today we taste mine."

"Heute versuche mür da früsche." "Today we taste the newly made," and on that one, watch out. That might be the milky way, wine less than sixty days old.

They played it very clever, they thought. They never walked away from church together. Each one went a different path to the cellar and each one arrived there at a slightly different time. They fooled no one.

On any Sunday in any one of the seven villages, several panels of samplers plotted to do their duty by the wines. They sampled only homemade, family wines, not the community wine. They were only interested in determining who in their group of friends made the best wines, the wines with the "clearest color, the best flavor and aroma." Those were the qualities they looked for in a wine.

Once at the appointed cellar that day, they went right to the tasting. They only had two rules. First, every barrel in that cellar had to be sampled by every sampler present. Second, they never helped themselves to wine. The host always did the honors. The host pulled the cork out of the bung hole near the top of the barrel and drew the wine out with a "thief," a tin tube, twenty inches long, an inch in diameter. It was inserted into the barrel and by sucking with the mouth, like drinking through a straw, eight to ten ounces of wine was drawn up into the thief. The palm of the hand was clamped tight over the end of the full thief to hold the wine in until it was released into the little sampling mugs. The host furnished the mugs. They were made of heavy glass and had a handle on the side. They looked like miniature beer mugs. They held about two ounces of wine. That had to be a sloppy maneuver at best. They didn't mess with a swallow or two of wine. They took their little mugs filled to the brim.

Sampling might start off real proper and sedate, but after a few samples, they skipped the sipping, smacking of lips and sloshing the wine around in the mouth, you know, the way wine tasting is supposed to be done properly to give the taster the full benefit of all the wine's attributes. Never mind ceremony, they quaffed the wine samples down in plain, old, hearty drinking.

There's no telling how many times a single barrel might have been tapped and sampled over the months it aged and matured. Each tapping set the stage for spoiling the wine. When the thief was used, it couldn't help but dribble wine over the bung hole and back down into the barrel. In all probability, the outside of the barrel was not perfectly clean, so the wine dribbles could have carried impurities back into the barrel, impurities that could contaminate the wine. The thief wasn't rinsed or cleaned between dips. It was used over and over from one barrel to the next. Just by drawing samples, they risked ruining whole barrels of wine. It was not the most sanitary procedure, but the old samplers I know deny they ever ruined any wine. I find that hard to believe.

In a community with few recreational outlets, the samplers made their own fun with the friendly competition among themselves and their wines. Each one wanted to outdo the others, to make a better wine. Their only reward was to hear their wine praised by their friends. Talk that accompanied their sampling was unpretentious compared to more stylish wine samplings. It was centered on the wine's merits and demerits, a subject of which they never tired. A wine might be said to be "merely good," but no matter, it always deserved "one more taste."

They'd taste and then they'd comment.

"This is a good wine."

"This one has a sting."

"This one is sour."

"This one is bitter."

"This one sure hits the taste."

"Let's top a good one."

"This tastes like more." That was the sure sign of a first rate barrel of wine.

They never said wine was bad, so bad they couldn't drink it. Some wines were just easier to drink, gave more pleasure than other wines, that was all. They did have one saying that tickles me.

"We don't drink the wine for taste," they said, "we drink it for feeling." That said it all as far as they were concerned.

They never tired of hearing how the wine was made, what formula ratio was used or was "thought" to have been used, the juiciness of that year's rhubarb, the age of the wine and so forth and so on. After all the barrels in the host's cellar had been sampled, they would agree which barrel was the best and then they stuck with that barrel for the remainder of that day's sampling.

After an hour of sampling, they were *bedrunken*, slightly drunk. It doesn't mean drunk, it means they felt easy, happy, mellow and relaxed. To us, it is sitting down, having wine with light, friendly talking. It is not loud and rowdy. When they were through sampling, they all went home.

By the time they got home, the Sunday dinner would have been picked up from the community kitchen, carried home and be ready to serve. It might be boiled beef with horseradish, Amana-style spinach, fried potatoes, bread and butter. If it was spring or early summer, there might be a radish or lettuce salad, too.

One sampler was also a pipe-smoker. He was an older gentleman and he was *bedrunken*, all right. After a sampling round, he lit his pipe and puffed on it all the way home. By the time he got to his house and went inside, he saw food on the table and he realized immediately that his family had been waiting somewhat impatiently for him to come so they could eat. His grandchildren were fidgety and cranky because they were hungry. The old man hurried to take his place at the table.

Food was passed, plates were filled and after they had been eating for a little bit, someone noticed a smoky haze rising over the old man's chair. There was a lot of hollering and his wife jumped up in a mad scramble and shoved the man outdoors! There was no serious damage, but his lit pipe had burned holes in a pocket of his Sunday suit pants. The family went back to the table and finished their dinner. After a big dinner, it was nap time.

Village women were quite accustomed to and accepting of the men and their Sunday wine sampling routine. The women understood. They saw there was nothing for the men to do on a Sunday. They didn't work. They weren't allowed to play games. There was no place to go, nothing to do, so why not have a little wine and take a nap?

Helen's grandfather was an elder in West. Other elders were often invited to their house for Sunday dinner. Before dinner was served, the elders had wine from the community wine rations in the main living-dining room, not in the cellar. The wine was served in a special set of glasses. Helen was excited when she saw *Oma* get those glasses down from the top cupboard shelf.

"Not because the elders were coming," she said, "although I was impressed with *Opa's* respected position in West, but even more than that, I loved seeing those dainty little glasses. I didn't see them very often. They were the prettiest things my family owned. They were fragile and pretty and only three inches high, on a short stem. The tiny bowls were etched with fine lines and held only two ounces."

It's surprising those glasses weren't sold along with other dishes and furniture after reorganization and during the Depression. Antique dealers came into the villages snapping up pieces families had brought from Europe. Folks in Amana had no idea what their things were worth. They had had no experience buying or selling household items. Anyway, it was hard times and regardless of the prices, they felt they had to sell.

Fortunately the little wine glasses were spared. Helen's mother gave them to Helen and me on our twenty-fifth wedding anniversary. We use them on birthdays, engagements and holidays.

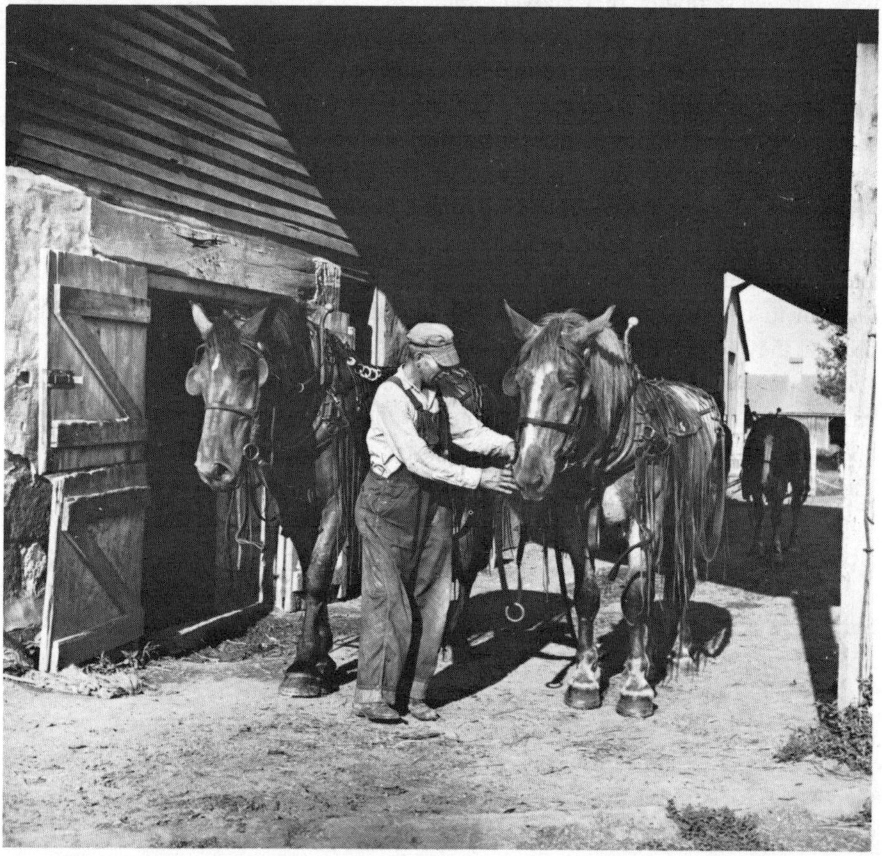

Henry Metz hitches a team of work horses at the Middle barns, early 1930's.
Rudolph Kellenberger photo.

11. Prohibition

In 1917, during World War I, Congress passed and sent to the states for ratification the Eighteenth Amendment to the United States Constitution. Iowa was among the first states to ratify the amendment, which prohibited the manufacture, sale and transporting of alcoholic beverages, including wine. The law did not go into effect nationally until 1920, but as soon as the Iowa legislature approved it, dumping orders were issued across the state. That was sobering news for the seven villages in Amana, each with a cellar full of barrels holding several thousand gallons of wine.

The news hit hard at first, but as leaders of a law-abiding community, the elders ordered all grapevines and all community wine destroyed. Nothing was said about the *Hinterlistiger wein,* on-the-sly wines. They weren't supposed to exist, so how could the elders order them to be destroyed?

To the villagers, Prohibition sounded like a law that would be vigorously enforced. They expected agents to come around with their sharp eyes, keen noses and heavy hands to get rid of the wine. In other parts of the country, or so I have heard, some people got the idea they would never be able to have another drink for as long as they lived, so they all went out and got drunk. That didn't happen in Amana, not here, not where these folks were so good at brewing their own beer and making their own wine. Sure Amana folks would miss not getting the community wine rations. Sure they would hate all the wasting of the wine, but they knew how to make wine and they weren't going to have to go without it for the rest of their lives.

In fact, I rather think that during Prohibition, people here got even more into making family wines. They continued to have beer and wine at Amana weddings all through Prohibition, so they weren't scared out by Prohibition.

Lots of stories circulated about wine dumping in Amana. My friend Carl Metz was a teenage kid in Middle at the time, but he was well aware what was going on. He tells how some were so dead set against losing the wine, that while the elders met trying to work out the dumping details, other fellows met to work out the salvaging details. They were determined to rescue the wine, their wine. Rumors spread that every single drop of community wine in every single village wine cellar had to be dumped. It stirred up a smoldering anger in the men until they got so mad, they were willing to risk getting caught stealing the wine, rather than see it lost.

Of course, they twisted the words, said it wasn't really stealing. They said they were "using the wine," or "borrowing the wine," and anyway, the wine was theirs; it really belonged to them. The community owned the wine, right? If they could get to the wine, drink it up before it was destroyed, what was the crime? As they saw it, there was absolutely no stealing involved. It wasn't stealing if you took what was already yours, what belonged to you, was it? My, they were good with the words.

They weren't so brazen as to go right into the wine cellar and confront the winemaker. And they weren't all that sure they could count on the elders seeing it their way. They had to figure out how to filch the wine without being discovered, so no one man could be blamed or held for breaking the law. They had to pull it off so it would never come out who the person or persons were that "saved" the wine.

Teenagers in those days were no different in Amana than teenagers today anywhere. They liked to get out of the house away from the family for a few hours every night to mingle with their friends. On one such night—it was a dark, moonless night—Carl met with a bunch of his pals.

They stood around talking when, all of a sudden, they heard a commotion. It was pitch black. There were no street lights in the villages then, so they couldn't see clearly what was happening. They crept closer to get a better look. They sneaked along in the shadows, sticking close to buildings and trees, inching their way toward the place where the ruckus was coming from.

They ended up down by the church. The door to the church basement, the wine cellar, was open and silhouetted against the lantern light, they saw what was going on. A team of horses hitched to a sled was pulled right next to the basement door. The sled was piled high with small barrels, ten, twenty and thirty-gallon barrels. Four or five men rolled the empty barrels into the cellar, filled them with wine from the huge, old community barrels and rolled the full barrels back out to sleds. When all the small barrels were full, off they drove.

Once the kids saw what was going on, they were scared. They didn't stick around and they didn't follow the sled. They didn't need to. They already knew what was going to happen to the small barrels of wine. They were dropped off, one or two at a time at the houses of the fellows who were in on the heist.

Discovering the heist put the kids on the spot. They didn't know whether they should tell somebody, or just pretend they hadn't seen anything. Carl says the kids convinced themselves not to do or say anything to anybody.

When the designated day rolled around, all the wine had not been "used" or "borrowed." There remained plenty of wine to be dumped. Every drop had to go.

None was held back, not even a few barrels for *Liebesmahl* services at church. It was a gloomy day in Amana. It has been estimated the seven Colonies ended up dumping some twenty thousand gallons of wine. They had been told that if the wine wasn't disposed of by a certain date, United States agents would come to Amana and personally tend to the dumping. People here didn't want outsiders coming on the premises anytime, much less outsiders who were coming in to dump their wine.

Then, too, if outsiders did the dumping, the folks in the villages knew for sure they would miss out on their last chance at swiping any of the wine.

"That was a real sad day," *Opa* said. "It was just like a funeral."

As Middle's winemaker, he was responsible for getting rid of the wine, the same wine he himself had made. It was hard, it was tough. *Opa's* friends gathered down in the cellar with him and witnessed his turning on the spigots of the huge barrels for the last time. One by one the barrels were emptied. The wine, their wine, splashed and spattered on the concrete floor, swirled and circled in an eddy over the drain grate, then disappeared down the sewer pipe.

Out beyond the building the sewer discharge pipe surfaced and ran in open trenches. Open sewers were a common sight in all the villages, but before you get too alarmed over that, remember that every house had its own outhouse, so the only sewage effluent that ever went into that trench was from the wine cellar and that was mostly water. Once in a while a little grape juice or wine ran in the drain, but mostly it was water.

As sad and sorry as the wine tipplers were, they weren't too sad to come up with one last effort to save their wine. They rigged up a real simple little wine reclamation scheme. In a passageway of the open trench, the open sewer, they dug a hole deep enough and wide enough to hold a big, wooden wash tub. They set the tub down in the ditch, then, as the tub filled with wine, they dipped the wine out of the tub with buckets and carried it off and put it in barrels back in their own basements.

For as long as the wine flowed through the trench, the bucket brigade was marching back and forth, back and forth for refills.

Carl doesn't remember the exact date of wine-dumping day, but he said it had to have been just before May, 1918. That was when his family moved from Middle to another village and he still lived in Middle on wine-dumping day. He was fourteen years old at the time, having been born in 1904.

Carl and his buddies stayed nearby and watched the wine being saved out of the sewer. The men hollered to the young guys, "Come help yourselves!" And the kids did. They got some cups and got their swigs of wine, too, whenever there was room to slip a cup into the tub in between the buckets. For Carl, it was a big day, the first time in his young life that he had been to a wine party. The men and boys hovered over the tub, dippin' and sippin' long enough so that they all got plenty cheered up over what otherwise was a real gloomy situation. Even Carl says he got a buzz on, his first.

It was a nice, sunny day. The whole operation took place in broad daylight. Nobody was afraid of anything or anybody at that point. They didn't care who saw them. They were out to get every drop of wine they could before it was lost.

The closing line on every wine-dumping story was the same.

"The morning after," it was said, "all the catfish in the rivers from Amana to the Mississippi River and on down to New Orleans were begging for aspirin for their hangovers!"

It was on a hot, humid, sticky, August afternoon in 1917 that a threshing crew drank the very last round of community wine that was ever issued to an Amana work crew. Threshing was a big affair here, so to me, it was fitting that a threshing crew should mark the end of an era, that the threshers should close out the village wine-break habit.

Wheat and barley bundles would have been cut and winrowed by horse-drawn reapers as the fields ripened early in July. Shocking crews propped ten or twelve bundles together, heads up, in shocks, to await the threshing marathon that made the round of the villages in August. Caravans of horses and hayracks hauled the bundles in from the fields and, one by one, bundles were pitched into the thresher's hopper. The machine, big as a locomotive, was belted to a big, black, smoke-belching, coal-fired steam engine and gears whirled shredder bars, shaker beds and bellows separating kernels of grain from the chaff and straw. A spout poured grain into a waiting wagon and pale, golden straw was blown out another spout.

Rigs were set up beside the barns. Amana had lots of barns. The barns were, you might say, segregated. By that I mean there were separate barns for every kind of animal: one for horses, one for beef cattle, one for milking cows, one for heifers and calves, one for sheep.

The thresher's straw spout telescoped, swung out in an arc around the back end of the machine and straw was blown twelve to fifteen feet high, side to side, for as far as the spout could reach. The fresh, new straw stacks were like big, half moons curved up against the barns. It was a neat thing to see. Kids and grown-ups alike watched threshing. Threshing time caused a big stir every summer.

By the time I was a kid, the thresher was run by a tractor with a gasoline engine, but it was still a great show. The circus never came to Amana, but we had threshing. It was the next best thing to a circus.

Watching was fun for the spectators, but for the crew it was hard, sweaty work. Handling barley was mean. The bristly beard of the barley heads stuck to clothes, pricked any bare skin it touched and scratched the eyes.

Come time for morning and afternoon breaks, the crew was ready. Usually a teenage boy brought the wine out to the field with a horse and buggy. He showed up just like clockwork. At two-thirty that last afternoon, the lunch wagon was met by a pretty quiet and docile bunch of men. Horses were tied up, engine shut down and the men lined up, tin cups in hand, to get their last fill from the wine paii.

Prohibition ended the making and dividing of community wine in Amana. But it was not the end of winemaking in Amana, far from it.

Village winemakers kept right on making wine all during Prohibition, but only for themselves, on an individual basis. With all the winemaking talent in the Colonies, some might wonder if Amana didn't have its share of bootleggers during Prohibition. No "feds" ever came snooping around. In fact, no federal agents even came here to oversee the dumping of the community wine.

Amana was a religious place, and the people would not have been suspected of having such an extensive wine and beer making operation. Never in a million years would they have been figured as a wine nest. Maybe it was lucky they weren't. It probably spared them a lot of trouble with crime and corruption that hit other places during Prohibition.

Ironically, while winemakers in Amana were getting lots of experience, increasing their skills, again it wasn't a skill they could publicize or brag about. They couldn't talk about how much wine they made or how good it was. Their own gardens, the meadows, fields and woods saw them through the Prohibition crisis. They were never without wine and they were left with some highly skilled winemakers. Usually in a family, one person assumed the job of winemaker. In my family, there was no question. *Opa* was our winemaker.

Prohibition was still on when I was growing up. I saw how anxious and uneasy *Opa* was each time he made wine. He was secretive about what he was doing and he locked the room in the cellar where he made and stored the wine. He wasn't breaking any state or federal laws. No one in Amana who made wine for their family was. It was legal for them to make it. It would have been illegal only if they had sold the wine.

As a child, I picked grapes and I pulled rhubarb. Of the three children in my family, I was the only one who took part in any wine work.

The last few days before Memorial Day, before *Opa* set the *Piestengel*, he was like a kid before Christmas, always anxious to get it going, always sure that year's wine would be his best yet. He pulled the crusher and press into the center of the basement, made sure they were in working order. Seeing him like that and then helping him make the wine were among my earliest childhood memories. When someone is excited about what they are doing, it rubs off on you. I caught his enthusiasm.

If I had ever dreamed that one day winemaking would be a business for me, I would have paid closer attention to what *Opa* did when he made wine. As a kid, winemaking wasn't a fun time particularly; it was work—more work that, as a kid, I didn't get paid to do. It had no reward, no benefit, not for kids, anyway. Kids didn't drink the wine. And if I had been given a nickel, there was no place for me to spend it. There was really no incentive in helping out, other than to do what you were told to do so you wouldn't be punished or scolded. As I look back on the whole set-up here in the old days, it seems to me that lack of an incentive was a big part of the trouble here.

Pulling rhubarb stalks was an undemanding task and it was well-suited to a child. The first time I did it, I was seven years old, but I was big for my age and had plenty of muscle strength for the job.

Mama took me down to our patch by the chicken coop, on the sunny south side of the coop where the snow piled up deep in winter but where the spring sun melted it fast and got the first rhubarb shoots up and growing. Mama instructed me.

"Don't pull all the stalks," she said, "you have to leave some of the smaller ones. They keep the plant alive and feed it so it stores up food for the next year's plant."

"Always pull, never break!" Breaking off the stalks leaves a stump of the stalk and the plant leaks juice there and that drains life from the plant and weakens it. Breaking the stalk also lets juice leak out of the stalk and that's bad, too. That means less juice for the wine.

"As you pull," Mama demonstrated for me, "give just the least bit of a twist to the stalk and it will come loose from the clump with a 'pop,' and be as clean as a whistle."

Putting stalks through the crusher—the same one I used to start the winery—was a job I helped with, too, as a kid. Juice squirted all over. The juice hit me right in the face and in the eyes, and how that juice stings and burns! I have to rub my arms even now talking about it. I can almost feel that sting and the burning on my skin. It was nothing serious, just annoying and messy! Oh, was it messy!

Mama warned me that the leaves of a rhubarb plant are poisonous. They contain oxalic acid. After I had pulled the stalks, it was also my job to snap off the leaves. Rhubarb leaves are great big, shiny green and they are lush, thick and heavy. It has always seemed to me to be a contradiction, in a way, that a plant could have poison in its leaves, but that juice from its stalks can become something as nice as rhubarb wine.

Stalks were picked early in the morning when the big leaves were slightly cupped, full of the morning dew. When the stalk popped free, I was drenched like a shower bath. In just a little bit, I was soaked from head to toe.

I was sent back to the rhubarb patch late in July or early August to break off the flower seed stalks which came up out of the center of the plants. If they weren't removed, they opened into tall, handsome, white plumes which were attractive but which weakened the plant if they were left to grow and mature. The plant needed all its strength to restore itself in getting ready to bear the next year's crop.

The only thing a kid ever got out of winemaking was that if he got sick or had a bad cold in his chest or head, then he got a dose of wine. Hot goose fat was put on a red, wool cloth—it *had* to be goose fat and it *had* to be red, wool flannel; then that was pinned to the inside of our underwear. We slept in our long-sleeved, long-legged wool underwear, not pajamas. We were given diluted wine, usually Concord grape or maybe wild grape or even black currant wine, which was heated a little, not enough to cause the alcohol to be lost to evaporation. Then we were put to bed and heavy wool blankets piled on top of us, up to our ears. Only our noses stuck out. We were to sweat out the cold. I can't say it was a sure cure. What I think happened was that the wine helped put us to sleep and after a good sleep, we naturally felt better.

Ratification of the Twenty-first Amendment to the United States Constitution in 1932 repealed the Eighteenth Amendment, but it had very little effect one way or the other on homemade winemaking in Amanas. The seven Amana villages had more pressing problems facing them.

12. A New Way

Amana's founders believed they had set up a sturdy and secure communal life style, one that would last past their own lifetimes and forever. Every member of the community pledged allegiance to the combined church and village governmental system. Each adult performed an assigned work duty for the community. In exchange, the community housed, fed, clothed, schooled and trained the people along with nourishing their spirits.

The life endured for three-quarters of a century with reasonable success under an arrangement of governing boards. Each of the seven villages elected its own board, the *Bruderrath*, which was composed of village elders and the village's resident Trustee, who also represented his village on the over-all Board of Trustees, the Great Council of the Brethren. The number of elders on a village board ranged from seven to nineteen, based on the population of the village. The Great Council handled all external and internal business for all seven villages and was vested with all powers, rights and privileges of a corporation under Iowa law. Each year, the Council elected a president, vice-president and secretary from among the Council's members.

As far as the rest of the county, state, or for that matter, the whole country knew, there were no troubles in Amana. They had no policemen. They didn't call in the county sheriff to settle any problems. They took their haggling, disputes, complaints and minor rifts to the *Bruderrath*.

Hearings before the *Bruderrath* were simple discussions. There were no lawyers. The board issued "rulings" in the general welfare. It was generally accepted that being an elder meant being part of the little power systems, the class struggles that went on inside Amana. Oh, yes, such things went on here. They had them even in the communal days. The elders had a lot of say. They were the ones who decided where the members lived and what jobs they held. Those two items were, after all, very personal and very important. They covered a lot of territory in everyone's life. In Old Amana, that meant power.

It was a life without money, as far as the villagers were concerned. The community owned the houses they lived in and the community furnished the food they ate. Anything else they needed in the way of essentials—clothing and household goods—was available merely by signing for them at the general store.

Money on the outside was another matter. The Colonies sold goods to outside businesses and with the money they got from those goods, they stocked the general store, equipped the mills, factories and shops with whatever goods they were unable to grow or manufacture for themselves. By the late 1920's and the early thirties, the whole country and the whole world was in a depression. It was a depression that penetrated even Amana. They couldn't sell their goods and get a decent price for their woolens, lumber or grain, not enough to maintain a cash flow. They were in just as deep economic trouble as were the people outside.

At the very time the Colonies were being jolted and rocked by the Depression, they were being jolted and rocked on the inside, too. Their isolation, a vital cog in keeping the machinery of their religious commune going, was gradually being eroded. Since the news of the original land sale broke, the curious had come to Amana. In the beginning, they came on foot and on horseback and then by train. They came in ones and twos. When Henry Ford rattled his Model "T's" and "A's" off the end of his Detroit assembly line at the rate of one car per minute, priced for Everyman's wallet, outsiders began coming to Amana by the carloads. They came to look, buy and sell. The radio, too, brought in more of the world's influences.

The more the villagers saw and heard about the "outside," the better the outside looked to them and the more they questioned the way they lived inside Amana. Money problems, loss of privacy, individual discontent—they all festered and spread. Things were not hunky-dory here. There was trouble inside, trouble that didn't go away with a few strong words from the elders. In place of the peace and harmony, there was a protest, a rebellion, strong enough to shake up even the firmest believers.

When there is trouble among people, it seems like trouble feeds on all their human flaws. Suspicions, laziness, contrariness, orneriness, lying, deceit—they all flared up and drove wedges between elders, between neighbors and even between fathers and sons and brothers and sisters.

Things came to a head in 1931. I was ten years old. I was young, but not too young to see how high emotions were running. The young people were less and less willing to accept the old restrictions their parents and grandparents had lived by. They broke rules to get what they wanted, to do what they wanted and to do it when and where they wanted. And the young people weren't alone in the push for changes. They had some support from some of the older generations. After all, there had always been rules against making the *hinterlistiger wein*, on-the-sly wine, but rules hadn't stopped the making of the wine. The young men wanted to play baseball. They played baseball. They wanted to play cards. They played cards. There were more and more things they wanted to have, to do and to have a say in and they meant to have their way. A change was bound to come to Amana sooner or later. The Depression just made it happen sooner.

As it turned out, the rest of the country was going through some of the same upheavals in the churches, towns and communities during the 1920's, too, but only a handful of Amana people knew about what was going on outside. They were too worked up over their own situation to pay much attention to outside problems.

A lot of small changes were made, but the talk for bigger and more changes got louder. Finally, the elders decided to find out how the members really felt. A committee was elected. All of the villages were represented according to their population. There were 47 members on the committee, none of them elders. That committee prepared a proposition to separate the church and the business affairs of the Colonies. The members voted on the proposition June 10, 1931. It passed with an overwhelming majority, 75 percent of the members wanting a change.

No one, from the oldest elder to the youngest worker, wanted the Colonies to go belly-up, to fail at the bank. They wanted to be able, somehow, to salvage the tillable land, the mills and any other industries and shops that could be turned into profitable businesses.

A sub-committee of ten and a staff of lawyers methodically and systematically sorted out the legal details and drew up the plans for incorporation for the new enterprise. The plans were submitted to a vote on Monday, February 1, 1932. The new charter was approved. Ninety percent of the members voted for it. The once all-encompassing single body that had administered and tended to every member's needs and to the public life of the entire community was split into two separate and distinct bodies. The Amana Church Society would handle church affairs and community benevolent functions. The Amana Society would be a modified stock corporation and would handle all business matters. June 1, 1932, was the date set for the change to go into effect.

After the vote approving the change, residents over twenty-one years of age were issued stock in The Amana Society signifying their ownership of a portion of the community's assets. The amount of stock each member received was based on the number of years of service by the individual to the community. Class A Common Stock, the voting stock, was non-transferable and could only be sold back to the corporation itself.

For the first time in Amana, wages were a factor in operating expenses. Wage scales were set for the jobs that were to be filled by those members who were to become the paid employees of the new corporation. The new corporation was structured to make a profit, to make money. In order to be a money-making concern, no business can afford to hire more employees than it needs and that applied to the new corporation, The Amana Society. The corporation could not justify hiring every man of working age in all seven villages. The Amana Society simply didn't have that many jobs available in the businesses it now owned and would operate if those businesses were going to make money. Some jobs were also eliminated by the merging of many shops, such as the wagon shops, blacksmith shops, cooper shops and other small shops that had been duplicated in each village.

The Amana Society was not going to be a landlord. Community-owned buildings which were unoccupied under the new regime went up for sale and all homes were eventually to be privately owned. By selling their stock in the corporation or by getting a job with the corporation, members had the means of getting together enough money to take care of themselves, to buy a house in Amana or to leave Amana, to go somewhere else and buy or rent a home and get reestablished, if that was what they preferred to do. If they left, and some did, at least they left with some money in their pockets.

Those who stayed, including my family, had to get jobs, find housing, and do all the things for themselves that the community and the elders had done for them. From the first of June 1932 on, they would make their own decisions, handle their own money, buy homes, install kitchens in those homes, buy groceries, pay taxes, buy cars, learn to drive and they would be endorsing insurance policies and other papers, some of which they wouldn't be able to read without help. Learning all of those lessons would have been tough enough in the best of times. They had to learn to do everything in the worst of times, in a country bogged down by a depression.

Now, they didn't get up the morning of June 1, 1932 and find that overnight their little world was all changed and now the good times were gonna roll. It took shape over several months. It was hard to forget the "we" spirit that had been so essential to the success of the communal lifestyle, but if they were to make it, they had to become self-reliant and self-directed individuals. They had to let the "me" spirit emerge and become stronger.

Out on their own, they were, in a way, a bunch of greenhorns, halfway afraid they were about to disgrace themselves. Yet the change was what they wanted. They had voted for it and they were going to try to make it on their own, heads up and proud of the chance to give it a try.

From the big things—where they lived, their jobs—down to the little things—what they ate, what they wore, what time they got up in the morning and what time they ate breakfast or lunch or dinner—all of those things they would now decide for themselves. No more would the village bell ring, calling them to pick up their food, no more would the elders tell them where to work and where to live. Old habits gave way to new ones. New customs were built, old ones torn down.

Neither Helen nor I heard any discouraging words about reorganization in our families. They were all for it and in a big way. My folks saw the change as a chance to get out from under somebody else's thumb. My grandparents had come to this country, to the land of opportunity, but they had never had much of a crack at all the opportunities. They thought that with the Change, maybe some of their family would now have a chance to take advantage of the opportunities. Talk of the Change made everyone in our families happy. They were pleased and they were optimistic that it would turn out to be a good thing for all of us. Of course, we children picked up on their good thoughts and their good words and we looked forward to the Change, too. We felt it was a brand new start.

The Big Change, that was the big chance!

Now that didn't mean they were going to get rid of every single thing from the old life. There was no need for them to get rid of the things from their past that they liked, like their wines. Their winemaking was taken right on into their new life. It was too good to leave behind.

People were like new immigrants in a new land for the first time instead of citizens whose families had been in this country, some of them for seventy-five years. Some of them hung back, avoided direct contact with anybody from outside. Others couldn't wait to get outside.

The public had a tendency both before and after reorganization to see Amana people as being all alike in how they thought, behaved, lived and worked. That's definitely not the case. Amana people weren't and aren't alike in those respects. Reorganization really brought out the differences. Many people became stronger and much more capable as individuals than they would ever have been under the old communal way of life. The Change turned out to be very good for most if not all of the people.

There was one thing that almost none of the workers had anticipated. No matter how good a man or woman might have been in a particular job in the community, few knew how to do a lot of different jobs well. When it came to mending a torn screen, repairing a broken hinge, fixing a loose board in the sidewalk, chopping firewood, any jobs of that nature, they had always just hollered for a handyman to come by and take care of their problem. Now there was no one to call.

When a child outgrew his or her shoes, they could no longer take them to the shoemaker for a new pair. If a mother wanted a son to have a new shirt or a daughter a new dress, she could no longer go to the general store and sign her name on the books to "pay" for them.

If a family made arrangements to stay put, even temporarily, right in the house where they had been living, they still didn't have a kitchen and they had few, if any, cooking utensils. They had never needed them before. After the Change, community kitchen wares were sold and families bought some cooking utensils, but the pots and pans that had been used to cook for a village were far too large for a family. Dishes and tableware each household already had. And furniture was not a problem either. Even though most of the furniture in every home had been made at the local community-owned furniture shops, at the time of the Change, it was just considered to be the property of the family. So they did not have to buy furniture, at least right away.

Scaling down old recipes that once fed a whole village to feed just one family wasn't a problem for women like Mama and *Oma.* They had had enough kitchen experience to judge proportions so they got along well.

And some families did seem to make an easier adjustment and made their own way quite nicely. No doubt it helped if a family had had someone who had served as an elder way back through the generations. In my own family there are examples of people from different backgrounds. My mother's parents and their parents and their parents were all longtime members. My father's family, on the other hand, didn't come until Old Amana had been established. After Papa and Mama married, they lived with Mama's family, the Schinnerlings, who stayed here after the Big Change. They influenced my parents to stay here, too.

Some of my aunts and uncles left because their personal attachment to Amana and to the old system was not strong enough to keep them from seeing more of the new country. They felt able, capable, smart enough to go out, find work and support themselves and their families somewhere else. None of them moved very far away. They are all nearby, close enough to drive over to Amana for Sundays and holidays. They are still very much a part of the family.

The Big Change and all the talk about money had not passed me by. In 1933, the summer I was twelve, I gathered lily flowers and sold them for ten cents a dozen. Other boys my age did it, too. We waded out fifteen or twenty feet into the shallow water and picked buds rather than fully opened flowers. Buds lasted longer for the customers. We didn't have a stand. We just stood along the side of the road with our pails of flowers and sold to the passers-by, tourists in their cars. We would each sell four to six dozen flowers a day, so we made forty to sixty cents. To an Amana kid, that was a fortune!

Whatever a kid wanted back then—a candy bar, a ball, a book, anything—the grown-ups begged off with, "There's no money for that." So we went out and earned the money for things we wanted.

Helen and I now realize that in many ways, we had the best of the two worlds in Amana. We spent our early years in Old Amana but we have had the opportunity to be a part of the New Amana, too.

13. Changing to the One-Family Home

Reorganization, the Big Change or the Great Change, brought changes that affected every man, woman and child in Amana. Even though nearly everyone wanted the changes, that didn't mean they weren't, in one way or another, afraid of the shake-ups in their lives.

If a man stayed in Amana, he was afraid he wouldn't have a job. If he left, he was afraid he didn't speak English well enough to get a job outside. Regardless of whether he stayed or he left, he was afraid he wouldn't make enough money to buy all the things he had been in the habit of receiving at no cost, for only his labor. If he bought a car, he was afraid to drive it. There were so many new situations and new things—a job, a house, food, clothes, learning English—it was no wonder a little fear crept into their hearts now and then.

But fear can be turned to courage if you get busy, get going, make decisions and take some action. And that's just what seemed to happen after the Big Change.

My grandfather Schinnerling wasn't a young man. He was fifty-nine years old in 1932, but even so, he took the Big Change right in stride. He got right with it about as quickly and as well as anybody, young or old.

Before the Change, *Opa* had always spent the long, slow winter months working at the village broom factory. No one told him he had to do that. He just needed to be busy, and in the winter, when no work could be done in the vineyard or orchards, he busied himself making brooms. After The Change he bought the machinery that was being dismantled at the broom factory, planted a small patch of broomcorn and went into business for himself.

He was a man who had never known any kind of life other than the communal system, but he took the plunge and made a go of his own business.

Broomcorn is an earless variety that looks like maize or milo. Straw for broom heads comes from the broomcorn's tassel-like seed cluster that grows out of a short stalk. *Opa* had the whole operation—he grew the broomcorn, made the brooms and sold the brooms. He made all kinds of brooms, all sizes and all styles, and they were good brooms. I wouldn't be surprised to find some of *Opa's* brooms still around and still in use.

And did his little shop ever smell good from all that broomcorn, especially when he used the gadget to shake out the seeds and fray the tassels into straw splinters to make the broom heads. I liked going to the broom shop and helping *Opa* sweep it out and bundle up his new brooms, ready for sale.

Papa didn't have to job hunt and that was one less worry at our house. His job at the woolen mill was assured when the new corporation, The Amana Society, decided to continue operating the mill. It was one of the Colonies' most successful operations and had an established reputation with a string of Eastern buyers.

So Papa had a job, one with a paycheck, and *Opa* had his business, and that left a house, a house large enough for two families, as the most urgent need facing my family. We could probably have continued living in the same quarters we had always occupied in the church, I suppose, since the Amana Church Society had hired *Opa* to stay on as caretaker of the church building.

Our quarters were far from spacious. Seven of us lived in five rooms on three floors at one end of the church. The first floor was one big room, a combination living-dining room which both families used. *Oma* and *Opa's* bedroom and parlor were on the second floor. The third floor, where my family lived, had a parlor, dining room and one bedroom. The bedroom was filled with beds—a double bed for Mama and Papa and three narrow, single beds for my brother, my sister and me. After the Change, we had to have our own kitchen, and it was installed in the basement. Both families shared it. It's understandable that my folks wanted a larger place and a place that gave them more privacy than they had living in the church building. They didn't want to rent; they wanted to own their own home.

Buildings which had been used as homes were put up for sale after the Change. In most cases, families who lived in those buildings tried to raise the money to buy them. Sometimes two or three families ended up with each buying one-half or one-third of a house. Then they remodeled, added separate entrances, partitions and stairways so each family had a completely separate home within the building.

There was a strong desire among the Amana people to have separate, one-family homes. It was one of the strongest of all the motives which were behind the push for change in the Colonies.

Residents were given a grace period to find housing. No one was put out on the streets. And they needed time to locate space and to raise the $500 to $1,500 it took to buy a place in one of the villages.

My folks couldn't make an overnight decision. Not many could. They all had a lot to learn about buying real estate. My folks made up their mind to stay in Middle, but Middle had a large number of families to be relocated and few structures that could be converted to housing.

Each village had a meat market, but after reorganization only the Amana, Homestead and South Amana markets remained in operation. South Amana's meat market later became a restaurant but the others still turn out smoked hams, pork sausage, bratwurst and the other meat specialties for which Amana is well-known in the Midwest.

In a closed bid sale, June 20, 1936, Charles and Helena Kraus, my parents, bought the meat market building at Middle. They hadn't toured the old market. They hadn't studied its layout to know if it was feasible to convert it into a home. But they did know, that like all buildings in Amana, it was solid and well-built. And it is. The outside walls are three bricks thick, making nice wide window sills and deep-set windows. Not only was the building big, roomy and tight, it was on three acres of land.

Built in 1861, the old meat market had three levels—basement, first and second stories and a smoke tower. It is set into a shallow hillside. The front of the building faces the street and is at ground level on the south. The basement entry, the back side of the building, is also at ground level on the north. The hill was carved away and the foundation and basement walls were set back into the slope.

The original Colony planners chose this particular site for a meat market because the animals could be held out back in catch pens, then driven up the hill, around the side of the building and into chutes that brought them right into the butcher shop.

The wagons that delivered meat to the village kitchen pulled up about where our front door is now to load the parcels of cut-up meat. In seventy years of operating, Middle's meat market processed an estimated 3,500 animals. Records show that Middle's kitchens used more than a quarter-million pounds of pork a year. These Germans were more used to pork than they were to beef and they liked their pork fresh or cured; it didn't matter. They had plenty of corn to fatten the hogs so they made nice, rich, juicy roasts and chops.

A section of the first floor of the market was once the cooler room where pork sides and beef quarters were hung to cool after the animals were dressed. Beef aged in that room and was later cut into roasts, steaks or ground according to the needs of the kitchen. A lot of pork was made into ham, bacon and smoked sausages. After it was cut, it was carried to the top of the smoke tower where it was strung from the rafters.

The smoke tower stands at the east side of the building. It is completely walled off from the other sections of the building and has its own stairways, two flights of them. They start in the basement at the fire pit and go clear up to the top of the tower. When the tower was in use, a fire was lit in the pit. Smoke curled up through the tower, smoking and curing the meats that were hung there. Then the smoke was vented on out the tower's cupola. On a quiet and still day, the smoke hung among the rooftops and treetops of the village. Oh, that was an enticing smell! Just thinking about it reminds me of that wonderful taste of good old Amana hickory-smoked ham. The hickory chips came from trees right in a nearby grove. Once the fire was lit, it was kept burning day and night for four to six weeks. It was maintained as a very low, very slow fire—it never blazed. They aimed for it to be only a bed of smoldering embers, just a red glow among the logs. That's when it created the most smoke.

In the many years of use, the fires coated the inside walls of the tower with a thick, shiny and hard soot. It is half to three-quarters of an inch thick, is coal-black and looks a lot like baked-on enamel.

Being a butcher in Old Amana was hard work. Running up and down all the tower stairs was work, but the butchers did it when they were saddled with hams, sides of bacon and yards and yards of sausage links draped over their shoulders.

Kids today have another idea about how the old smoke tower might have been used. A boy about nine years old asked if the smoke tower had once been a hideout and whether soldiers peeked out of the little windows at the top so they could see to shoot Indians.

Papa tackled the remodeling of the old meat market with hammers and saws borrowed from neighbors. He was up at five o'clock in the morning and at the mill at six. He worked his full shift six days a week and when he got off at the mill at two-thirty in the afternoon, he went to the house to work. He worked until it got too dark to see to hit a nail on the head. *Opa* helped, too, mostly by cleaning up during the day so the place was ready for Papa the next afternoon. Separate apartments were made for the two families.

I tagged around after Papa as he worked and got the layout of the rooms figured out, not from anything he said, but just by seeing how many rooms there were and where they were situated. The day I counted five bedrooms, F-I-V-E bedrooms, I knew that meant a bedroom for my folks, a bedroom for my grandparents and one for each one of us kids. Boy, that was a surprise! Until then, I had never known an Amana child who had his or her own room. Then I couldn't wait to move. I had wondered how the old meat market could ever be a house. I had been in it and had seen the sides of beef and pork hanging in the cooler. I had seen the cold, cement floors and high ceilings. It looked like a big, old barn of a place. I wondered how it could ever be a house. Knowing I was about to have my own room got those thoughts out of my head.

I did hate being stuck over at the new place helping Papa in the summertime when school was out. I would rather have been out in the pasture playing baseball with my buddies. But I helped. I handed Papa tools, fetched the hammer or saw, held the tape measure, got Papa a drink, picked up scrap lumber and nails, swept up sawdust. I made sure I did enough work so I didn't feel guilty when I did get away to the ball diamond.

The Middle Amana Meat Market with the smoke house tower at right. This building was remodeled to become the Kraus family home and the Kraus Old Style Colony Winery. From The Amanas Yesterday, *© 1975, The Amana Society.*

The Kraus winery today.

Camping in the Amana woods, fishing and hunting were favorite recreational activities of the Amana people. Circa 1915.

On the nearby Iowa River, circa 1915. George Kraus's grandfather, Carl Schinnerling, had a boat.

The remodeling didn't change the old meat market a great deal on the outside. The four different roof elevations are the same. The smoke tower is the highest at thirty-five feet. The other sections are twenty, eighteen and sixteen feet high. The original building is 100 feet long. We added a breezeway and double garage, making it 160 feet long.

Papa had to remove sections of the brick walls in a couple of places to put in new windows. He erected partitions, hung doors, plastered the walls and laid oak flooring over the old concrete slab floors and transformed the wide open interior into rooms.

In the 1930's, a network of poles and wires were being strung in Iowa as a result of the Rural Electrification Associations that were set up nationwide to lend money and guarantee loans to bring electric power lines to all rural areas. Amana, a newcomer to the morass of government agencies spawned in the thirties, had shied away from FDR, Franklin Delano Roosevelt, and his hand-out programs. But a promise of a light bulb in every room was one new deal they couldn't pass up. Amana officials were willing to run the marathon of interviews and interrogations, fill out forms and sign statement after statement to get the loan that would assure the Colonies the opportunity for a brighter future.

Folks in Amana weren't about to miss getting electricity, even though it meant they had to borrow money. They had been behind the times on indoor plumbing and telephones—we didn't get a phone in our house until 1940 or maybe it was even 1941—but electricity, they went for. It was approved in December 1936.

Until that time light had come from kerosene lamps and lanterns or hissing gas lamps, the kind that had cloth mantles that the bugs were always flying into, wrecking both the mantles and the bugs. With electric lines coming, stores in nearby towns had a run on electric irons, lamps, toasters and radios. The villagers were in a hurry to catch up. The big power hook-up took place in March, 1937.

My folks couldn't wait. They bought us an electric radio for Christmas in 1936, three months before the juice was on and even before we moved into our new home.

REA had come to Amana at a very good time for the remodeling. Papa struck a good deal with an electrician and got the new place wired for probably less than a hundred dollars. So we knew, once we moved, that we would be able to use our new radio. It was a Philco table model, the size of a big shoe box. My Aunt Mina, the only one of Papa's sisters who stayed in Amana after the Big Change, already had electricity at her house, so we carried our new radio to her house and plugged it in.

We had had an old battery-operated radio for a few years. The batteries in it were always running down right in the middle of some good program—like Jack Benny's Sunday night broadcast, or Bing Crosby with Bob Hope, George Burns and Gracie Allen, Fred Allen, Charlie McCarthy and Edgar Bergen. . .

I just realized something. All of those shows were comedy shows! Well, in Amana, I guess everyone was ready for some laughs. They had some catching up to do on laughing, too.

My favorite summer radio listening was the play-by-play of the major league baseball games, if I could happen to pick up a Chicago station on the old radio and if the batteries were strong enough to last until the end of the game. Once the old radio battery started to go, the volume got weaker and weaker, until it faded out. If the radio was turned off for a little bit, the battery perked up, so when the radio was switched back on, you could catch a quick play or maybe hear the box score at the end of an inning. I'd stick my ear right up against the speaker, switch off the radio, then switch it on trying to catch what I could until finally, it wouldn't come back on at all.

Announcers for the Cubs games were Bob Elsen, Pat Flanagan and Quinn Ryan. It would be nice if I could say I used to listen to Ronald "Dutch" Reagan when he was on the air doing baseball, but I can't because I never heard him. I would never have expected a baseball radio announcer to become president of the United States. That would have seemed as unreal as expecting that I would ever be a baseball player or a winemaker someday.

Not only was our new home going to have electricity, it was going to have indoor plumbing, and that meant a bathroom. Saturday night was bath night at our house and it was always a hassle. Mama had to heat up the big wash boiler full of water four and five times to get through the weekly scrubbings for four adults and three children. We took turns bathing in a big, round, galvanized tin wash tub. It was put in one of the already cramped bedrooms.

A bathroom, my own room, electric lights, an electric radio—those were just some of the things I was looking forward to when we moved into our new home. I would be glad to get away from all the people that surrounded our home in the church. With eleven regularly scheduled services at the church every week, not to mention the extra ones during special seasons, it seemed like we were never alone.

There still remained a lot of finishing and painting work to be done by spring of 1937 but Papa knew he would be able to work later into the evenings once we had electric lights. Mama and *Oma* thought they could stand to dodge his sawhorses and paint spatters all summer if they could just get moved into the new place where each family would have its own home complete with kitchen.

14. The Right to Dream

If reorganization had not hit Amana, formal schooling would have ended for me in the spring of 1935 when I completed the eighth grade. I would have been out of school and on the job at fourteen years old.

Amana children had very limited goals before 1932. They didn't dare to dream about what they wanted to do when they grew up. It was an accepted fact that a boy would do the same work his father did and all girls would work in the kitchen and garden. There was no need for us to waste time thinking about what work we would do when we grew up, no more than we should bother to think about where we would live, what we would wear, eat or anything else. When we grew up, we could expect to look, think, act and be pretty much like our parents. As adults, many of us would even live in the very same house in which we had been born. It was the pattern in Amana. Children followed in their parents' footsteps. The pattern seldom changed.

Before 1932, only those students being groomed as the next doctor, dentist, druggist or teacher for their village went on to high school. When the elders looked ahead and saw that an opening in one of those positions was coming up, they picked the student who would be educated to fill the position. In order to qualify for college and pass the entrance examinations at the University of Iowa at Iowa City or Iowa State Teachers College at Cedar Falls (now the University of Northern Iowa), Amana students had to be sent to Marengo or Williamsburg for four years of high school.

Immediately after reorganization radical changes were made in the Amana schools. Well, the changes were radical if compared to the old Amana schools. The newly formed Amana school board made arrangements for ALL students who had just finished the eighth grade in any Amana school in June 1932 to enroll in the high school of a neighboring town in September 1932.

The board also hired the first superintendent for the Amana School System, John R. Neveln. He was in charge of all Amana grade schools and responsible for establishing the first Amana High School. They couldn't have found a better man for the job than Superintendent Neveln. He was from the outside—none of the Amana resident-teachers had the required educational training or experience to qualify them to administrate or to teach at the high school level. Neveln was born at Victor, Iowa, and received his higher education at William Penn College at Oskaloosa and Iowa State Teachers College in Cedar Falls. His family background was German. He had had several years experience in small town school systems at Swea City and Manly, Iowa.

He strongly favored the teaching of foreign languages, even at the elementary level. He had no objections to the German that was still being used in Amana schools, although he did want French, Latin and other foreign languages also taught, and he wanted English to be the main language, the one that was used in all classes other than the foreign language classes.

The present teachers were not fired. They were Amana residents and Neveln retained them on the staff even though they were limited in how well they were able to teach under the new system. Most of them did not speak English any better than their students, but Neveln made the best possible use of their experience and teaching abilities by rotating them among the Amana grade schools. They had jobs here until they retired.

Changes were apparent in the grade schools the first fall Neveln headed up the schools. The standard five-day school week and a September-to-June school year was adopted. Amana schools took the same holiday and vacation breaks taken by all Iowa elementary schools. Courses of study for each grade were brought up to the same level practiced in other Iowa grade schools.

I was a sixth grader at Middle and Helen was a third grader at West. Neither of us at the time could possibly have visualized the consequences of the changes in the Amana schools. Later we did realize that of all the changes in Amana after reorganization, none was more important to the children of Amana than the changes in the schools.

The first few months after the Big Change and for the next few years, the new school board had its hands full. At the same time the grade schools were upgraded and high school was made available to all who finished the eighth grade, plans were drawn up to establish a high school by converting one of the two existing grade school buildings in Middle into larger classrooms so freshmen, sophomores, juniors and seniors from all seven villages could attend one high school. It was a two-story brick building, built in 1874, as near as I can make out now from the inscription in the cement plaque near the peak of the roof. Later, the building was no longer used as a school. It was sold and converted into apartments.

Amana High School officially opened for the 1935-1936 school year. I was a freshman and a member of the first class of graduates that attended all four years at Amana High School. Those students from Amana who had been at Marengo and Williamsburg high schools since 1932 transferred back to Amana. They made up the sophomore, junior and senior classes at the new high school. The first graduation exercises were held in the spring of 1936. I graduated in 1939.

The faculty of the new high school consisted of the superintendent and two teachers. Neveln, himself, taught the mathematics classes—algebra and geometry. Despite a limited faculty and facilities, he made every effort to provide a well-rounded curriculum, one that prepared students for college or for taking their places in the working world without further education. He stressed extra-curricular activities. My favorite was baseball. Our coach was Howard Durner. He had taught under Neveln in the Manly, Iowa, schools and was attending law school at the University of Iowa. In Amana, he taught history and commercial law besides coaching the baseball and softball teams.

Fortunately cars were quite plentiful in the Colonies by then and students from the other villages car-pooled to the new high school. The high school ball teams were hauled in cars so we could play the teams at other high schools. Cars also made it possible for our fans to follow the team and give us their support. Amana high school teams still have great fan support.

Coach Durner hoped to start basketball teams here, too. He had an idea to turn Middle's old woolen mill, which had stood vacant since 1932, into a gymnasium. The roof and walls of the main structure were in excellent condition. All they needed to buy and install were the floor, lights and bleacher seats. It would have been a very inexpensive gym.

During the winter months and on rainy days, I already used the old mill as a gym. I was a pitcher on the high school team. I would get our team's catcher to go to the mill with me so I could keep my throwing arm in condition and work on my pitches on the off-season or on days when we couldn't use the practice field because of wet weather. We young guys figured if Bill Zuber could get away with using the old mill, we could, too. No one ever chased us out.

Before Coach Durner's idea could get off the ground, Durner finished law school and left Amana. Howard—now I call him "Howard," though I always called him "Coach" or "Mr. Durner" when I was in school—is a lawyer in St. Paul, Minnesota. We have remained good friends. We keep in touch and we see each other quite often.

Baseball wasn't the only thing Neveln instigated at Amana High School. He increased the faculty to five and in 1936, he convinced the board to build an auditorium by connecting the high school and the grade school. That provided the stage for plays, operettas and musical concerts by the glee club, band and orchestra. Each year the freshman German class did a night of one-act plays in German, the sophomore English class did an English-speaking play and the junior and senior classes together did a three-act play. I'll never forget "The Little Clod-hopper." It was a comedy and it brought down the house. The senior class did a springtime operetta. "The Windmill of Holland" was one of the biggest and best remembered productions. The school shows were a big deal for this whole community. For the first several years, I think just about everyone of every age saw every performance staged at the high school.

The senior English class also began to publish a school newspaper. Called "*Die Posaune*," "The Teller," it was written in English and was mimeographed in the superintendent's office by the students. At first, the paper only came out four times a year, but it was popular and it was well-read. There had never been a newspaper in the Colonies and the parents were as eager to read "*Die Posaune*"as the students were. It was passed around to parents and grandparents and they got a chance to practice reading English.

A regular feature of the newspaper was a column from the German class that pointed out ways to improve German-to-English translations. In one column, the writer used an incident as an illustration of how to avoid mixing German and English words. This had really happened. A thirsty tourist was puzzled as to why, when he pumped a hand pump to get a drink of water, no water came out. In all seriousness, believing he was answering correctly, the writer said, "You can't pimp because the pimp's kaput."

On at least one occasion, the newspaper had a censorship problem. When the German ambassador to the United States visited the Amana Colonies, a program was presented in his honor. The high school chorus did several old German songs. Words to the verses of the musical selections appeared in an article in "*Die Posaune.*" Two lines in one verse offended some local people and they called a quick conference with the superintendent. Before the newspapers were circulated, those two lines had to be blacked out with ink in every single copy of that edition.

In 1969 the new, modern consolidated school was built by Middle's lily pond. It has classrooms, laboratories, an auditorium, a full-sized gymnasium and an Olympic-size swimming pool. The baseball field, the same field where the teams I played on played all of their home games, is near the new school, only now the old ball diamond has built-in dugouts and bleacher seats. A fleet of school buses has replaced the car pools.

The high school brought the young people of all the Colonies together after reorganization and that did a great deal to unify the community. It also made it possible for friendships to develop, friendships that could not have existed before the Big Change. Since Helen lived in West and I was from Middle, we might never have met or gotten together if it hadn't been for the high school.

Almost from the beginning, a high percentage of Amana High School's graduates have gone on to college. Some of them return to the Colonies after college and others pursue careers elsewhere. Many Amana graduates have had outstanding careers as doctors, lawyers, college professors and in just about every area of the business and professional world.

When Amana schools went from the old, eight-grade country school to a full-fledged school system complete with its own high school, Amana children were given the opportunity to choose their own occupation and to attend college if the field they planned to enter required college. But the most important thing reorganization did was give Amana children the right to make a choice. We found out we could now make some plans. We had a right to dream. We had a chance to make those dreams come true.

Young men in Amana worked on the farmland both before and after the Great Change from communal life to free enterprise. Rudolph Kellenberger photo.

15. Baseball Fever

Baseball was one of the adult games that were forbidden in Old Amana. Even so, the young men, those in their late teens and early twenties, went to great lengths to play their version of the great American pastime anyway. By the time I was in grade school, just before reorganization, the younger members of the Colonies were more outspoken and were more willing to push for what they wanted. Baseball was one thing they wanted. If they weren't playing it, they were talking about playing it. I heard all the talk and I was curious. What was so bad about baseball?

The excuse the elders gave was that playing games was kid stuff and once a young man was old enough to work, he was no longer a kid and, therefore, he should not play games.

Know what the kids did? They just gave the game a new name, called it "Ground Ball." They made a ball diamond in an open area in the timber a mile and a half south of Middle where they played the game surrounded by trees. They couldn't be seen or heard by the elders. They had equipment—bats, balls, gloves and mitts. Bats were of oak and willow and were made by the village cabinet makers in the furniture shop. Turning a baseball bat on a lathe wasn't that different from turning bed posts or chair legs and backs.

Before 1932, balls, gloves and mitts were ordered out of the Sears and Roebuck catalog. Things were pretty cheap in those days—baseballs were seventy-five cents apiece and gloves and mitts sold for a dollar to a dollar and a half. When Amana was a communal set-up, people could, in an emergency, order items the general store didn't stock if the items sold for under one dollar. The store manager had to approve each order and he did the ordering. Each family was supposedly limited to thirty dollars worth of special orders in a year. Baseball equipment was in the right price range.

Evidently it qualified as an "emergency" in enough families that eventually each village was able to field its own baseball team. Regular nine-inning games were played among the Colony teams every Saturday afternoon from spring until fall.

Baseball is, I think, a great way for young guys anywhere to let off steam. They can be rowdy, boisterous, entertaining each other with their high jinks and showing off their physical skills. I also think, for the young guys in Amana, baseball was even more important because the communal system made it just about impossible for the individual to be recognized for his own individual talent and ability. But if a guy could hit a baseball, steal a base or pitch a strike-out, boy, he was a star, at least on his own team.

Middle and Amana had the largest populations and fielded the best baseball teams. Of those two villages, Middle had the largest number of men in the sixteen to twenty-five year old bracket, so Middle naturally had the better team. Every day but Sunday, Middle's guys were throwing, catching or hitting a baseball somewhere. As soon as they got off the job in the afternoon, they headed out to the baseball field to try to get in a game before the sun went down.

Gradually, the rule against baseball was relaxed. The teams even had uniforms. Folks in Middle went for their team in a big way. They sent away for regulation baseball caps in blue-black with a big, felt, white "M" above the bill. The uniforms were homemade in navy blue with big white letters spelling out "M-I-D-D-L-E" across the front of the shirt. The letters were often lopsided, unevenly spaced, crooked—they were lucky if "Middle" wasn't misspelled. No two suits looked exactly alike. All in all, it was a pretty ragged-looking team. But that never took away the fun of a baseball game.

It took a while for the teams to build up a following of fans. *Opa* was one of Middle's most faithful and avid spectators. By then, Middle's diamond was laid out in a pasture—it was a poor excuse for a diamond, with gopher holes that tripped the outfielders, but it did have a backstop of chicken wire. *Opa* couldn't walk clear out to the pasture, so he borrowed a team of horses and a spring wagon and drove out to watch the games. He took me along. When the team needed a bat boy, I got the job. I was nine years old.

It was a big deal for me to be part of the game of baseball, to hang around the older guys, the Saturday heroes. Sometimes I played in practice innings or pre-game warm-ups. Usually I was stuck out in the outfields to shag fly balls or to pig tail—back up the catcher. I didn't care where I played, just so I played. I wanted to be good enough to make the team when I grew up.

As time went on, it was obvious all the old rules against baseball had disappeared and a large percentage of the total community participated in the game, either as players or spectators. There were no more efforts to stop the game from being played.

Middle's big rival was Amana. A Middle-Amana game always drew a big crowd. An ordinary Middle game attracted fifty or so fans but a Middle-Amana match-up pulled in two or three times that many. They flocked in by the wagonloads. They pressed against the backstop screen or sat on the grass along the third and first baselines. There were no grandstands or bleachers. The fans were mostly men. A girl might go to the games to watch a certain player that she admired. Helen saw me play when I was on the high school team before we had ever dated.

There's one game between Middle and Amana that's still talked about today. Middle was always number one in the village league but that particular year, it came down to the last game of the season, to the game between Middle and Amana, to decide which team would be tops in the league. Middle's team really believed Amana could never beat them but just to tease the Amana team, get them mad and riled up before the game, some of the players on the Middle team rustled a Holstein heifer calf out of the dairy barn and tied her to a stake out in left field with a sign around the calf's neck that read, "Middle beats Amana and this is no bull!"

After a ballgame, the baseball players got together to rehash the game and to have a little wine. Baseball and wine drinking—those two pastimes just seemed to go together in Amana. After a game the players needed to celebrate a win or console themselves for a loss. Most of the time, the guys from Middle were celebrating.

After the Great Change in 1932, baseball moved from the cow pasture to the school playground. The second year after the Change, the Colonies league went into a rapid decline. Entire team rosters were all but wiped out. Many young players either moved away or took jobs outside the Colonies and no longer had time to practice and play baseball.

By 1934, the smaller villages couldn't even field a team. But there were enough good players left to form one Amana team. They called themselves the Demons. Can you beat that? A bunch of guys from this little church-going colony were a baseball team with a name like that! That team played teams from nearby towns.

After Prohibition, the players no longer had to sneak around to drink wine after the games and that ended the after-game partying. It was more fun for them when they had to do it "on-the-sly."

I started on the Amana high school baseball team when I was a freshman. I played my first two years under Howard Durner and my last two years under Charlie Selzer. By the time I was a senior, I was six feet tall and weighed 185 pounds. I was a pitcher, but I couldn't pitch every game, so when I wasn't on the mound, I played in the outfield. I had a good strong arm and it was good in those positions, too, because I could throw the long ball to home plate and pick off a runner tagging up to score after the long fly ball.

I was a good hitter and usually batted third or fourth in the line-up, which was another reason the coaches always made sure I was in a game playing some spot so I could hit. I was never a benchwarmer. I hit home runs, lots of them. Once I hit three home runs in one game. It was a big day for me!

"What's your pitch?" That's the question always asked of a pitcher.

The Amana Athletic Association league champions in 1928 included (front row, from left) Carl Hahn, Henry Roemig, William Rettig and Rudolph Hergert. Standing (from left) are William Hahn, Carl Metz, William (Bill) Zuber, Carl Heinze, George Deuchler, William Hoppe and Fred Schinnerling. Bill Zuber later had a remarkable career with professional ball clubs.

"FAST!" was the word I gave to describe my best pitch. I got plenty of strike-outs in every game. There weren't any radar speed guns in the 1940's to measure how fast I threw the ball. Batters who faced me said I threw the ball "lightning fast."

About the time I graduated from high school, the Cleveland Indians had just found Bobby Feller warming up with his dad down behind their barn on the Feller farm out by Van Meter, Iowa. From then on, it seemed as though every high school or American Legion baseball coach in the whole state of Iowa thought he was a major league baseball scout. The Indians were especially hot to find another kid like Feller out here in the Iowa cornfields. Well, Coach Selzer thought he had a pretty good country pitcher in me and he passed the word to Ollie Marquardt of the Cedar Rapids Raiders. An agent was sent to Amana to check me out.

At the time, I wasn't aware that I was being observed, so I was surprised when the agent came around after the game and invited me to Cedar Rapids to work out with the Raiders. I pitched batting practice for the team. The coaches evidently liked what they saw and the agent offered me a contract for the following year to pitch for a Cleveland Indians farm team. I have newspaper clippings telling that I signed that first contract and clippings relating that I went off to spring training camp.

I played the next seasons in the Northern League with the Fargo, North Dakota-Moorhead, Minnesota, Twins before going to the Ohio State League where I was with the Findley, Ohio, team.

During my second season with Findley, I was plagued by a back injury. It did not respond to rest or therapy and I quit the game of baseball but not without a lot of wonderful memories of some great times.

My first contract to play baseball was for $80.00 a month. At the time, I thought that was a fortune, not to mention the fact I was getting paid just to play the game. The contract is packed away with all of the newspaper clippings from my playing days and I take it out and look at it every so often. Just looking at it gives me a thrill. It was my dream to play baseball and I did. I didn't play as long as I would like to have played, but I don't look back at it as a dream that was shattered. I look at it rather as an opportunity. It was an opportunity that I took a crack at. I really believe, when an opportunity comes your way and there's a chance for you to get something you want, you have to try to make good on that opportunity, you have to give it everything you've got. I had a chance to play baseball and I took it. I gave baseball a hard try, I threw my best pitch and I will always be glad I did.

George and Helen Kraus (center) on their wedding day, September 30, 1944. With them are John Berger and Colette Fischer.

16. After Baseball

Late in 1942, only a few months after I was back from playing baseball, I was called to take a physical for the World War II draft. Because of my back injury, I didn't pass.

At that point I was hired by a Cedar Rapids farm equipment manufacturer. I worked for that firm fifteen years.

In 1957, after I had done just about everything from clerking in parts to service and sales with the firm, I started my own equipment distributorship. Five years later, Al Frieden and I formed a partnership to purchase a bankrupt plant. We manufactured fertilizer blenders, spreaders, conveyors and bulk feed delivery systems. It was the right time for that kind of business in this agricultural area. Small farms were beginning to disappear. Farmers were using more and more equipment to work more and more acres of land in order to produce higher and higher yields. It was no longer efficient, practical or cost-effective to spread barnyard fertilizer on the fields. The farmers needed commercial fertilizers with accurate, laboratory controlled nutrients which could be applied more quickly with the kind of machinery we were making.

All day long I dealt with people—people on the phone, people in person across the desk from me, laborers out on the line in the plant, suppliers, truckers, salesmen. At night and on weekends, I made wine. I made it all by myself down in the cellar where it was calm, quiet and secluded. It was a nice change of pace for me after a day at the office.

Both businesses did well financially and between the two, they kept me very busy but in a nicely balanced way. When I was in Cedar Rapids on the job, I knew the winery was in good hands, thanks to Helen and our children. Each day, they all did whatever jobs needed doing down in the cellar or in the wine shop. Together we got the wine made and sold.

In 1972, Helen and I were ready for a slower work pace. We wanted more free time to travel and take more vacations. My partner and I sold our manufacturing business. Under the sale agreement, I served an additional five years as president of the Kraus Division of that corporation.

Five years was enough. I found out running a division for a big corporation wasn't for me. After years of making my own way in the business world, I had become used to making quick decisions. I wasn't comfortable in a large, industrial company.

In the corporate structure, it seems to me, the higher the person gets in that structure, the farther removed he gets from his buyer, the end user of his product. That bothered me. When I was in the equipment business, I had the chance every day to either talk to a prospect on the phone or to see him in person out in the field and to find out directly from him if he was satisfied with the machinery we were manufacturing.

In the winery, I am the winemaker and anytime I want to hear from my buyer, all I have to do is go upstairs to the wine shop and talk to the customers. I like having that close contact with my customer.

For every business man or woman in the world who has to suit up, spend hours each day at a desk, talk on the phone and see people, or maybe has to pack up, hit the road, race for a plane, I recommend they start their own little winery. Making wine would take away from the jangling telephone, the traffic, the hub-bub. It sure did for me.

Harvest scene on Amana lands. Rudolph Kellenberger photo.

17. Our First Sale

After I miscued on the inspection, and from then on, I made sure I followed all the laws, rules and regulations spelled out in the little booklet the United States Bureau of Alcohol, Tobacco and Firearms furnishes a new winery.

After Prohibition was repealed, wineries came under government agencies at both the state and federal levels. To operate a bonded and licensed winery, you file an application with the nearest Regional Commissioner for the United States Government's Department of Internal Revenue Service. The Bureau of Alcohol, Tobacco and Firearms is under that department because it collects taxes. The application includes a description of the facility, a drawing or blueprint of the plant, detailed lists of all equipment used in the winery such as crushers, presses, vats, tanks, barrels, right down to the smallest utensils. Formulas for the wines you plan to make are part of the application and must include the length of fermentation and the anticipated percentage of alcohol in the finished wine. A sample label is filed. The label must show the kind of wine, the alcohol content, the name and location of the winery and the brand name of the wine. The winery must also post a bond guaranteeing payment of federal taxes, the sum to be no less than the total tax due on all wine in the winery's possession at any given time.

When that paperwork is done, the winery is subject to an "on site inspection." It was at this point that I had been out of step when I started the winery.

An inspector wants to see the premises just as it is going to be used. Tanks and barrels must be marked as to whether they will be used for fermenting or for storage. He wants to see that all supplies and materials will be handled in a safe manner, that the winery has the correct temperature and good air circulation, and that all wine, regardless of whether it is in tanks, barrels or bottles, has safe, clean surroundings.

Once approved, the winery is given an identification number. That number goes on file and applies only to that winery for as long as the winery exists. The number must appear on all records, documents and letters submitted to any governmental agencies thereafter.

That's only the beginning of the paperwork. Records are kept on materials received and used, such as sugar, fruits, vegetables and any other supplies. A perpetual inventory is run on the gallons of wine in fermentation, in storage, in bottles and when it is sold. We are allowed a three percent loss due to shrinkage, evaporation or leakage when we compute the final figures we must submit each month. Fiscal year totals are submitted on June 30th and December 31st each year for as long as the winery operates.

The only time we see an official now is when agents make unannounced inspections. We are supposed to get those once or twice a year. In those visits, not only does the winery get the once-over, but all the books and records must be opened, too.

The winery records are the basis for the wine tax paid twice a month, on the 15th and the last day of the month. Movement of every gallon of wine throughout the year must be on the records. Wine in fermenting or storage tanks is not taxed. As soon as wine is bottled, sealed, labeled and moved to the sales room, the tax must be paid on it.

We pay a per gallon federal tax. There is no Iowa state tax on wine. When the wine is sold, then we pay the state sales tax. The state also collects a manufacturer's fee. The federal tax includes one rate for wine under fourteen percent alcohol and another rate for wine over fourteen percent and up to twenty-one percent alcohol. Kraus wines fall in both ranges. The rates have not changed since we have been in the wine business.

All wineries operate under the same rules. As of October 1982 there were 1,084 wineries in the United States. Our little winery obeys the same laws that govern larger California and New York wineries.

Each state has its own set of laws on marketing, selling, advertising and otherwise promoting liquor and wine. In Iowa, every winery is controlled by the Iowa State Liquor Control Commission. Under Iowa law, native wines made in Iowa may be sold only on the premises where the wine is made. It is possible, however, to sell such wine outside Iowa by obtaining an Iowa manufacturing license and by complying with the wine laws of the state into which the wine is being shipped. We are not allowed to ship or mail wine to an individual. An Iowa winery may not sell wine by the glass. Only restaurants or bars with a state retail liquor-by-the-drink license may do that. We are allowed to give free samples, however, from a bottle of the kind of wine the customer may be interested in buying. Under Iowa laws, a winery is not allowed to sell at retail more than five gallons of wine to an individual in one sales transaction. Recent changes in the law permit the sale of wine on legal holidays, election days and Sundays.

By February 1950, our first big batch of *Piestengel* was finished. I filled several one-gallon jugs and carried them up from the cellar to a clothes closet just off the living room, near the front door of our house. With every trip I made up those stairs with the box of wine jugs, I was reviewing all the laws, making sure I was in full compliance and ready to sell the wine. When I was positive everything was in order, then I began to wonder how long it would take to sell four hundred gallons of wine.

"*Grosse gusch und nix Da Hinter.*" I couldn't help being reminded of that old German slang expression which means, "Large mouth with nothing behind it." It was a thought that had come to my mind every now and then since we had decided to start a winery. Well, I had made the wine—four hundred gallons of it—and now it was ready and I would let it speak for itself.

The front closet was our upstairs storage for the wine and the top drawer of a three-drawer walnut chest in the front hall held our cash box—a cardboard cigar box with a hinged lid. That may not sound very business-like, but we made do with what we had. The closet still had to hold our coats and jackets. We couldn't build a separate shop for wine right at the start and we sure couldn't afford to go out and buy an adding machine or a cash register to keep track of the little dabs of money we expected to handle. We did take the time and trouble, though, to keep careful and accurate records of all our sales and the daily receipts so we would be right on line to meet the state and federal regulations on paying taxes on what we sold.

We decided to start selling wine on March 1, 1950. It was a Wednesday. The night before, I dug a hole straight out from the front door, next to the street, to set the post that would hold the new sign which read "WINE FOR SALE." The four-inch black letters were painted on a white board and underneath in smaller letters were "Rhubarb" and "Grape."

The next morning I headed off to Cedar Rapids to work. Helen waited anxiously to see what was going to happen. While she waited, she tried to go about her usual house-work, but she couldn't help glancing out the window toward the street now and then.

"Nothing happened all morning," she told me later. "No one stopped. The front door never opened once." Helen began to think she wasn't going to make a single sale on that first day. Then about two o'clock in the afternoon, in comes Ray Koepple from Cedar Rapids. He was a traveling salesman who made regular calls to the Amana Refrigeration Company office here in Middle. He had been to their offices that day, had had lunch with some of the men there and he drove by our house to see, by chance, if I had started to sell wine yet. Ray called on the firm where I worked and we had become acquainted. He knew I had made wine to sell. Ray was glad to see the sign was up. He was ready to buy some wine. He bought a gallon of rhubarb wine for $2.50. That was it! Our first sale!

For the first few years, we sold wine only in gallon jugs. Half-gallon jugs were added later, and in 1968, we began to use the fifth bottles, bottles that hold one-fifth of a gallon.

Every day from then on, Helen sold four or five gallons of wine. Oh sure, there were some days when nobody stopped and she sold nothing. But there were very few of those days.

Ray Koepple spread the word around Cedar Rapids about Kraus wines. He helped our business to grow.

From the start, we gave out samples of the wines, right in the front hall. We set a tray of eight small glasses on the chest of drawers and always invited our customers to have a sample before they bought. Actually those little, stemless, cranberry-colored crystal glasses were prized souvenirs of a visit to Ebenezer, New York, the place where our forefathers once lived. The glasses were made at an Ebenezer glass factory. We passed out thousands of samples in those glasses. For a long time, we had only the two wines, rhubarb and grape. Sampling doesn't take very long when you only have two wines to sample.

Right from the start, the demand for the wines grew. It grew so fast and kept Helen so busy, she soon discovered she preferred selling wine to operating a beauty shop. When we expanded and remodeled, she didn't mind giving up the space her shop had occupied in order for us to make the present wine shop.

I have been asked whether I would still make wine just for our family if we didn't have a commercial winery. I honestly think I would. You see, I am a winemaker who really likes to make wine. More than that, I really like having others enjoy the wines I make. I get a great deal of pleasure and satisfaction from making and from selling wine.

The rhubarb and grape wines sold out so fast our first year in the winery, I boosted the total volume to a thousand gallons the second year. A thousand gallons was all I had time to make and to take care of at that time and that was all the basement would hold then, too.

In the first year, the winery business brought in about $1,500—pretty nice for "pin money," I'd say. The next year, that figure jumped to $2,500 where it held steady for several years until we expanded the winery.

18. The Making of Kraus Wines

Wine wasn't invented. It just happened. No one knows who the first winemakers were but sketchy hieroglyphics of grape clusters on goblets connect wine to the ancient civilizations. There is a theory that the very first batch of wine was an accident. Juice with just the right balance of sugar and yeasts was forgotten and was shoved back to the corner of a cave or tent. There, without any help or interference from man, it slowly turned into alcohol. When the scum covered mess was discovered months later, it was tasted, no doubt reluctantly. Imagine the unexpected jolt and pleasure the very first wine taster got! Wine was an instant hit! From then on, juice "accidents" were encouraged. They were intentionally and deliberately set.

In the beginning, people not only liked drinking the wine, they soon found out drinking wine was a practical and sensible thing to do if they wanted to avoid being sick. There were no sanitation engineers or pollution control centers, and the connection between careless disposal of wastes and impure drinking water had not been discovered. But people did realize that those who drank wine instead of water were sick less often than those who drank only water.

Drinking wine in place of water is still a common practice in many parts of Europe and the rest of the world.

"Don't drink the water" is the slogan you hear when you travel. I say that is as good an excuse as any to drink wine.

There are no records or stories tying other-than-grape wines to a particular place or time in history, but it is believed they were made not only as "happy" beverages but also for tribal ceremonials and religious rituals in much the same way grape wines were used. History does show that there were times when vineyards were struck with disease and drought and whole sections of Europe went without grape wine. If they were to have any wine during those periods, they had to resort to other sources. Other extracts may also have been used when grape wines were preempted by landlords, political and church leaders, leaving the peasants to their own winemaking devices.

There are, after all, only a few choice spots on the whole planet earth that are superior for growing grapes. Grapes require a climate that is not too hot, not too cold, not too wet and not too dry and they like soil that would generally be considered poor—a soil that is sandy, flinty and loose, land that is usually not suitable for other crops.

Iowa's soil was a prime asset when the Inspirationists moved west. The land here was good for grain and hay, but too rich for grapes. The climate here wasn't the best, either.

Even in areas where grapes thrive, they can be harvested only once a year. Many other wine sources are available almost any month of the year; therefore, making wine from sources other than grapes has more flexibility.

I would bet there is not a place in this country or in the world, for that matter, that doesn't have some fruit, berry, flower, vegetable or some other plant material that will make a juice capable of becoming wine. You don't have to be rich and own a vineyard to make your own wine. Nature furnishes many other products from which wine can be made. Some of those products are used to make Kraus wines.

Other-than-grape wines have been around probably for as long as grape wines. Long before the first settlers arrived in this hemisphere, American Indians were fermenting berries and grains. In what is now the southwestern part of the United States, cactus was the source of alcohol. It still is today in Mexico and elsewhere.

Religion was a strong force behind the spread of winemaking. Monks tended vineyards and ran some of the best and certainly some of the largest wineries in Europe, where wine was part of every meal. Wine comforted the aged and the sick. It cheered and refreshed the weary. It was a gesture of friendliness and hospitality. It was a gift. It was a thank you. It sealed pledges between sweethearts and ambassadors. A cup or a glass of wine was part of the daily lives and the celebrations and festivals and feasts for the rich and the poor alike.

That is how wine is still used today.

In Germany, the link between the monastery and the winery was well-known. The winemakers must have been very good at their job and they also did a good job of teaching others. German wines have always had a good reputation and are popular all over the world. German winemakers had to have been a hardy lot of farmers. They were able to produce great wines in spite of less than favorable weather. Rain never came at all or it came in downpours. The sun was seldom seen. They tilled soil that wouldn't support any other marketable crops. When grapes ran short or failed altogether, the Germans turned to their gardens, orchards, fields and woods for their wines.

Amana's winemakers came from such a background. They had brought those old winemaking lessons with them to Amana. The lessons were all in their heads. Even though there had been some scientific breakthroughs which greatly improved the quality of wine and reduced the number of yearly failures, news of those laboratory findings did not reach the winemakers here in this little, secluded and isolated community. Winemaking here continued to be somewhat chancy.

Some say winemaking is an art, others say it's a science, still others say it's a craft. To me, it's all of those things plus years and years of experience. When it comes right down to it, winemaking is really an act of nature. The winemaker is nature's helper. If nature does all the work, how come I'm the one who gets so tired?

Winemaking is not for the lazy. There's a good deal of strenuous, physical labor involved—unloading fresh produce, pushing it through the crusher, the grinder and then the press, stacking boxed bottles of wine for storage and later hoisting them up that long flight of stairs from the basement to the wine shop—it's all grubby, sweaty work. I am always pulling, tugging, pushing, shoving or lifting something. But I no longer worry that my hard work will be wasted if a wine fails. Wine losses simply do not need to happen today. All aspects of winemaking are now much more controllable than they were in the old days. From start to finish, from crushing to pressing to fermentation to bottling, we are rid of the guesswork.

The winemaker and the wine drinker both have the world of science to thank for improving winemaking procedures. They should also thank the United States government for demanding that winemakers operate according to the rules and regulations.

While it's sure not easy for most winemakers to say it, the truth is that it has been a very good thing for winemakers to know they were going to be inspected and to know they had to follow government-approved and standardized methods for making wine. It has been good for the industry and it has been good for the consumer.

Wineries are classified as "standard" or "other than standard." The classification is based solely on the method used to make wine. A "standard" winery must use a specified amount of grape juice, no water, to make wine. Sugar may be added in very limited amounts if the grape juice falls below a specified level of sweetness.

An "other than standard" winery makes only formula wines, wines made by using specified amounts of juice, water and sugar as allowed in an approved formula. An "other than standard" winery may make wine from many different juices, including grape juice.

Maybe it sounds like a winemaker has only to follow standardized formulas and procedures and he'll turn out top quality wine every time. That's not the case. The winemaker is still left with plenty of day-to-day decisions that only he can make: When to rack? How many times to filter? When to bottle? The wine industry has gained a great deal from technology over the years, but many things remain a judgment call for the winemaker. Technology hasn't completely taken over nature's role in the juice and that's where winemaking really starts—in the juice. The juice determines how fast and how thoroughly fermentation will progress and when the wine will mature. Even with set formulas, fermentation still varies with every batch of wine.

It takes time to transform juice into a dark, clear, fragrant red wine or a glittering, pale gold wine. Fermentation cannot and must not be hurried. For me, the long wait adds to the anticipation of what is to come. Everything is so rush, rush, rush today, but now more than ever, we must accept waiting. In the end, we are waiting for something wonderful to happen. For the wine to be its very best, it has to have time. The winemaker just has to wait it out.

No matter how patient I am or how hard I've worked, the work and the waiting could be blown away by sloppy, careless sanitation. I make sure that doesn't happen. All the way through every single step of winemaking, I have one rule and I harp on it—KEEP IT CLEAN! Some folks picture a wine cellar as a dark, dingy dungeon, full of cobwebs. That's not what they'd find at this winery or at any other winery that is striving to make first rate wine.

The cellar work here is usually a one-man show. If I can handle the work by myself, I like it that way. I may be the owner and operator of Old Style Colony Winery, but I might also be the janitor who pushes a broom sweeping up the place or the muscleman on the press jack or the friendly clerk in the wine shop. I hire help only for the busiest days when I am extracting juice or bottling. It is a small winery but it is efficient. Everything has to be in place all the time, especially when equipment is being operated. If one thing is out of place, it's like everything is out of whack.

The winery is either going full force or it is sitting completely quiet. During extracting and formulating, it is a flurry of noise and commotion. Filtering and bottling are quieter and seem slow-motion by comparison.

Thirty percent of my cellar time is spent making the wine. That includes all the steps necessary to extract the juice, press and formulate. Another fifteen percent is spent filtering. Fifty percent is spent bottling, labeling and stocking the wine shop. The remaining five percent goes to paperwork, tax and sales records and ordering supplies.

In the early years, if I needed help down in the cellar, all I had to do was holler and Papa came or Helen came or one of the kids, if they happened to be home. It's perfectly legal for offspring to participate in a family-owned winery. But I could not hire anyone else under the legal drinking age in Iowa to sell wine.

Donna, Kandyce and Dennis all picked blossoms, yanked rhubarb, lugged supplies around in the basement and did whatever needed doing. They've helped out in the wine shop, too. They have seen the wine business inside and out, bottom to the top and from all sides.

When Kandyce married Neil Hannon and Dennis married Margaret Fawcett, you can be sure Kraus wines were on the menu for both wedding receptions.

Opa lived to see me make wine to sell and I know it made him happy to see how folks took to the old wines he used to make. If he felt badly about any of it, it was that he couldn't get around well enough to help me make the wines. He would have been right down there in the thick of all the cellar work if he hadn't been hobbled by arthritis. He would have loved seeing the basement full of wine and winemaking equipment. He wouldn't have liked all the record keeping that now has to be done. I didn't like it at first, but I have done it so long, I do it automatically.

I only mark the "starts" on my winery calendar. That's when a wine is actually formulated and put into a fermenting tank. Once wine is started, I look ahead to determine about when I can expect to be filtering and bottling that batch. I mark those dates on my calendar after the wine has worked and matured for a while. Once it's in the tank, wine doesn't work on my schedule. It doesn't have a tight, fixed schedule at all. It makes up its own schedule as it goes along. I don't tell the wine when it's done, it tells me. I may have all the way from twelve to fifteen, sixteen wines, all in different stages of their development, working at the same time. People wonder how I can keep track of them all.

I've got the simplest, easiest system there is. I write it down on a card taped to the outside of the tank, just like you would write on a blackboard. I put down the name of the wine, the government's formula number, the starting date and the number of gallons in that tank. Later, when the wine is filtered, that date is marked there, too. If it's finished wine that is in storage, the alcoholic content is written there, too.

Any time of the day, any day of the year that I go to the cellar, I can be busy. There's always something that needs to be done. To the casual observer, I may look like I'm taking a stroll around the winery but as I go from tank to tank, I read my notes. The notes remind me of what is happening with each tank of wine and what is going to be happening with it. In a glance, I can tell which wine will be the next one up for filtering or bottling.

Making as many wines as I do is really an advantage, because the wines all have different timing patterns. I start a wine, bring it to a certain point, such as into fermenting or holding in storage, and from then on, the wine just takes care of itself and I am free to start a new batch of wine or take care of those already underway that need my attention.

My winemaking year begins in March and ends in October.

Down through the year, month by month my starts go like this:

March—grapefruit and orange.

May—dandelion near the first of the month and rhubarb near the end.

June—red clover around the middle of the month and blackberry at the end.

July—cherry right after the Fourth, and later in the month, blueberry. If June clover picking ran light, I might need another clover picking about the middle of July.

August—beet.

September—tomato.

October—grapes in the early days and cranberry near the end. Grapes have to be harvested before frost hits. There have been years when some of the grapes were picked in September.

It is vital that I stick to a precise timetable on two procedures—formulating and pre-fermenting.

Once I have the juice, then I want formulation to move right along, smoothly and quickly. It's important to get it off to a good, clean, fast start into fermentation so it has a lively and a bubbly start at a strong, even pace, not slow and sluggish. An active send-off means more flavor and a clearer color in the finished wine a year or so later.

In the case of pre-fermenting on grapes or soaking of blossoms, I make sure the top layer is broken up with regular, punctual agitation. The top layer needs to be stirred all the way down, over and through itself, so the pulp never dries out, forming a cap. That would invite mold or spoilage.

That isn't to say other winemaking steps aren't just as important. It just means the other steps aren't timed to the minute as much as formulating and pre-fermenting are. Those two steps need careful watching. There is a little more leeway and flexibility as to the day or the week that I do some of the other steps.

Many of the wines move from produce to juice to formula all in one working day. Pre-fermented wines take longer, some as much as a week longer. The size of the batch, the number of gallons being set, doesn't affect preparation time very much. Preparation time is determined by the number of steps involved and their degree of complexity.

From the mixing vat to the bottle takes ten months for some wines and up to twenty months for others. Rhubarb has the shortest maturing time and blossom wines the longest.

Each kind of wine is made every year in quantities sufficient to replenish the sales stock and to allow for any projected market increases.

19. First Comes the Produce

Kraus wines really start in the vineyard, the garden, the grove and the field. I want to know my wines from the ground up, from the garden to the glass. In the case of rhubarb, that's easy. It grows right in our own back yard and I am the one who sees that it is fed, cultivated and, if necessary, watered. As for the rest of the products, even though they aren't under my direct supervision, I do advise and consult on them as much as I possibly can.

I have been in the fields of every grower I deal with. The fields are scattered in many states. After I have once contracted with a grower and he knows the kind of produce I want, the degree of ripeness and, in some cases, the sugar content I have to have, then I feel that he will ship me the pick of his crop. A grower will call on the phone and give me a report on the fruit when he thinks it is ready. I say "Ship," and within hours, his produce is unloaded at the winery door and is put on flat bed carts or the small hand trucks. From then, it's all up to me.

Wines can't be any better than the juice they start with, and the juice can't be any better than the produce it comes from in the first place. I ask the grower to ship me his best at its peak and I go from there. If I don't short-change nature, nature won't short-change the wine. There's no way to get out any better than you put in, so I don't skimp. I put in the very best that I can buy.

Nature holds only a promise of what the wines can be. It's up to me to guide and guard the juices along their way to becoming wine. Wine is a living thing and like all living things it may encounter some risks as it flourishes and matures. That's when the winemaker lends his protection.

A strong, active vitality during fermentation depends on the sugar content being balanced by acids, allowing a full, natural interaction of the yeasts that are already present in the produce. That calls for the juiciest, sweetest, ripest product, so ripe that it is just short of being over-ripe and on the verge of spoiling. The most juice and the best quality juice comes from produce that has had the best care—spraying, feeding, pruning, cultivating—and all done thoroughly and on time. The best farmer in the world can't totally eliminate threats of bad weather. Irrigation systems can alleviate shortfalls of rain and can, to some extent, make minor temperature adjustments when temperatures fall below normal prior to harvest. Other than that, crops are subject to the changeable whims of the weather.

Some years, even before the season starts, or after it is underway, a shortage can be predicted. When that happens, I have a chance to adjust how much I buy or where I buy. But a violent storm can take a crop out overnight. A hail storm can wipe out a crop when it is right on the brink of picking. Since I have had the winery, there's never been a complete crop failure in any of the produce. A few times, an early frost has put a dent in how much of one particular kind of grape wine I am able to make for that year. When that has happened, I adjusted by making more wine from grapes that weren't cut short so my total grape wine volume for that year remained the same.

Even on minor, day-to-day decisions, the weather determines what I might be doing in the winery. The weather controls when dandelion and clover blossoms are picked, when rhubarb is pulled, when the blueberry grower will call to say he is ready to pick. Weather won't wait, and a winemaker must be flexible. Schedules may have to be varied every day, hour by hour.

No two seasons are alike. Some are cold and wet. Others are hot and dry. Some years there are blights and insect infestations. Frost may come too soon. Rain at harvest is another problem. Wind and hail cut down yields and damage produce. That slows down harvest and processing. And that can happen anywhere, in Michigan in the vineyards or right in our own back yard.

One year, there was a heavy hailstorm late in May, just before the rhubarb was ready. Hailstones as big as golf balls pelted down. A strong wind tossed the big rhubarb leaves. Usually the leaves act like a big canopy that shelters the stalks. But the leaves were no help in that storm. The stalks were damaged and scarred. They had holes knocked in them.

The storm had come up late in the afternoon and it passed through rather quickly. After it calmed down, the sun came out. You know the kind of an evening, where there is a big beautiful rainbow off to the east against heavy, gray and blue skies. Well, I got the whole family—Helen, the kids, Mama and Papa—out there and we all pulled the rhubarb as fast as we could. With the stalks split and bruised, the juice would have leaked out and been lost. If we had let the stalks lay there until morning, we would have lost that year's rhubarb wine. We made the *Piestengel* a little early that year, but it turned out fine, just fine.

Hailstorms aren't as devastating to dandelion and red clover blossoms. Hail might cut down on the number of perfect blooms but the plants recover and send up another round of blooms.

Another year on a May night, after a very quiet, very still and warm day, we had gone to bed under a sky full of stars. There was no breeze at all. The bedroom window was open and the curtains hung limp. In Iowa, those conditions make us suspicious. Sure enough, about midnight I woke up to a clattering. It was hail. Lightning ripped the sky and the whole house trembled from the thunder. The sky was lit up like floodlights. I could see hail piling up.

There was nothing to do but watch and hope it didn't hurt the rhubarb. The next morning, I found that a few stalks had been hurt but not enough to cut the yield. The leaves had shielded the stalks.

The growers I buy from all know I make wine from their produce. Growers are always on the lookout for new places to sell their crops. When I take them back bottles of wine made from their blueberries or cranberries, it may be the first time that grower has tasted that kind of wine. Making wine from their crop was, at first, a brand new idea for many of them, but it has given them a new appreciation for their crop and for my business.

Growers get rid of decayed, bruised, green, immature, blemished, mildewed and inferior culls before they box or package their goods. They all have processing plants, packing and shipping sheds right in or near their fields.

I have requested that the produce trucks arrive at the winery during daytime hours. Big trucks, semi-trucks, tractor-trailer rigs are a curiosity and a noisy intrusion in Middle even in daylight hours. If they rumbled in here in the middle of the night, they would really shake the local people up. It would probably shake up the drivers, too, if they had to find the winery at night on these narrow, country-road streets. The drivers need all the help they can get to negotiate some of the turns.

Trucks back up to the lower, ground level winery door. The tractor is unhooked and driven away. Then the driver heads out to one of the fine Amana places to eat. He fills up on sausage or ham or pie, while I unload the goods. That is usually when I yell for a friend to come help me get the stuff unloaded and stacked in the basement. Then the driver comes back, hooks up his trailer and drives off.

For the grower, harvest is the end of his season. For me, the winemaker, harvest is just the beginning.

20. Four Main Steps

There are four primary steps in making Kraus wines—extraction, formulation, fermentation and racking.

Extraction of the juice from the originating product may also involve secondary steps, such as soaking, cooking, grinding, crushing, squeezing or pre-fermenting prior to pressing.

Formulation is the mixing of the juice, sugar and water in the proportions stated in the approved formula.

Fermentation is the natural biochemical reaction of yeast slowly turning all sugars present in the juice and in the formula into alcohol.

Racking is the removal of the evolved wine from one barrel in which the wine fermented into another fresh, clean barrel. It is a clarifying process. It draws off the clear wine and leaves behind the "lees," the solid sediments, flecks of pulp, skin, yeast and tartrate particles that are thrown off during fermentation. Racking used to be done just by siphoning off the clear wine but since I now use a filtering machine when racking the wine, I refer to this step as filtering.

None of the steps are ever abbreviated or skipped. As time-consuming and painstaking as some of the operations are, they are done over and over, again and again, the exact same way, every time. Winemaking requires that kind of precision, that kind of attention to the details. It is the only way to be sure the wines are always right.

Nearly every piece of winery equipment has been outfitted with rollers or casters. Large vats and heavy machines can be scooted quickly and easily around the basement. Lightweight, easy to clean, stainless steel pails, measures and tubing have replaced heavy wooden and rubber items. With the exception of a few wooden barrels still used to store wine from short runs, stainless steel has replaced wood throughout the winery. Any equipment that touches the juice during crushing, pressing or mixing is stainless steel. Stainless steel is superior because it does not interact with acids in the juice and therefore it has no effect on the flavor of the resulting wine. Copper, iron or galvanized metals are avoided. Stainless steel meets the criteria and is a breeze to clean.

Wooden barrels can be a headache. They have to be replaced and they aren't easy to find any more. They are a pain to clean and sterilize. Barrels are sometimes flawed and they leak. When there is leakage, fermentation doesn't proceed at the smooth, steady pace that is desirable. I use a few wooden barrels and only on a very limited basis.

To anyone who has ever visited a big, commercial winery, our winery hardly looks like a winery. There is no permanent assembly line of machines and equipment with conveyor belts that start at the door where, say for example, a truck load of grapes is unloaded.

A large volume winery housed in a building designed and constructed to be a winery may resemble such a description. But it doesn't happen quite like that here. Not when your winery is being operated in what once was a meat packing plant and was later converted into a family dwelling. I have 3,000 square feet of winery space and it does double duty, even triple and quadruple duty.

The area is divided mainly into three large rooms. In the first one, I receive the produce. In that same room, it is crushed or ground or whatever before it is pressed and formulated. In the middle room are the fermenting tanks and the filter machine. That's also where racking, filtering and bottling are done. The third big room is for storing finished wines before they are bottled. There are smaller rooms for storing supplies and one for keeping records.

Each Kraus wine has its own step-by-step recipe now. Variations in each recipe have to do with extraction and that in turn affects the order in which the machines are used. I will give details covering each variation when I get to the individual wines and how they are made. For now, I will cover the processes and the equipment—vats, press, tanks, filter—that are common to *all* wines.

I can walk and talk and take an imaginary batch of wine through the winery. My equipment is a mix of old and new. Each piece serves a particular purpose and together, they get the job done. Some of the equipment is available and is on the market from commercial winery suppliers. Some I have designed just for a specific job or to fit the space I have to work in.

There are vats in all shapes and sizes. Some are like lidless boxes, 36′ x 33′ x 48′ and others, round, three feet across and three feet deep. All of them hold up to 200 gallons of liquid and all are made of stainless steel. They are used interchangeably for soaking, formulating or pre-fermenting and they are all on rollers. Even when they are loaded, they are light enough for one person to handle. I work alone so much of the time that I have found rollers to be a big help, a big back-saver.

It wasn't long after we had started the winery that I realized one of my biggest bottlenecks was the old, two-ton press. It had to go. It was small, slow and it held up the processing. Yet there was the problem of limited space. The wine presses that were available from press manufacturers were all too big for the basement.

In 1956, I enlisted the help of a carpenter friend to build a five-ton press with a tub three feet deep and three feet across. The side of the tub is made of oak slats three-quarters of an inch thick, bevel-edged, and two-inches wide, banded by three stainless steel rings. Pressure comes from a hydraulic jack mounted on top of the press.

The old press was screwed down on the pulp in the tub by a horizontal lever. When the tub was full of thick pulp, getting that lever down was one tough job. It took a lot of muscle to pull it tighter and tighter, getting every last drop of juice out of the pulp. Working the jack down on the new press is a little work, too, but not too much for one man. And it does a much better job and it does it faster.

When pulp is dumped into the tub, the juice comes running out through the stainless steel screen at the bottom. Juice runs into the catch pan in a flat stream, like a little waterfall. The screen holds back tiny seeds, skin particles, anything that isn't juice.

By the end of the first day of pressing, pulp will appear to be all through oozing out. Then the jack is set into position. The bulkhead, a round, wooden disk, is fitted snugly down into the tub over the pulp and pressure is manually applied, very slowly at first. I take it down barely enough to get juice slowly running again. Juice must never gush out of the press, but it should come out not much faster than a good steady drip. Attempts to hurry the process can damage the press and, surprisingly, the juice yield from hard, fast pressing is substantially lower.

Tighten and wait. Tighten and wait. Tighten and wait. That's how good pressing is done. That goes on for hours, even days, until no more juice comes through the screen. Those very last few hours of pressing must not be cut short. Those last drops of juice are loaded with flavor. They make all the difference in the wine you will be drinking a year later. You have to take all the time it takes to get them all. Getting those last drops, the juice will be going plink-plink-plink-plink and then it just stops...stops altogether...there's not one more plink.

Then the jack is pulled, the wooden disk removed and all that is left in the bottom of the press is a virtually dry, compact disk of pulp. The looks, color and texture of disk varies depending on what was being pressed.

Throughout pressing, as juice collects in the flat, stainless steel catch pan, it is dipped up and measured into a larger formulating vat. By the time step one, extracting, is done, work goes directly on to step two, formulating.

The components of a wine formula can be expressed several ways. My method specifies pounds of sugar per gallon of liquid. For example, if 2½ pounds of sugar are dissolved in one gallon of combined juice and water, then the proportions according to that formula would be 2½ pounds to one gallon. Each formula has an allowable range established at the time the formula is approved. The formula for a fifty-gallon batch of wine may read "115 pounds of sugar to 20 gallons of juice plus water enough to total 50 gallons." Ranges allowed in approved formulas eliminate paper work that would be necessary on each new batch of wine in the event growing conditions or other harvest problems affect the sugar or acid content of the produce. Sugar and acid are vital factors in winemaking. Those two factors become one single consideration when making formula wines. Because sugar is part of the formula, the amount of sugar added can be adjusted to accommodate higher acids. This is particularly true with high acid products like rhubarb and tomatoes.

All products contain acid. It is the sharp, sour taste we all notice, say, in an unripe cherry or a stick of rhubarb. Yet you don't want to eliminate acid altogether when you make wine. If there were too little acid, you would get a flat, insipid, even bitter, medicinal tasting wine. Just the right amount of acid gives a bit of a bite and a tang that's right and natural for each wine.

Taste alone can't judge acids. Our taste buds can be fooled. Most fruits and berries have a fairly heavy acid content but the acid content is often masked by the large quantity of sugar also present in fully ripe fruits. The water that is added to formula wines also dilutes acid.

Cane sugar, ordinary household sugar, is used in the formulas. Juice does not resist sugar granules in the way water does, so the amount of sugar needed is first dissolved in part of the juice to make a very light syrup. It is so light you can hardly tell it is a syrup. Then the water is added.

I have even managed to mechanize part of the formulating with an industrial size, electric food mixer which can be clamped to the side of a formulating vat. It has a one-third horsepower motor that powers two stainless steel paddles on the end of the rotor blades. They whip up the solution. The hardest part is hooking the mixer to the side of the vat and that takes all of two seconds. This machine was made to be used in the food business. I doubt very much if the manufacturer ever thought it would be used in a winery, but for me, it is a slick deal and makes quick work of formulating.

It is important to agitate the solution enough to be sure all the sugar is thoroughly and quickly dissolved. Once the rest of the juice and water are combined and added, fermentation gets going. It starts right away. There's no stopping to wait for sugar crystals to finish dissolving. Just a few buzzes with the mixer and that's done. Hand-mixing that used to take me a couple of hours and leave my arms and shoulders aching is now done in seconds. It all happens as fast as it takes me to open up and pour out a fifty-pound sack of sugar. And that's fast.

It is important to be accurate on the sugar. During fermentation all sugars present turn to alcohol and that in turn determines the final alcohol content of the finished wine. Winemakers use another device from the food industry to get a sugar reading. It's a saccharimeter. It is a self-contained device with a bulb that floats in the solution and gives an instantaneous reading. There is no formula to be computed, no measuring to be done. A saccharimeter is a kind of polariscope that arranges light waves in an orderly fashion according to the amount of sugar concentration present.

Water is another important ingredient in formula wines. It is essential that it be the purest water available. Our water comes from Middle's town well. By the time it reaches our house, it will have gone through all the treatment and testing the state requires to certify it fit for public consumption. At our house, it is circulated through a water conditioner located at the point where water enters the house. That removes trace elements, chlorine in particular. Later, at the time wine is being formulated, the water passes through a charcoal filter to further purify it and knock out any off-flavors or odors. Periodically, I have water samples checked at a laboratory to make sure all the systems are functioning properly.

I really go after chlorine. Of course, chlorine kills any bacteria that is present in the water and that is good, but after chlorine has done its job, then I want to get it out of the water before I make wine. Fast, active fermentation is vital to the wine getting off to a good start and chlorine hampers that fast start.

Some folks around Amana make their own family wines with rain water. They catch rain from the roof in a barrel under the downspout. They feel that the soft rain water is free of chemicals, additives, rust and dirt sometimes found in water lines. Maybe rain water used to be pure, but I don't think anyone can be sure any more with all the talk about air pollution and contamination.

During my first years in the winery, I moved the formulated solution into the fermenting barrels by buckets. I was a one-man bucket brigade. Fifteen years ago, I made the operation easier—a flick of an electric switch activates a pump that moves solutions from vats to tank, tanks to tanks—whenever and wherever it is needed—and it does it at three gallons per minute. A job that once took me all day is now done in an hour or two. The pump moves from room to room on a rolling stand.

The second basement room has all four walls lined with huge, sleek, stainless steel tanks. It is the fermenting room.

A fermenting container, whether it is a tank or a barrel, should not be filled clear to the brim. In those first, wild days of fermentation, the formula gets foam riled up and that foam has to have room at the top for expansion. That wildness may go on for thirty days. If the tank is too full, it would boil over. It would spill down the sides and could become a bed where unwanted bacteria could start growing. That could lead to spoiling. Newly set wine is vigorous. You have to give it room to work.

During the third step, fermentation, nature does its wonderwork. Slowly, yeast changes sugar into alcohol. Slowly, juice becomes wine. As the yeasts act on the sugars to make ethyl alcohol and carbon dioxide gas, there are other by-products, too, such as glycerol, acetic and lactic acids, and so on, but basically, winemaking is a simple thing.

When I say my wines are "naturally fermented," that means no chemicals are added to the juice or to the formula. I do not put in additives to speed up fermentation. Fermentation is done by the yeasts already present in the extractions from the fruits, vegetables or blossoms. Those yeasts occur in very minute amounts, yet the action they generate is usually sufficient to bring out full fermentation. Weather during the growing season can cause some variations. If this should happen, the product's own yeasts can be supplemented with a very small amount of natural yeast to make sure the fermentation goes along steadily so the wine finishes in its appropriate time frame.

To me, fermentation is a miracle. It's a magic act. It never ceases to amaze me. I doubt that wine drinkers, not very many of them at any rate, ever give a thought to or fully appreciate the miracle that is behind their favorite wines.

Few are aware of the hard work done by the tiny, tiny, microscopic, rounded, slightly egg-shaped yeast cells as they labor by the millions to turn sugary juice into an alcoholic potion. Yeast works until a predictable concentration of alcohol has formed. If more sugar exists than the yeast can convert, the finished wine is "sweet." If all, or nearly all, of the sugar is converted, then the finished wine is "dry."

When yeast works, it generates heat. If it gets too hot, above 90 degrees Fahrenheit, some yeast cells will be extinguished and the outcome is a diminished flavor and body in the wine. The fact that basements and cellars offer a cooler working environment for wine makes them a natural location for a winery. There is an old saying that when wine is fermenting, it is talking. To start with, it ferments fast and wild and there is a faint hissing, a sizzling sound that can be heard even if you are standing a few feet away. By pressing the palm of your hand to the side of the tank, you can feel the slight vibrations and tremors the fermentation causes.

As little carbon dioxide bubbles surface, they come up with a little burst, a little "pop." It is like the sound you get when you flick your thumb against a finger. It's a gentle commotion, more like a seething foam, not rambunctious and noisy. That first stage usually lasts a month, sometimes a little longer.

To start with, all of the wines were fermented in fifty-gallon barrels. I purchased used barrels from a whiskey distillery. The distillery would have charred them on the inside before they used them and after they had used them, the high alcohol content of the whiskey acted as a sterilant, so I did not have to sanitize them or do anything except to rinse out the charcoal and fill them with wine. The charring treatment sealed the wood so it didn't flavor the wine.

The work of fermentation is done by living organisms. They must have oxygen and they must have room to breathe. Wine fermenting in barrels draws what little air it needs through the pores of the wood. The "bung hole," the opening at the top of the barrel where the wine is poured into the barrel, has a *Stopfer*, a wooden bung. If the bung is too tight, the barrel might explode from the gas pressure building up inside. I have never had a blow-up but I have had some close calls, especially the first few years I had the winery and used only barrels. At the start of fermenting, enough gas is generated to rip the barrel apart if the bung was hammered in tight. Several times, I caught a barrel with its ends bulged a little. I loosened the bung and it didn't blow. Fermentation progresses faster in a small quantity than in a large amount—I would say almost twice as fast in a fifty-gallon barrel as in a 400-gallon tank.

The stainless tanks have air locks over their top openings. The locks vent out the gas and allow a minimal amount of oxygen into the tank. There are no valves on the air lock. In fact, the only gauge on a tank is the volume indicator that helps me keep track of how many gallons of wine are at work in the tank.

The whole idea of a closed container during fermenting is to capture all the essences of the wine within the developing wine, and to prevent them from being dissipated into the atmosphere. In my opinion, tanks do a superior job of that in addition to maintaining a uniform temperature and stabilizing the rate at which sugar becomes alcohol. It is that slow, steady exchange that yields the more natural, fresher tasting wines.

I am a regular walking commercial for stainless steel tanks. When I saw from my own experience, all of their advantages not only in sanitary matters but their effectiveness in fermentation, I ordered them. With their legs on, they are over seven feet tall. They are almost forty inches in diameter and each one holds 400 gallons.

When wine gets to the fermentation stage, all it needs is time. I give it all the time it wants. I believe time itself should be considered an ingredient in winemaking. Today, it is instant this, instant that, but some things should not be speeded up. Wine is one of those things.

Once the wine is in fermentation, I am not so much the winemaker as I am the wine sitter. I don't push. Wine is not to be hurried. My job is to sit, watch, wait and see how it turns out.

As time wears on, you barely hear the "pop" of an occasional bubble. The closer the wine gets to maturing, the slower it works. When it is all quiet, that means the yeast has expired and fermentation is over.

There is a lot of sophisticated testing equipment available today in the wine industry, but there isn't any of it that replaces the judgment and skill of the winemaster. At no time is this more important and more apparent than in the critical days near the end of fermentation. During those last few days, I feel the wine is really born. That's when wine is brought silently, secretly, slowly to its peak in taste, character, body, aroma and color. That point is reached by different wines in different lengths of time. Kraus wines take twelve to eighteen months to mature and a few may go slightly longer some years. Fruit wines with a high acid content, such as rhubarb, ferment faster than berry wines or those made from blossoms or vegetables. There is no problem in letting wines go a bit beyond their maximum fermenting time if that should become necessary in order to fully utilize winery space and equipment, but fermenting time is never shortened on Kraus wines. Premature racking, stopping the fermentation, gravely reduces all of the wine's qualities. When wine is racked and filtered, fermentation is stopped once and for all. That's it for that wine, it can't get any better, it can only get clearer.

An old way to check to see if fermentation was over, was to strike a match and hold the flame over and slightly down into the open bung hole. If the match was blown out, that meant carbon dioxide was still being produced, the wine was still working and fermentation was not over.

Length of fermentation can also contribute to the sweetness or dryness of a wine. Wine that is not racked or filtered at the end of the first fermentation but is allowed to remain in the same container in which it fermented, on top of the old sediments, will start up another fermenting cycle all on its own. That will happen once each year the wine is permitted to remain with the original yeast since yeast regenerates and reactivates itself. Each time wine goes through a new fermenting cycle, its color, flavor, taste and aroma are all slightly changed. However, once the alcohol content is established in a wine, it never changes regardless of how many times the wine recycles.

Naturally fermented wines are best right after they complete the first fermenting stage. They are ready to drink right then. That means, they are ready to be filtered for aging or bottling. The magic act is over.

Even though I go by the same formula year after year for each wine, when each run of that wine finishes, the wine, to me, tastes just the slightest, littlest bit different. Some runs go a bit sweeter, others a bit dryer. That's because I don't attempt to control the acid or the yeast in the juice artificially. I let the wine distinguish itself with those little differences. I have found that the more natural the action, the better the balance in the wine. Nature does it better than any winemaker could.

21. Into the Bottle

Newly racked wine will appear, at least to the naked eye, to be completely clear and free of all stray solids. After it stands in the second container another few days, another dust-like settling shows up on the bottom of the tank, indicating the wine needs at least one more racking. Wines are racked at least twice. Each time, as more precipitates settle out, the wine becomes more stable, more clear and closer to its own true and natural color. Some wine is lost with each racking. It is left with the sediments. That's a small price to pay for improved clarity and quality of the wine.

Iowa's cold winter weather is an advantage in helping wine to settle out. Storing wine in a cool room promotes settling and speeds clarification. When heat is shut off in the cellar and outside temperatures go to twenty below zero, the inside cellar temperatures go no lower than 45 to 50 degrees Fahrenheit. That gives a boost to the clarifying wines. The cellar temperature never gets warmer than the upper fifties even in the summertime. With less than a fifteen degree difference between winter and summer cellar temperatures, the wine is maintained at a fairly steady temperature. What's even more important, when the temperature does climb or drop, it does it very gradually. There are no sudden fluctuations which would disturb the fermenting or resting wine.

Each wine has its own natural life span. It has a youth. That's when it is through fermenting. And it has a prime time. Naturally fermented wines come into their prime after they are filtered and racked. That happens somewhere around a year or a year and a half after fermentation started.

My filtering machine looks more like an apparatus than a machine. It isn't very large and there doesn't appear to be much to it. As wine is racked, it goes from one container to another, and as it is being moved, it passes through the filtering machine, a closed, air tight, pressurized filtration system. A three-quarter horsepower motor pulls the wine silently through the tubing, through a vinyl filter pad and into the fresh tank. The eighteen-inch-square filtering pads come in varying densities. Thin, light ones are used for the first or rough filtering. Thicker, tighter pads are used for the final polish filtering. The very last filtering is sometimes called "fining." I call that last step "polishing the wine."

It is a simple procedure by a pretty simple looking machine, but it is a very important step. It calls for a nice, easy flow through the tubing. The wine should pass through the tubes and and be spread over the filter pad in a steady, controlled flow. I say it should flow along like a river when it runs bank-full, you know, smooth, steady but clear full, bank to bank, with the top of the fluid smooth as glass. Getting the wine through the filter at an even rate disperses the wine over the entire area of the pad, so the pad does a better job of straining out particles. If wine runs too fast, or in uneven spurts, then sediments will slip past.

It may not look or sound like this contraption is doing anything or could do much of anything for the wine, but the pads show how much the filters really clean the wine. The filter machine puts my wines right up there with the best of them for clarity.

After wine is filtered and stored, there is no time limit on how long it can be held at its peak. Air locks on the tanks are covered with a thin film of plastic, shutting off all air movement. Any scant dusting of sedimentation which may be cast to the bottom of the storage tank will be left in the tank at bottling time.

Once it is bottled, the wine needs no further aging. When the wine is ready for the bottle, it is ready for the glass.

"Does a winemaker taste the wine as he works it?" I am often asked.

"Absolutely!" I answer. I don't go after it like the Sunday samplers did in Old Amana. I do have to keep track of the wine, though, to see how it progresses. After it has fermented six to eight months, I taste.

Before wine is bottled, it is tested for percentage of alcohol. Once tested for alcohol, stored wines are not tested again at bottling time. Alcohol content does not change once fermentation has stopped and the wine has been racked.

It is assumed by many who visit the winery that state or federal agents test for alcohol. That's not the case. The procedure is handled by the winemaker with the aid of an "ebuilliometer." That is just another simple apparatus. I bring a specific measure of wine to a boil. The temperature at which the wine boils is compared to a chart that transposes the degree reading into an alcohol percentage.

I know my wines so well that I can predict their alcohol content. I hit it on the head about every time. I can almost test for alcohol in my sleep.

"Proof" of the wine is double the alcohol content. For example, wine with 14 percent alcohol by volume is approximately 28 proof. Proof is the "strength" of an alcoholic liquor.

When the wine is as clear and as stable as it can be and the bottled stock for that kind of wine tells me it is time to bottle, then I bottle. Bottling is the best part of making wine. It is the culmination of all I worked for and waited for in all the months before.

Some might think any person who sells wine should say the day he sold the wine, the day he made some money, would be his best day. I like that part, too, but not as much as I like knowing I am bottling a good wine.

I keep the supply of new glass bottles and jugs stored in their cardboard shipping cartons until I am ready to use them. The cartons are stacked as high as my head and fill one corner of the first large room in the basement.

Bottling day is another time I call on my reliable neighbor boy for help. We fill the bottles and set the caps. It's a short assembly line. Empty bottles are lined up on the floor near the tank of wine that is being bottled. When a bottle is filled and capped, the sealing paper is smoothed down over the cap and bottle neck and the label is slapped on. Bottles go right back into their shipping cartons. That's a good, safe way to store filled bottles. As a team, we are pretty speedy. We can bottle 150 gallons of wine in an eight-hour day.

Screw-capped bottles should be stored upright. A corked bottle is stored on its side to keep the cork moist so it doesn't dry out and lose its seal. Upright storage makes storage easier here at the winery and I should think it would be easier for home storage, too.

I sometimes add to the label with a rubber stamp to show if the wine is "sweet" or "dry." It isn't always possible to tell ahead of time, ahead of tasting and testing, especially on grape and rhubarb wines, how dry or how sweet the finished wine will be. With naturally fermented wines right out of fresh produce, it can be different year to year, batch to batch, even though I follow the same formula. I taste right before I bottle. If the wine has a noticeable tendency to be one or the other, I mark it. That helps the customers get the dryness or the sweetness they want in a wine.

22. Cleaning Up

Clean-up follows every step of winemaking. I never consider myself through with any part of winemaking until the winery is clean and everything that has been used is back in place and under cover, draped with sheets of industrial weight vinyl. The entire basement is kept as clean as it can be all of the time.

After a batch has been extracted, pressed, formulated, filtered or bottled, all the machinery, buckets, measures and stirrers—anything that was touched by the produce, juice or wine—is scrubbed with brushes and washed under hot, running water, lots and lots of hot water, steaming hot and under force. Slackness on cleanliness can ruin wine before it ever gets set. Cleanliness is vital to successful winemaking.

Our cellar has never been used for any other activities since it became a winery. All the rooms are well-ventilated, which is important to wine. On hot, damp summer days, a dehumidifier keeps the steel tanks from sweating. Excess moisture can be a welcome mat to mold and fungus. Both are unwelcome in a winery.

23. Start with an Idea

The formula for a wine as it is set down on paper and submitted for approval is over-simplified. To bring a wine to the point where you can write down a formula takes a lot of work, a lot of study and a lot of experimenting. The simple equations don't show all that goes into a wine.

Whether the idea for a new wine comes from a suggestion made by someone else or out of my own head, it is only an idea. The idea is a start, a bare start.

To make formula wines from whole, fresh produce by natural fermentation, I don't pull out a recipe card. I don't look it up in a book. I start, first of all, with what I know in general about making formula wine. If the person who gives me a new bottle of wine, for instance, is the same person who made the wine, then I ask questions—how many pounds, or gallons and so on. More than likely that person only worked with a couple of gallons of wine. The least amount I work with is fifty gallons, so I adjust whatever figures I might have been given. It really comes down to what I know plus a little trial and error. So far, I have been able to eventually work out the correct proportions and to guess right on the fermenting time.

All of my formulas are for fifty gallons but forty-eight gallons of finished wine is a more realistic yield because of evaporation and racking losses. If someone wants to try only two, three or five gallons, the same juice-sugar-water ratio must be maintained as listed in the original formula.

While I am often asked to give out my formulas, I believe the customers really plan to let me keep on making the wines for them. I rather think they like knowing how the wines are made, but I think the most fun for them is pouring the wine into a glass. I understand that. It's a high point in winemaking for me, too.

People who want to make small batches of wine as a hobby and for their own personal use should remember that the United States government monitors all production of alcoholic beverages. But the government's attitude toward the home winemaker is, by comparison to the commercial winery, quite generous. Any nineteen-year-old who is the head of a family can obtain a federal permit to make up to 200 gallons of wine in a year for his or her household, all tax free. The only requirement is that the wine be consumed by members of the immediate family. There is no charge for the permit. It is simply a declaration wine will be made for personal use. It is titled "Registration for Production of Wine for Family Use." It can be requested as Form 1541 from the nearest Alcohol and Tobacco Tax Division, Bureau of Internal Revenue. An application must be filed in duplicate five days prior to making wine. The supervisor stamps the copies. One is for his files, the other is returned to the applicant. When wine is made, the applicant records the number of gallons and the date. Should that form ever be demanded by an Internal Revenue agent, it can be presented.

The license is good for only one calendar year. It must be renewed annually. It is a license that is freely given, but if you are making wine, failure to have a license is breaking the law just as surely as the mountain moonshiner breaks the law when he runs a still hidden in some out-back, under-the-hill thicket. It is a generous law, open to any citizen. There's no need to violate it.

For aspiring winemakers who might try my formulas, there are some general reminders.

All the recipes will yield well-balanced, superior wines with their own individual characteristics. Those characteristics will seldom seem to have any obvious connection to the plant material the wine came from as far as color, flavor or aroma is concerned. The leeways I give in the formulas allow for seasonal changes in the produce and also for personal taste.

If someone likes a sweeter wine or a drier wine, with more or less bite, then they can alter the recipe to get the taste that they prefer in a finished wine. I would suggest, however, that only slight variations be made in the recipes as they are listed. The ratio of juice-water-sugar must not get too far out of line or the result will be a fruit punch concoction rather than wine. If the original formula is followed, the wine will have the correct balance in taste, body, bouquet, aroma, alcohol content and it will have good storing qualities.

A special word of caution on filling the fermenting container. When newly formulated wine is put into a barrel, tank or some other container to ferment, the container should never be completely full. On a fifty-gallon barrel, I hold back three to five gallons of the formula water and add it thirty days later, at the end of the initial fermentation. The liquid level should always be three inches below the top of the container.

After following someone else's directions and having some success, I think every winemaker eventually wants to strike out on his own and try to come up with something new. As new wines were added to the Kraus line, I worked them out first in my head and then did experimental runs before I finally put the formula and the procedure down on paper.

Since I made the first run of rhubarb wine in 1949 to start Old Style Colony Winery, sixteen other wines have been added. Listed in the order of their approval dates, they are:

1949—Rhubarb, Concord grape.
1952—Catawba grape.
1958—Delaware grape.
1963—Dandelion.
1966—Cherry.
1969—Red clover.
1973—Beet, wild blackberry.
1974—Tomato, Fredonia grape, Ontario grape.
1975—Niagara grape.
1977—Blueberry.
1978—Grapefruit, orange.
1979—Cranberry.
1983—Riesling grape.

24. Rhubarb

Spring takes a long time to come to Iowa. And when it comes, it is often gray, slushy, wet and drab. One subtle, almost secret sign of spring may be the wrinkled edges of rhubarb leaves breaking through the garden soil. When the frost is out of the ground and the last of the snow has melted, rhubarb shoots may already be two inches high. A couple days of warm sunshine is all rhubarb needs to be coaxed out of the ground.

Rheum rhaponticum, its botanical name, is a long-lived, hardy, deep-rooted perennial. It's called a vegetable because only its stalk is edible, but it is used most often as a dessert.

The common name for rhubarb in Amana is the German slang word, "*Piestengel.*" In the rest of the county, it's called "pie plant," because of its popularity as a pie filling. Rhubarb can be canned or frozen, but it is more popular fresh.

The plant migrated from Mongolia to Europe to the United States. It grows in areas where the ground freezes to a depth of several inches in the winter. Iowa qualifies on that score.

Rhubarb is best transplanted in late fall when it is dormant, or early in the spring, as soon as the frost is out of the ground. The gnarled roots of the rhubarb plants were dug up from the gardens of the first Inspirationist communal settlement in Upper New York state, packed in straw for the trip to Iowa to be re-set in little backyard plots. They weren't going to leave the rhubarb behind.

The new starts are yellowish, only a few inches long and about as big around as my finger. Each main root has a mass of white feeder roots. It's a good idea to leave some dirt sticking to those little roots. Plant the whole thing two to four inches deep. Iowa has the perfect soil for rhubarb—rich, loose with lots of humus. It needs a location where it gets sun all day long and it should be a spot where the rhubarb can stay put and not be disturbed for several years. When a bed is first started, it's possible to divide a clump and re-set it every three years. It takes four to five years for a plant to reach maximum growth. Iowa's spring, fairly cool with plenty of rain, is perfect for rhubarb. The wetter the spring, the juicier the stalks, the longer the stalks and the higher the sugar content.

There are jokes in Amana about rain and rhubarb.

"Do you think the rain will hurt the rhubarb?" That's a joke, because rhubarb is one plant that can't get too much rain.

One answer is, "Only if it comes in cans." That means, if the *rain* comes in cans, the falling cans would cut and bang up the rhubarb stalks, the juice would be lost, and if the juice was lost, the wine would be lost. If they lost the wine, that would hurt!

In the spring when the soil has dried out enough to be tilled, rhubarb plants need a deep cultivation. I use a small garden tractor. It works between the rows, but stays far enough away from the plants that it doesn't disturb the roots. A week later, the patch gets one more machine cultivation. After that, the stalks come on so fast and the leaves get so big, the rows are closed and it's impossible to get the tractor through. If the soil gets packed down by heavy rains or a few weeds show up, the ground has to be worked by hand with a hoe. That point usually arrives before the first of May. A month later, about Memorial Day, stalks will be ready to harvest, just seven weeks after the first leaf broke ground. By then, the thick, dense leaves shade the ground so well that they prevent weeds from growing and there's no need to hoe or cultivate.

When rhubarb is ready, when it's ripe and full of juice, I can tell it's ready just by looking at it.

"Time to pull the rhubarb!" I'll say and we head for the patch, which by that time will be, from all appearances, nothing but leaves—great, big, broad leaves, one to two feet across and cupped to hold the morning dew. The stalks don't show because of the leaf cover. You have to work right down in among all those leaves to wrench the stalk free from the plant, so you end up getting a morning shower bath while you work.

Rhubarb stalks from the first crop of the season can be as big as a baseball bat. They are long—thirty to thirty-six inches long—thick and ridged and somewhat square. The lower part of the stalk, the part that would be the hitting part of a bat, is two to three inches in diameter and is a pinkish to bright red. The upper part, the handle of the bat, is an inch and a half in diameter and it is mostly green. A mature, well-established plant will produce up to forty stalks which can be harvested. Some stalks must be left to help shade and nourish the plant for the rest of the summer while the root system stores food for the next crop. Plants will restore themselves so they can be harvested again about the middle of August. But that second crop will have smaller stalks, so you get less juice and the juice will have less sugar and more acid. I make all of my wine from the first crop. Helen might make a little rhubarb sauce or pies from the second crop, but that's all.

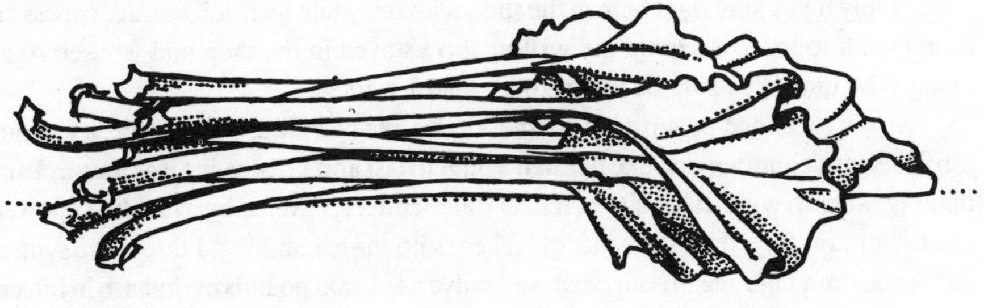

If the climate and growing conditions have been right, the fast growth of the stalks makes them very brittle and easy to break off. Never use a knife, scissors or any tool to cut rhubarb. In fact, cutting the stalk means losing juice and the juice is what you want. By taking hold of the stalk right where it comes up out of the ground—just like Mama taught me—and giving a slow, steady sideways tug, the stalk snaps right off at the base of the plant. It comes off slick as a whistle, without pulling up or in any way damaging the roots. When a stalk snaps, it cracks. It sounds just like a fine china plate breaking.

If spring rainfall is below normal and it's dry, the rhubarb will not be as large and the juice will contain more acid. Weather affects all the fresh produce I use, but it affects the chemical make-up of rhubarb the most, I believe. A season with less than normal rain will delay harvest a week or two.

Our patch has been planted in the Sutton Seedless variety of rhubarb plants for thirty years. Sutton Seedless does not send up flower stalks like the old-fashioned rhubarb does, and though the old-fashioned rhubarb thrived and produced just about as much juice as the Sutton Seedless, I prefer to make wine from the Sutton Seedless. Its sugar and acid levels are more uniform and that makes it easier to balance the wine formula.

I am on my third patch of rhubarb since I began to make and sell wine. The first patch was replaced when it was twelve years old and the second one at fifteen.

Rhubarb is relatively free from insect attacks and suffers few diseases. Root fungus is the only trouble I have ever had in a bed and that happened about five years ago. I was able to quickly control and eliminate it and only a few plants were lost.

Once rhubarb is picked, it is wonderfully easy to process for winemaking. The leaves are snapped off down by the garden, the stalks are hauled on a flat-bed pickup truck to the backyard, and they are hosed down to knock off any loose soil. That's it. There's no peeling, coring, pitting, stemming—all I have to do is run the stalks quickly through the crusher.

Each year the rhubarb wine sold better and I had to crush more and more stalks with the old crusher. I was selling more wine and felt I could afford to replace the old crusher after a few years. I drew up an idea for a new crusher, took the sketch to a friend who had a machine shop and asked him if he could make a crusher from my drawing.

"Only if you stay right here in the shop with me while I work," he said. I guess he didn't want to try to decipher my writing. So I stayed in the shop and worked right along with him to be sure he understood what I wanted.

So what I ended up with is a crusher that is one of a kind, a prototype, a custom job. There isn't another one like it. But it's built to last and I'll be using it as long as I am making rhubarb wine. It has six-inch steel roller-cutters powered by a five-horsepower electric motor. Boy, does it do the job! There's no more cranking. I throw the switch and it goes into high gear. It can crush and pulverize 1,000 pounds of rhubarb in fifteen minutes.

It's a quiet machine. All you hear is the crackle of the fat and juicy stalks as they get hammered until they look like sauerkraut—pink sauerkraut. The stalks are crushed so fine, they can go right into the press. I no longer have to allow three days for the rhubarb pulp to stand and soak after it is crushed. That stainless steel crusher makes it possible for me to make and set 400 gallons of rhubarb wine in just two days.

After pressing is completed, a thousand pounds of rhubarb pulp will have been reduced to one big, compact disk, six inches thick and thirty inches across. It is discarded and I am ready to formulate the juice.

Formulating is the fastest part of the job. I can do it about as fast as I can tell how I do it. In no time, I've got a fresh, new start of rhubarb wine in the tank. Rhubarb wine can finish in nine months, but for the 400-gallon batches I make, I give it a full year to ferment. If rhubarb wine is to be fermented in a barrel, it should be a fresh, new barrel, one that has not been used to ferment or to store any other wine.

My formula for fifty gallons of rhubarb wine is ten gallons of rhubarb juice, eighty pounds of sugar and water sufficient to make fifty gallons.

It takes approximately thirty pounds of crushed rhubarb to make one gallon of juice. Since I get about sixty pounds of rhubarb out of the forty fat stalks from one rhubarb plant, I can plan on about two gallons of juice from each plant each year.

Anyone who enjoys many different wines is sure to like rhubarb wine. The more experienced wine drinkers who come to our shop tend to pick rhubarb over the other Kraus wines. Drinking rhubarb wine can be habit-forming. You can acquire a taste for it that no other wine can ever completely satisfy.

During fermentation, all or nearly all of the sugars present in rhubarb goes into alcohol, creating a very dry wine. The reason some of the Kraus *Piestengel* is made sweeter is that the average customer prefers a sweeter wine.

Rhubarb wine is a crystal clear, white wine with a crisp finish, a fresh springtime bouquet, pleasantly but not overly sweet, and it may sometimes be dry with a pungent flavor that whets the appetite. It is a zesty wine, a big, original favorite in the Amana Colonies. It may be sweet, dry or very dry.

This is the wine we started with in 1949 and it's still one of my own personal favorites. It was part of my family, part of my childhood in Amana. It is one I especially feel very good about sharing with new visitors to our wine shop.

25. Grape

For the *Trauben* or grape wine, I located a source for Concord grapes, prepared a formula and sent it off for approval the summer of 1949. By fall, eight barrels of grape wine were fermenting in the basement right next to the eight barrels of *Piestengel.*

Now I make six different kinds of grape wine. Two are white—Niagara and Ontario. Two are red—Concord and Fredonia. Two are pink—Catawba and Delaware. The five new ones were added between 1952 and 1974. They offer a wider appeal and are more in keeping with the preferences of midwestern wine drinkers. Some go for dry, others sweet and still others prefer semi-sweet.

All the grape wines are made from what are called "table grapes," meaning they are grapes sold primarily to be eaten fresh or to be made into jams, jellies or juice. They make high quality wines, too. When they are fully ripe, Niagara and Ontario grapes are the color of the first new blades of grass in the spring. Catawbas are pink and might go up to a red. Delaware grapes are pink also. They are small, half the size of most grapes, but they are nice, firm and juicy. Fredonias are the darkest grape, a blue, almost black. And Concords! Everyone knows the Concords' familiar dark blue, almost purple color.

Grapes raised in the village for community wines had not done well because the soil was too rich and the climate was not the best for grapes. I knew I would have to look somewhere else for a supply of grapes. The grapes visitors see growing in Amana today on the trellis supports on the side of some homes end up being spread on hot biscuits as jam or jelly. I doubt that any villagers bother to make even a gallon of wine from Amana grapevines any more. The earlier ripening of the Iowa-grown grapes also affects the amount and the quality of the juice from those grapes.

Where the grapes grow makes a great difference in the wine. My grapes come from the Benton Harbor area of Michigan. If that surprises people, I remind them that Michigan ranks fourth in grape production in the United States.

Michigan's version of California's Napa Valley covers some 16,000 lake-front acres across thirty-five miles in the southwestern part of the state where the soil is light and sandy. Cool breezes blowing off the lake keep the grapes from scorching in the summer. Heavy snowfalls insulate and protect the sleeping vines in the winter.

The growers start their new vineyards in the early spring when the vines are dormant. New roots are placed seven feet apart down rows also seven feet apart. The porous, well-drained soil is regularly cultivated to keep it loose for easy root expansion. That way, the plants get all the moisture that is available. Cultivation controls weeds. Weeds draw on the already scant soil nutrients and limited moisture, and if left to grow, the weeds interfere with the harvesting machinery.

Two strands of smooth wire are strung between stout posts which are set at each main grapevine stem. The wire runs the full length of the rows, up and down and over the hills. One strand of wire is placed thirty inches above the ground and the second is thirty inches above the first. In a few weeks, new shoots are clinging by their own strong tendrils to the wire trellis. Branches extend twenty-five feet in each direction from the main stem.

Opa and Papa never saw grapevines growing like that here in Iowa. If Iowa grew grapes like that, it would never have become known as the corn state.

Scientifically named *vitus*, long-lived, hardy, woody vines of the grape are susceptible to many insect problems: the leaf-hopper, grape-berry moth, grape root worm, phylloxera and root pest, to list a few. At least four different fungi spell trouble in a vineyard. All except the root pest can be treated and controlled by dust or spray. A plant infected with root pest needs quick diagnosis and fast removal from the vineyard. It should then be burned to prevent the pest from spreading.

A valued employee in any vineyard is the pruning specialist. The new crop of grapes rides on every snip of his shears. Established plants are pruned in the dormant stage, near the end of winter, and should be reduced by one-quarter to one-third. All dead wood and the twiggy growth is cut. One-year canes are spared as they will bear the fruit for the coming season. A strong plant can support four canes. Each cane is as big around as a pencil.

My grower knows I want the grapes ripe, dead ripe, a bit beyond what he would harvest for table use. The longer the grapes stay on the vine, the better they are for wine. They will have collected all the juice they can hold and that's just the way I want them.

By the middle of the summer, I check my sales and inventory records and let the grower know how many boxes of which kinds of grapes I will need to replenish my stock. If the grower has an outstanding quality in a particular variety, he tells me and I might order a little heavier that year. If he is running a low yield on another variety, he tells me and he also lines up grapes for me from another grower in that area to make up the difference.

Going to the Michigan hills for grape harvest is a heady experience. The atmosphere for miles is filled with the fragrance of the ripe grapes. That smell plus the sight of the triangular clusters of the colorful little baubles hidden among the gold, russet and scarlet grape leaves is wonderful! It's a picture!

By September, the grapes want all they can get of the last warm rays of the sun plus a few rain showers to complete ripening and filling up with juice. Rain that delays harvest, however, cuts down on the size of the grapes and their juice and sugar content. Cool weather or an early frost lowers sugar content, too. Fortunately, with formula wines, I can add sugar and, in that way, compensate for some of nature's irregularities. It may take a little more time to restore the balance, but the wine still comes out fine.

Mechanical pickers are now used in the vineyards. A grape harvester has a shaker rod that agitates the vine just enough so it releases whole bunches of ripe grapes intact. Any leaves that might be jarred loose, too, are lost in the breeze as the conveyor belts swiftly deposit the fruit into the picker bin. The machine is faster than hand-picking and it has another advantage—it works just as well at night as it does in daylight hours, so grape harvest can be done in the cool of the evening when grapes are not exposed to the heat of the sun and they will retain their plump, just-picked freshness better.

At the packing shed, grapes are hand-sorted and go into forty-pound lugs that stack together for a safe, fast, non-crush trip to Iowa in a semi-trailer truck. It's about a ten-hour ride. By the time those ripe grapes cover the miles from the vineyard in Michigan to the winery, the floor of the trailer is slick with grape juice dripping out of the boxes. That's good. That's just the way I like grapes to come in—dead ripe and oozing juice. Then I know they are ready to make into wine.

And are they pretty! Just like a picture, from the dark blue Concords to the pink Catawbas. Grapes all have what is called a "bloom" on the skin. It is a faint, dusty look, like the mist of your breath on a cold window pane. Grapes are never washed before they are processed because you don't want to lose that bloom. It contains yeasts that play a big part in fermentation. The bloom is actually a build-up of the microscopic cells of windborne wild yeasts and molds.

The first thing I do with the grapes is to put them through the de-stemmer and crusher machine. It is one machine but it does the two jobs simultaneously. It is not the same crushing machine I use on rhubarb or the other fruits and vegetables. It's another rig. It is totally stainless steel and is run by an electric motor. It is manufactured especially for wineries and other food companies that process grapes. It is one fast machine. It handles grapes, box after box, just as fast as the boxes can be opened and the grapes poured into the machine's hopper. The hopper is a big twelve by twelve by sixty inch box with sloping sides to funnel grapes into the rollers. It is mounted on a tall frame, high enough so rolling vats can be positioned directly under the drip tray which catches the crushed pulp and juice. As the grapes go through the rollers, the stems are knocked off first. You have to get rid of stems. Otherwise, in the five to seven days of pre-fermenting that grapes go through, the tannins in the stems would be drawn out and would give the juice a bitter, woody taste. Flipper fins on an auger guide the chewed-up stems to one end and they drop into a plastic bag to be discarded.

The crushing part of the operation tears open the grape skin so the pulp is exposed. The seeds inside the pulp are so hard, they go through the processing unscathed. Nothing penetrates them. The big disk that is left after grapes are pressed is full of tiny grape seeds. They are still whole.

Grapes have a high sugar content and I need to know what that reading is. It's called the "balling reading," and it is the amount of sugar in the juice. The grower furnishes that information with each shipment of grapes.

Only on grapes do I need the balling reading. Other fruits, vegetables or blossom extracts do not contain enough naturally occurring sugar for it to be a major concern in formulating. Sugar readings are expressed in degrees roughly equal to a percentage of sugar based on the weight of the grapes. The anticipated alcohol content of the finished wine will be between 12 and 14 percent by volume.

The high natural sugar content of grapes, their ready supply of yeasts in the bloom and the fact they contain sufficient acid to prevent spoilage make grapes perform especially well in a pre-fermenting stage. Pre-fermenting is where they stand and soak, drawing out all available juice from both the skin and the grape pulp. Pre-fermenting lets grapes stew in their own juice. Their own natural yeasts and sugars get fermentation going and within hours the grapes' own distinctive odor fills the cellar. When grapes are pre-fermenting, you know it! Concords have a sweet aroma but the most dominant individual fragrance of any of the grapes is that of the Niagara. I'll bet I could smell that grape a mile away. It is a very pleasant honey-like smell. When you smell grapes pre-fermenting, all you can think of is the wonderful wine that is going to come from them. Pre-fermenting enriches the color and the flavor of the finished wine.

For the week that pre-fermenting goes on, the mixture is visibly active and frothing. There is a quiet hissing along with the popping of a few intermittent bubbles as gas is thrown off. The juice becomes an opaque liquid. Skins, seeds and pulp rise to the surface and float as a "cap." The cap must be broken up twice a day with a wooden paddle much like a canoe paddle plunged down deep to fold the pulp back over itself to keep it all thoroughly moist. When the pre-fermenting no longer shows any life and there are no more gas bubbles breaking on the surface, the pulp goes into the press, is formulated and pumped into the tank.

The formula for fifty gallons of any of the six Kraus grape wines is eighteen to twenty-five gallons of juice, one hundred to one hundred thirty pounds of sugar and sufficient water to total fifty gallons.

It takes twelve to fifteen pounds of grapes to yield one gallon of juice.

Generally speaking, red grape wines require a somewhat longer fermenting and clarifying period than white or light colored wines do. I believe whites finish faster because of their higher acidity.

Ontario is a light gold wine with a rich, intense bouquet with hints of a fresh nectar-like flavor.

Concord grape wine is a rich red, full of flavor from America's choice of home-grown grapes.

Niagara is a light gold wine and is full bodied with all the flavor of ripe and rich white Niagara grapes. Some folks like this wine after a meal or they like to just sip and relax with it.

Fredonia, a dark bluish red wine, is the heartiest and the driest of the Kraus grape wines. It has a crisp flavor that matches its bright color.

Catawba and Delaware are both pink wines and both carry strong grape hints in their flavors and aromas.

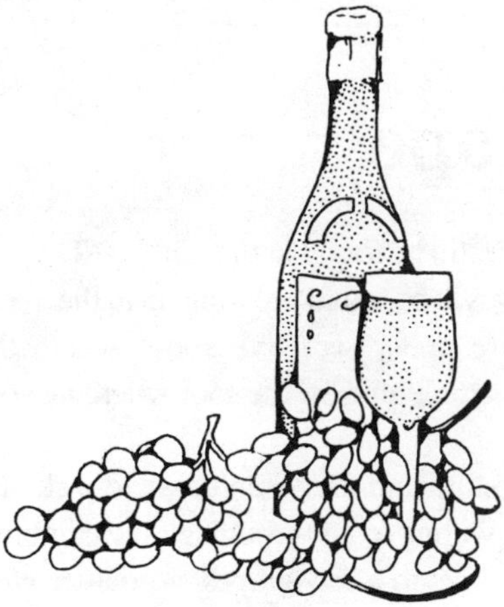

26. Wild Grape

Some wild grape vines can still be found in the timbers. They might run along on the ground but more likely they will be found growing up in the trees or on fence rows. People who hunt for them are pretty secretive about where they find the wild grapes—like a fisherman who won't tell you the spot where he goes to catch the big ones.

Wild grapes aren't easy to find and they aren't easy to pick once you find them. It's even harder to find pickers willing to go through all the climbing, scrambling and maybe even some poison ivy to get to a few grapes, no matter what wages they are paid. But if you can find the wild grapes, you can make an excellent wild grape wine.

Vitus riparis, the wild grape, is a distant cousin to the highly bred and cultivated species used for most of the world's commercial grapes. *Riparia* are tough. They can survive brutally cold winters and summer droughts. They fight off mildew, fungus and insects and they are very good at losing themselves among the trees, plants and shrubs that surround them. Not only are they scarce and well hidden, but the bunches of grapes and the individual grapes themselves are very, very small. It takes many, many, many of them to make fifty gallons of wine. When I'm lucky and get enough grapes, the best way to handle such a small quantity of such tiny grapes is by hand. Those little bitsy things would be lost in a machine.

We pick off the stems by hand, and squish the grapes in our hands to crush them. When they are well-mashed, the skins are open and the pulp is out. Then the pulp is mixed with a small amount of warm water and allowed to pre-ferment for a week.

Then the pulp is pressed and the juice is formulated with a little more water. The formula is one part juice to two and a half parts water. That's total water, including the warm water added to the pulp before pre-fermenting. Wild grape juice is potent. It takes two and a half pounds of sugar for every gallon of wine you expect to get, or for fifty gallons of wine, that would be a total of one hundred twenty-five pounds of sugar.

Wild grape needs a full year to properly ferment. It makes a semi-sweet, very dark, almost black wine.

Back in Old Amana, this was one of the most popular wines for doctoring colds. You were supposed to heat the wine to a simmer, drink it while it was hot, and then go right to bed and to sleep. I don't know that it was a cure for a cold, but it sounds to me like it would be a good way to treat a cold and give yourself a nice little treat, too.

Wild grapes bear only every other year and they have been known to skip a crop for two consecutive years. If you make wild grape wine, you'd better be prepared to ration it out, using it very sparingly and making it last. It is a rare wine.

27. Dandelion

There's nothing more plentiful in Iowa in May than dandelions. Bright, yellow earth-hugging flowers face toward the warm sun and sprinkle the lawns and fields with yellow. They are beautiful and they are scorned and maligned as a troublesome weed that is a foe of grass lawns and is difficult to control. People who despise the dandelion go after it with poisons and they slash it with knives, but it survives and even seems to increase in numbers.

In Amana, the dandelion gets another shot at respectability. I tell folks to stop fighting the dandelions. I tell them to make wine. That's the best way to get a kick out of the dandelions.

More and more wine hobbyists are doing just that. Many are making one, two or five gallons of dandelion wine. It has become a spring ritual for them to gather this year's blossoms to make next year's wine.

The dandelion came to America from Europe. Some believe the plant was deliberately imported, because in many parts of Europe the plant has long been considered delectable and edible. If the leaves are cut before the first blooms, they are tender and may be used fresh in salads or blanched as a vegetable. But the leaves must be picked *before* the plant blooms. After it blooms, the leaves are bitter. Leaves show up about the middle of April and can be picked for the next two to three weeks. Dandelion salad, *ziggorie salat*, is a delicacy in Amana, just as it was years ago.

Dandelion leaves contain vitamin A and iron. The leaves' smooth surface with sawtooth edges is said to resemble the teeth of a lion. This caused the French to tag the plant *dent de lion*, meaning tooth of the lion. In Germany it is *löwen-zahn*, lion's tooth.

A few east coast farmers raise dandelions primarily for sale as fresh or canned greens and some make wine, but only for their own use. Several wineries in the

Amana Colonies make and sell dandelion wine. But I know of no wineries outside of Amana marketing dandelion wine.

In Iowa, there's no need to cultivate the plant. If rhubarb likes the weather here, dandelions love it. After I started the winery, some Amana folks asked me why I didn't make *ziggorie*, dandelion wine. Some called it *blumen wein*, blossom wine. They remembered it along with *trauben* and *piestengel* wines which their fathers and grandfathers once made. They were curious. They knew it was held in great affection and they just wondered what it looked and tasted like. For them, I tried it.

In 1963 I wrote out the formula, got it approved and started making it.

References to dandelion wine are found in literature from various countries, yet its origin is unknown. There are strong indications that it was first fermented in this country by Yankee housewives during the early colonial years.

The dandelion's botanical name, *Taraxacum officinale* roughly translates from Latin as "official remedy for disorders." Old records in many languages attest to its medicinal qualities.

Dandelions are self-perpetuating with strong, deep root systems. If for any reason the roots don't make it, the seeds will. The white, cottony seed puffs are carried by the winds and start new plants.

I will not accept blooms from a place that has been sprayed with herbicides in an attempt to eradicate the dandelion. I say "attempt" because you may thin the stand, but you can't kill the dandelion. When I see a spot that has millions of dandelion blooms, I know that area hasn't been sprayed and that it will be a safe place for pickers to gather blooms I will use to make wine.

Often the flowers bloom before the bluegrass lawns in which they live are mowed for the first time in the spring. Two weeks after the first flowers show up, the blooms peak. That's when there are the biggest blooms and the greatest number of blooms. The peak lasts only a few days. I've noticed the peak bloom period has come earlier and earlier each year over the last ten years. Ten years ago, the peak was May seventh to the tenth. Now the peak comes the last couple of days in April and is over soon after the first of May. There'll always be plenty of dandelions. I'll never have to have those shipped in to make wine.

My pickers scout the territory for the biggest, thickest patches of dandelions. They pick from lawns, school yards, pastures, roadsides or ditches. Dandelion picking doesn't call for a sunrise start. The best time to pick dandelions is from ten in the morning until two or three o'clock in the afternoon. It must be done on a sunny day. Flowers don't fully open until the sun is on them full force, and they begin to close as the sun drops and temperatures cool.

The bloom is all I want—no stems and no leaves. It's also important that the petals be fully opened and spread apart rather than closed up in a tight little ball. An open flower will put all available petal surface in contact with the water during soaking, so that the flower's flavor can be drawn out.

The first six or seven years I made dandelion wine, ours was the only Amana winery making it. Now others make it, so they buy blossoms, too.

When the blossoms reach their peak, Helen calls the school principal's office and a call goes out over the loud-speaker.

"Kraus winery will take dandelion blossoms Saturday!"

We have children as young as two years old and going on up in years to *Omas*. They pick side by side. It's nice to see them working there together.

We may buy pickings from fifty or more individuals in a season. An experienced picker can get twelve to fifteen or even sixteen gallons a day. You should see the garb they come out in! They come out in everything from sweat shirts and jeans to shorts with T-shirts and halter tops. Early in the summer, some younger ones are anxious to start a tan. Older women, mothers and grandmothers, cover up with long-sleeved shirts, sunbonnets and straw hats. They don't wear anything they would mind getting grass-stained and they shouldn't because they are sure to get on the grass and probably get wet, too. Each picker has a style of picking—some are down on their knees, others squat, sit, crawl or bend over from the waist. They comb the neighborhood, the whole village, on their dandelion chase. It's quite a show.

We have counted pickers lined up fifteen to twenty deep at the receiving counter we set up on our driveway under the shade of the linden tree near the side entrance to the winery. They wait to get their blossoms measured and to collect their pay. We once paid a dollar a gallon, and raised it to $1.25 in 1982. The little ones are happy that they will be able to buy a small trinket for their mothers. Fortunately, dandelion picking comes just ahead of Mother's Day, so if they need to earn some money, dandelion picking is one good way to do it.

As they check in, we ask if they have plans for spending their money and usually they will say it's for a gift. Some want a toy or a new book. Some work until they have earned just the amount they need for their purchase and then they quit. Others tire of picking and play "Blow Out the Lights." That's where each one finds an old, mature dandelion head, one that's fluffy, like a white ball, with all the seeds, each with its own feather-like arrow. Then each child blows on a seed head to see who can, with one big breath, blow away all the little seeds. Another version is for each one to make a wish, then blow away as many seed heads as possible. The number of seeds left on a head means that's how many days will have to pass before the wish comes true.

Then there's the one where you pick a fresh, new dandelion flower, and rub it under someone's chin. If yellow rubs off, that means the person likes butter—just nonsensical children's games. Anything to give the kids an excuse to play with the sunny dandelion blooms.

We don't turn down any flowers. We wouldn't dream of turning any of the children away. If a little three-year old comes with only a sand pail and has only the bottom of the pail barely covered with blooms, we still pay that child a dime or a quarter to reward the youngster for the work and encourage him or her to pick again another year.

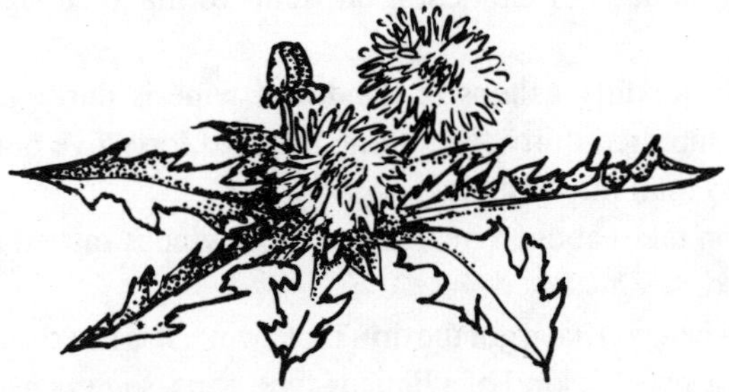

The pickers have counted and they claim they can tell us exactly how many heads are in one gallon. The figures run all the way from 335 to 370 heads. The number of flowers in a gallon container also tells me something about how long it took the picker to fill the pail. The slower the picker, the longer the flowers are in the pail and the more they shrink down, so naturally, there's room for more blossoms in a slow picker's pail.

The average time for a young boy or girl, say nine or ten years old, to pick a gallon of blossoms is forty minutes. Adults, if they have picked before, can get a gallon in twenty minutes. What a picker earns rests pretty much on the age and the ambition of the picker. One thing for sure, poor picking is never due to the lack of dandelions.

Either Helen or I teach the youngest and the newest pickers how to pick. We take them right to a plant and show them how to pick only the flower head. The dandelion has a smooth, slick, straight hollow stem that contains a white, bitter, milky juice. We must avoid getting any part of the stem with the flowers. By gripping the blossom between the forefinger and the middle finger with the fingers around the stem and up under the flower head, all it takes is a little pressure from the thumb against the fingers and with one quick tug, the bloom pops right off the stem.

When I get the blossoms down in the basement, I measure them again for the record in a quick, lightly packed measurement and I also look them over for stray leaves. Then they are put into a large vat and sprayed with hot water, 180 degrees Fahrenheit, water deep enough to cover all the blossoms. Every blossom must be submerged so every petal is saturated with water. They soak for three days, but no longer. Otherwise, the blossoms darken and mold could ruin the wine. The blossoms tend to float. If they aren't stirred down twice a day, the top would dry and form a dense layer. I cover the steeping container lightly with a sheet of plastic to keep air out. Air also contributes to the top layer turning brown and I don't want that discoloration to come out in the wine's color.

After soaking, the entire contents of the vat—water and blossoms—goes into the press. The juice pressed out is called an "extract," and it is then measured and formulated with more water and sugar. Water that was measured into the steeping vat is calculated as part of the total water in the dandelion wine formula. The mixture is then pumped into a fermenting tank.

It takes 180 pounds of dandelion blossoms to make enough extract for fifty gallons of wine.

The formula for fifty gallons of dandelion wine is thirty gallons of blossom extract, plus one hundred thirty-five to one hundred forty-five pounds of sugar and water sufficient to total fifty gallons.

Fermentation takes about a year. Dandelion wine is racked and filtered twice before it is bottled.

And that's when you have got the drinkable wine. It is a very unique, pale golden yellow wine. It's a sweet, a kind of a liqueur-type wine, slightly heavy. It's actually a pale golden color, but it's categorized as a white wine. It has a fresh, springtime bouquet that's pleasantly but not overly dry, with a pungent flavor.

The dandelion is one of nature's more versatile plants. What more could you want from a weed?

28. Cherry

Cherry wine was added in 1966. The best known of old-time Amana wines were rhubarb, grape and dandelion. All had been well-received on the market.

Then I remembered another family favorite, cherry. *Oma* and Mama made pies and desserts with the cherries, but they'd leave some fruit on the tree until it got very ripe, full of juice and real squishy. Then they'd make a little wine.

Birds liked the ripe cherries, too, and they raided the trees. So Mama got netting, the kind used at a cheese factory, and draped it over the branches so the birds couldn't freeload.

There remains only a scattering of cherry trees in Amana. No cherries are sold locally. I went to the orchards of Michigan in the southern part of that state and to northeast Wisconsin for my supply of fresh cherries. Both areas have a climate that is kind to cherry trees—not too cold in the winter and not too hot in the summer.

I make wine from Montmorency cherries, a small red, sour cherry, and from the larger, dark red Bing cherries. There are differences in the trees as well as in their fruits. The trees have distinctive growing habits and highly individual pollinating practices.

Sweet cherry trees are spaced twenty-five to thirty-five feet apart down orchard rows and grow tall and straight with trunks more than a foot thick. Fruit is borne on the upright branches only if the pink and white blossoms are pollinated by some other variety of cherry tree. Several varieties of sweet cherry trees are planted in a grove to provide for the transfer of pollen between the varieties by bees.

Sour cherry trees are smaller and are planted closer together, eighteen to twenty-four feet apart. They have a horizontal branching pattern with small pink and white flowers. Blossoms may be self-pollinated or may receive bee-carried pollen from another cherry tree of the same variety.

Both the sweet and sour cherry trees are related to the famous Washington, D.C., ornamental Japanese cherry trees, but the trees in the orchards have been grafted to hardier root stock so they can be grown in other climates and are less susceptible to pests. Cherry trees are in the rose plant family and are found around the world's moderate climate zones. They thrive in deep, well-drained, slightly sandy soil. Cultivation of them as a food crop likely began in Asia. They are heavy bearers. A single tree may yield several hundred pounds of fruit.

Cherry picking was a surprise to me the first time I saw it. With all the mechanization that has taken place in the agriculture industry the last few decades, I shouldn't have been surprised to see that it has affected cherry harvest, too. It's a speedy method and it is completely safe. It doesn't hurt the cherry at all. A motorized shaking machine is strapped to the trunk of a tree. When the motor is on, the whole tree vibrates just enough to cause ripe cherries to fall, stemless, from the tree. A catch cloth suspended beneath the tree's lowest branches collects the cherries and funnels them directly into a container. Filled containers go onto conveyor belts leading to a flatbed truck. At the packaging plant, the cherries are washed under a fine water spray, pitted, and put up in thirty-pound metal containers. They wait in a quick chill room until it is time for a refrigerated truck ride to Iowa.

Right after we've celebrated the Fourth of July and had a little rest from making rhubarb and dandelion wine, I can expect to get the word from my grower.

"The cherries are coming!"

All the grower does for me is pick and pit the cherries. No sugar is added. They come to me fresh and unprocessed.

There are two ways I can make cherry wine. One way is to begin by crushing the cherries and then formulating the cherry pulp immediately with sugar and water and pumping the formulated pulp directly into a fermenting tank. With this method, I skip the pressing step. Racking and filtering eventually produces a wine that is just as clear as if I had pressed the pulp and fermentation had taken place with cherry juice.

The other way I make cherry wine is to crush the cherries, let them pre-ferment two days, then press them and formulate the juice. Both ways work equally well. I have wines to set, press, pre-ferment or filter almost daily throughout the summer, so I really appreciate the flexibility cherry wine gives me in the day-to-day operations. I decide which method to use on the cherries depending on what is the best use of the winery space and equipment on the day the cherries arrive.

The formula for fifty gallons of cherry wine is sixteen to twenty-three gallons of juice, one hundred to one hundred twenty-five pounds of sugar and water sufficient to total fifty gallons.

Freight and labor costs make cherry one of the more expensive of the Kraus wines. It can be formulated to become a sweet wine from the sweet Bing cherries or a dry wine from the Montmorency cherries. Both wines have a beautiful, clear red color.

There is one fantastic cherry wine made from Pitter's Juice. Few people even know about it. I wish I could make more of it.

Pitter's Juice wine is made from collecting the one or two drops of cherry juice that drips from each cherry as it is collected from the pitting machine. Most processors do not bother to catch those precious drops of juice. Pitter's Juice wine is a luxurious nectar. It is completely different in color and texture, and possesses a much more pronounced cherry flavor than it is possible to achieve with more conventional juice extractions.

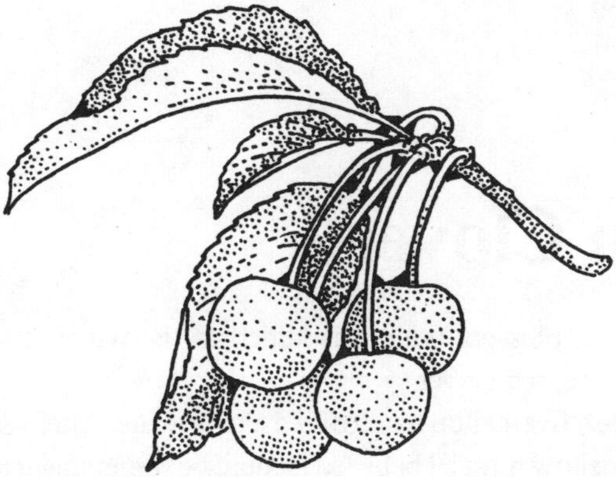

29. Red Clover

After dandelion blossom wine was added to the winery's stock, I learned of another blossom wine, red clover.

A friend made a five-gallon batch of red clover wine. After I sampled it and saw how smooth and mellow it was, I believed it could be something really unique to offer wine drinkers. Going by my dandelion formula, I played around with clover blossoms, sugar and water and made a small batch. Everyone who sampled it raved about it. It was a truly different, very enjoyable wine.

I sent the formula in for approval and started making red clover wine in 1969.

Red clover is a legume from the plant world's pea family. It's used as pasture and for hay which may be cut and stacked or cut and baled for livestock feed during the winter. Clover is also a good soil builder. It restores soil nitrogen that other crops deplete. Many farmers plant clover every few years as part of their crop rotation plan for some fields. It's also used as a nurse crop for alfalfa. Alfalfa and clover are seeded together in the same field. Clover, being a weak perennial, grows vigorously the first year while the alfalfa gets rooted down. The second year, alfalfa takes over the field. The clover blossoms gathered to make wine come from a field that is in the first year of growth.

Clover does very well in Iowa. It likes rain, sunny and warm summer days and a good, rich soil. Nothing special has to be done to clover in order for its blossoms to be used for making wine. When clover is one to two feet tall, the fields turn a purple glow with all the nice, fat and fragrant flower heads. That's when the farmers want to make hay. I talk them into holding off a couple of days until my pickers have a chance to pick the blossoms. Then we all hope and pray the weather stays nice until we get the flowers and the farmer gets the hay.

It's pretty easy to find fields of red clover close by. Most years I get permission for pickers to go into fields owned by the Amana Society, just outside of Middle, only a few miles from the winery. I have been assured that in no way does it harm the hay crop if a few blossoms are removed. Farmers don't mind having the pickers go through the fields. Clover is a sturdy and erect plant with plenty of stamina. It bounces right back up and isn't easily trampled.

Hay is cut from a field two or three times each summer. The first cutting is usually during the first two weeks of June. The second cutting is six weeks later in July. If there is a third cutting, it is in September.

I like blossoms from the first growth for winemaking. The heads are larger and fuller and they rise up on taller stems, which makes them easier to pick. The first crop of the season bears more blossoms, too. The pickers like that better because with the bigger blossoms, they can get the necessary number of gallons faster.

I make red clover wine every year, so that means I need over a thousand pounds of blossoms.

Clover can be vandalized anytime by the weather but it is more vulnerable when it is nearing peak bloom periods. In a matter of minutes, hail, rain and wind can flatten an entire field of clover. In a dry spring, the blossom crop will be slight with fewer and smaller blossoms. Once clover comes into bloom, the blooms last over two weeks before they turn to seed so that gives me some allowances in scheduling pickers.

Lining up pickers is the biggest problem in making red clover wine. Picking is hard work and it's a short term job. Youngsters old enough and willing to work can find better jobs. I try to line up the ones who are just a little bit younger, those who are just getting into high school and who aren't working any other part-time jobs yet.

When I grew up, hoeing the garden and pulling weeds wasn't a lot of fun, but if we earned a few cents doing it, we felt good about it. I try to find kids with that spirit to pick clover for winemaking.

Picking clover blossoms is hand work and it's also stoop labor. It can't be done while kneeling, crawling, squatting or standing fully upright. The picker must look at the flower, see the exact spot to take hold of it so only the bright, freshly opened, deep purple flower head is picked. I want only the flower, no stem and no leaves. The picking motion is a quick, straight up pull with the flower head held firmly between the thumb and forefinger. The picker has to lean forward from the waist and duck his head if he is to see to pick only the flower head in just that way. I don't want any browned, damaged or faded flowers. Those stay on the stem.

Picking is hard and it's even hard work just to walk through a clover field. The stems are so thick and so tough, it's like cutting through a small jungle. After pickers have been in the awkward picking position, they have tired and aching backs besides sore, aching thumbs and fingers. The clover field harbors other hazards, too. Red-winged blackbirds hide their nests in the field and blossom time is when the baby birds are newly hatched. The parent birds get mad, swooping down, and "dive-bombing"

the pickers who get too close to the nests. Bumblebees love clover blossoms, too, and they may sting an unsuspecting picker. When I see a kid swatting with his hat or waving his arms and yelling, I know the bees are after him. For that reason, the kids should wear caps or hats. They should wear long-sleeved shirts and full-length jeans, not cut-offs, so they offer as little skin as possible to the bees. Whatever they wear, it's going to be soaked by dew since they start as soon after seven o'clock in the morning as possible. Later in the day, they'll be soaked with perspiration.

Picked flowers go into one-gallon pails and then into giant plastic bags for a quick trip to the winery before the flowers wilt.

Red clover wine is made the same way dandelion wine is made. Blossoms are rinsed and checked for stray leaves. Then they go into a vat of hot water, 180 degrees Fahrenheit, where they steep three days before being pressed to get the extract. The extract is formulated and fermenting begins.

The formula for making fifty gallons of red clover wine is thirty gallons of blossom extract, one hundred fifty pounds of sugar and sufficient water to make fifty gallons.

Red clover wine tastes as rich as a field of clover in bloom, with just enough piquancy to give visions of blossoms waving gently in a light breeze. It is a truly unique wine and one of my favorites. It was an exclusive when we started it in Amana and it still is.

There are three statements we make over and over in the wine shop about the red clover wine.

"Yes, the wine is really made from clover."

"Yes, it is made from the clover blossoms."

"No, it has nothing at all to do with the lucky 4-leaf clover."

30. Wild Blackberry

Wild blackberry wine was kept ever-ready in the back of cupboards in many homes in Old Amana. Both Mama and *Oma* hunted the scattered wild berries in the woods near Middle and made an occasional gallon of the wine. They wanted it for its well-known medicinal powers. It was the so-called "cure" for many disorders, but some speculated that the pleasure of the cure may actually have triggered many disorders it was claimed to cure.

Ever since we opened the winery, people asked, "Do you make blackberry wine?"

In 1973, I added it to our list of wines.

Blackberries haven't been seen around here in any amount for a long time. I knew I had to buy them from somewhere else. They are in good supply in Oregon, but they are such a fragile and perishable fruit, I didn't want to risk shipping them that far. The freight from there would be prohibitive and the quality of the berries, the really ripe berries like I need for making wine, would be questionable by the time they got to Iowa.

I started asking around, letting people know I was in the market for blackberries. I happened to mention blackberries in a conversation with a friend from Miami, Oklahoma. He told me wild blackberries were still gathered near his area and in fairly large quantities. They grew in timber on heavy, trailing vines, massed among thick tangles, thickets and brambles so they were very hard to get at and very hard to pick.

It takes a lot of berries to make a gallon of juice and I wanted enough berries to make at least a fifty-gallon barrel of wine on the first run. My Oklahoma friend rounded up some youngsters wanting a summer money-maker and they took on the blackberry hunt in July.

They got 'em all right. They turned out to be the biggest, juiciest blackberries ever! They were as nice as any domestic berries I have ever seen.

Few blackberries ever make it to the supermarket. Growers freeze or can most of their crop. In some parts of the country, there are woods where a few wild blackberry bushes can be found, but only the staunchest pickers will go blackberrying anymore.

The hardy blackberry plant is from the rose family and has the botanical name of *Rosaceae Rubus occidentalis.* It likes a warm, moist climate. Each spring, the branches drip with blooms of white tinged with pink. By mid-summer, clusters of cylindrical-shaped, purple black seedy berries are clinging to the underside of the stalks, waiting to be picked. Where the bushes are grown as a crop, the canes are cut away and burned as soon as the fruit has been harvested. The plant then sends up new canes from which next year's crop will be harvested.

The berries are still handpicked. That delicate little berry can't be harvested with a machine. There's a scarcity of pickers, particularly ones willing to fight their way through the scratchy and prickly bushes. The labor obstacles on top of shipping costs makes wild blackberry wine expensive, but it's rare and that rarity gives it a great deal of appeal for the customer.

I had a fairly easy time writing out the formula for blackberry wine. I just went to *Oma* and Mama and asked for their advice.

I got help from them, all right, help on how to make one gallon. But it did give me enough figures to get me going. I did it pretty much the way they had—sorted and rinsed the berries before I mashed them—except, they mashed the berries by hand and I put them through a grinder. I had the berries pulverized for fifty gallons of wine faster than Mama and *Oma* could have done it for a gallon of wine.

Sugar and water are added to the berry pulp and the entire mixture is stirred and then pumped, pulp, seeds and all, into a tank to ferment. At first the heavy pulp may tend to float around on top of the solution but since it is in a closed tank, there is no concern about a dry, sealed cap forming, not like there is when pulp is pre-fermented in open vats. By the time fermentation is over, the pulp settles to the bottom of the barrel and the clear wine is drawn off the top in the first racking or first filtering. Like any wine fermented in the pulp, blackberry wine may require extra filtering before it becomes sufficiently clear and can be bottled.

Wild blackberry wine can be a dry, semi-sweet or a sweet wine depending on the amount of sugar used in the formulation. For a dry wine, use two pounds of sugar for every gallon of juice. For a semi-sweet, two and a half pounds of sugar. For sweet, two and three-quarters pounds of sugar.

Having the word "wild" as part of the name of the wine gets that wine plenty of attention in the shop. However, it is a true use of the word "wild." Even though the berries are now harvested as a crop, and therefore might be considered domesticated, they are the same variety as the wild ones.

Wild blackberry wine is tart and fresh. It is a red dinner wine with a character that complements any meal and with a delightful heartwarming aftertaste.

31. Beet

Beet wine came as a gift. A friend brought me a bottle of beet wine he had made. It was a beautiful deep, dark red and so clear. It tasted sweet and smooth.

Well, that was a challenge to me. I had to try to make some of that beet wine.

That summer, the summer of 1973, extra rows of beets were planted in our family garden so I could try a run of the wine. Now neighbor boys grow the beets for me in their 4-H garden projects. By giving the youngsters a small business opportunity, I let myself have more time for winemaking. I like to make wine more than I like to garden. Each spring, the boys check with me to see how many pounds of beets I'll need.

It takes eight pounds of fresh beets to make one gallon of juice. As a rule I make one hundred fifty gallons of beet wine each year so I need a minimum of six hundred pounds of beets. This offers the boys some practical education. I let them do the arithmetic. They use the projected yields the seed company prints on the packet of seeds, and figure how many rows they have to plant to get that many beets for me. Of course, weather, rain, temperature can affect their crop, too. They soon learn that taking risks goes along with farming and being in business and they allow for any weather-caused shortages. If they get a bumper crop, extra beets are sold to local housewives.

In May, after the ground is warm, seeds are sown directly into loose, rich garden loam in rows twelve to fifteen inches apart. The plants have to be thinned when they are well leafed and two or three inches high. Each beet needs plenty of room to grow unhampered in full sun, so they get big, fat and round, about three inches in diameter.

Through the years I have come to rely on either Detroit Dark Red or a King Red as the best beets for making wine. Both have a deep, dark red color and are sweet yet large and uniform in size with a strong fibrous pulp that holds plenty of juice. For the beets to reach their peak, they need a steady growth pattern with plenty of sunshine and normal rainfall.

The beet is from the goosefoot family. The tops and the roots are edible. The succulent dark green, red-veined leaves are used fresh in salads or cooked as a vegetable. The red, bulbous, slightly globular roots also may be eaten raw in salads or cooked.

Beet harvest is late in August. The boys call me to come check their beets. When beets are considered ready to pickle or to can, I have to say, "Let them stay in the ground another two weeks." Extra time in the soil lets the beets get bigger and juicier. The more mature beets are not as tender, but tenderness doesn't matter in winemaking.

When I say the beets are ready, the boys pull them, chop off the little slender root tail and upper leaves, making sure to leave a one-inch stem where they cut off the leaves. Leaving just that little bit of the stem prevents loss of juice through the stem by "bleeding." After the beets are pulled and trimmed, the boys deliver them to the winery and collect their pay. At that point, the beets get a thorough scrubbing and are rinsed under running water.

Beet was a different kind of wine for which to figure out a formula. I knew of nothing comparable, but I did have the wonderful memory of the beet wine I had been given. My first problem was to figure out how to get the juice out of the beets. A beet has a tough outer skin and a tight structure of inner fibers that hold the juice tight.

I knew I couldn't put raw, whole beets in the press and expect juice to ooze out. Usually when beets are to be eaten, they are either cut or pierced to break the skin or they are cooked to soften the skin and the inner fibers. To cook enough beets to make fifty gallons of wine would have taken days in the kitchen. I knew the machines that crushed the grapes and the rhubarb wouldn't handle the big, round hard beets. Then I spied the old meat grinder. It was more than fifty years old. It had been used to make sausage and hamburger.

I thought, "Why not give that old grinder a try?"

It has six different dies and I used the finest one for the beets, the one with the smallest openings. Helen and I cut the beets in half, cut off the last of the stem and root cuttings just as the beets were fed into the hopper, and sure enough, the old grinder did the job.

It stands four feet high and has a three-foot handle for a crank. It took plenty of muscle to turn it, but now it's powered by a small electric motor.

It's like a great, big food chopper. The beets are dropped into the hopper and onto a rotating cylinder. Its flanges push the beets onto a four-sided, knife-edged cutter blade on through the die.

I experimented by grinding both raw and cooked beets and found that grinding first and then cooking yielded the most juice. After it is ground, the raw beet pulp

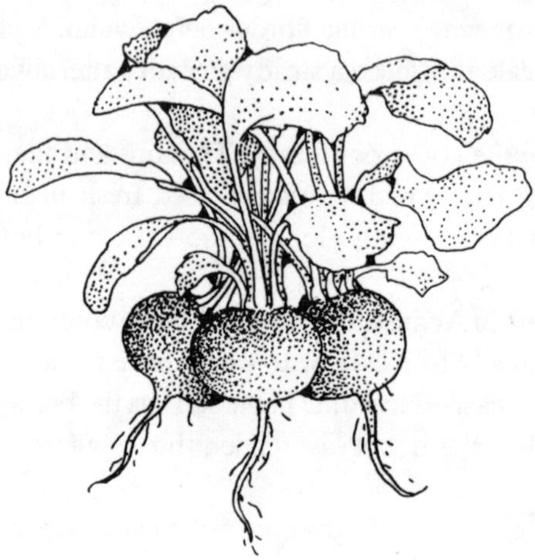

looks pretty much like raw hamburger and it keeps that fresh, bright color all the way through cooking and fermenting. Right from the start, beet wine is a rich, ruby red.

Beet pulp is cooked in another leftover from the Colony days—an old round black cast-iron thirty-five-gallon wash kettle. I mounted a gas burner under the kettle and the cooking is done outdoors. The pulp is brought to a boil and maintained at that temperature for fifteen minutes. Escaping steam lowers the water content and intensifies the flavor of the juice. After cooking, the beet mixture is cooled and then goes into the press. Cooling may take twenty-four to forty-eight hours, depending on the weather. At the start of cooling, I add part of the formula water to speed up the cooling.

Beet pulp is pressed longer and harder than other products. The residue from beet pressing is so dry and hard it's almost brittle. But I have to get every drop of juice if the finished wine is to have the body, flavor and color that distinguishes it. Once I have the juice, the hard work is over. I formulate it and get it pumped into a fermenting tank.

The formula for a fifty-gallon barrel of beet wine is twenty to twenty-five gallons of juice, one hundred to one hundred thirty pounds of sugar and sufficient water to total fifty gallons.

The first barrel of the new beet wine was quickly accepted by our customers and I have made the wine every year since 1973. Annual production gradually rose to one hundred fifty gallons, the lowest annual volume of all the Kraus wines. It's the only Kraus wine that lists "cooking" as one of its processing steps. From the garden to the bottle, beet wine has one of the longest work schedules of all the wines. Before it can be pressed and formulated there is a great deal of hand work—pulling, trimming, grinding, cutting and cooking the beets.

For the most work, I get the least amount of wine, but beet wine is worth it. It has been a lot of fun to introduce beet wine to tasters in the shop. They can't believe it. At first they are surprised that wine comes from a vegetable. Then they can't believe it comes from the beet. They are surprised to see the wine's clear red color, and are surprised again when they taste the sweet wine and they like it. It's a good after-dinner drink.

If a sampler is a first-time visitor to the winery, any of the Kraus wines may provoke questions, but the beet wine stumps them all.

"Is it made from the leaves or the roots?" they ask.

I can understand why they would ask that. After all, we do eat both the top and the root of the beet. I just tell them it comes from the root and I may also say something about all the trouble I go to to make the beet wine for them. As long as they like it, I'll make it.

32. Tomato

A Michigan visitor became a fancier of red clover wine. Over the years, he would stop here when he traveled in Iowa. On one trip, he confided that he, too, was a winemaker. He made wine in small quantities, one or two gallons in a batch. He asked me if I had ever tasted tomato wine.

I hadn't, but I had heard about it. I told him that I would like to taste it, so he gave me a bottle. When I tasted it, I thought it was real good! With all the tomatoes that are grown commercially in southeastern Iowa, along the Mississippi River, down near Muscatine where the soil is so rich and fertile and moisture always plentiful, I thought I should give tomato wine a try.

As a commercial garden crop, tomatoes can be risky business. Every season brings its own set of battles—blights, wilt, cutworms, white flies, root rot—any of which may leave an entire field a withered disaster overnight. The best protections against such disasters are within the farmer's control. The best thing he can do is to buy the hybridized varieties that resist insect and climate threats.

In spite of all the hazards, there isn't another garden crop that is a more beautiful sight in the field. When round, red, fully ripe tomatoes are nestled down among the dense, dark grey-green foliage, it's a picture. The tomato foliage is rough and hairy and it gives the plant protection against sun scald and the tiny, almost invisible leaf hairs deter insects. Although the bushy plants are called vines, they aren't. They sprawl but they don't climb. Folks may tie them up to stakes or put them in support boxes in backyard gardens, but out in the open field, the plants are barely a foot high when they are loaded down with tomatoes.

Tomatoes need long; sunny days to peak. Growers plant seeds in March in greenhouses. Seedlings are transplanted to the fields in May. They are spaced two feet apart in rows three feet apart and get monthly feedings and plenty of rainfall or irrigation the rest of the summer. The first pickings are available the latter part of July.

After testing several varieties, I now request only Burpee's Hybrid Better Boy tomatoes. They have a healthy, vigorous growth that the grower likes, and produce large, round uniform tomatoes that I like. I want the last pickings of the season. I want them dead ripe, mushy to the touch but not spoiled. End-of-the-season tomatoes are not only the biggest and the juiciest but they are also the most plentiful and the price is the best. I don't mind waiting until September to make tomato wine.

Tomatoes are hand-picked into the same bushel baskets in which they arrive at the winery a couple hours after they are picked. At the winery, tomatoes are rinsed under running water and are dumped into the old meat grinder's hopper.

I didn't start out doing them that way. I went through several false starts and headaches before I tried the grinder. When I started out to make the trial batch of tomato wine, I thought it would be a breeze. It turned out to be my most difficult wine assignment.

First of all, getting the juice wasn't the snap I thought it would be. A tomato is such a soft thing, with a thin skin, I thought I could put the fresh tomatoes right into the press and get the juice right away. But that didn't work too well.

So Helen and I quartered every tomato by hand with a knife just as we dropped it into the press. What a mess that was—those tomatoes squirted and spurted juice and seeds all over us and all over the basement.

Next, I tried running them through the grape crusher, and that was still a mess.

Then I tried the old meat grinder. It was better and that is how I still process the tomatoes before they are pressed. In all honesty, it is still messy. Tomato wine is the messiest of all the wines to make. The pulp sticks to the machinery, to the floor, to your hands, arms, clothes. It dries and sticks to everything it touches. Tomato skin is like wet tissue paper. When it dries, it clings.

Even after the crushed pulp is in the press, it is still so slippery, it is hard to apply pressure to get a slow, even stream of juice oozing out of the bottom of the press. With the least bit of pressure from the hydraulic jack, the pulp slides and skids around so much that seeds slither under the screen and into the juice. Who would ever think that the gorgeous, succulent tomato would be such a stickler to juice?

Even devising the formula had me scratching my head. With the high acidity in tomatoes, I didn't hit the sugar ration the first few times I tried it. I finally got an okay on the formula in 1974 and I have been making it every year since.

The formula for tomato wine is eighteen to twenty-two gallons of juice, one hundred ten to one hundred twenty pounds of sugar plus sufficient water to make fifty gallons. Sixteen pounds of fresh tomatoes will make one gallon of juice.

If getting the juice and the formula were chores, I was in for a double chore when it came time to clean up after making tomato wine. It takes two to three times longer to clean the equipment and the basement after that wine is set than it does for any other wine. Tomato pulp and skin hang and stick everywhere. They can't be flushed away with water pressure. It takes stiff brushes, elbow grease and lots and lots of hot, running water under a pressure nozzle to jar it all loose.

But tomato wine is an unexpected reward, a big payoff for all the work I go through to make it. It is an extraordinary wine. I really get a kick out of the reaction it gets in the shop from the samplers.

"No way could this come from a tomato!" They expect tomato wine to be the color of tomato juice or catsup. It isn't. The red color of a tomato is all in the skin and pulp. The juice itself is a golden color.

"Next time you cut a fresh, ripe tomato," I tell the samplers, "look at the juice that leaks out from the cut. Don't press the tomato, just look at the little droplets of juice on the knife and on the cutting board. See what color the juice really is."

When we ask folks whether they want to sample tomato wine, some say, "That doesn't sound good, but maybe I'll try it just to see what it's like."

After they have tried it and some of the other wines, they try tomato again. That's when they say they like it. If a person likes tomatoes, tomato juice, Bloody Marys or the vodka and tomato juice cocktail, they will like tomato wine.

Helen was tending the shop one morning when a group of people came in. One man was poking along behind his wife and the other couples. While the others sampled, he complained to Helen about having a hangover from a party the night before.

"How about a little tomato wine?" Helen asked him.

He took the sample, and he just went crazy for it. So now we recommend tomato wine for hangovers.

It has a golden color and a distinctive flavor that hints of tomato juice. It is a very uncommon wine that surprises and delights. It has a subtle aroma and its own distinctive taste. It is a perfect way to end a meal.

Tomatoes were found growing in the Andes Mountains of South America. They were carried by sixteenth-century explorers back to Europe, where they were found to be poisonous. Indeed, the leaves and stems are toxic, but not the fruit. It was called "Love Apple" because of so-called aphrodisiac powers. The name probably came about simply in the translation of its botanical name, *Lycopersicum esculentum* from Latin to French to Italian to Spanish to German and Greek. The Greeks called it "Wolf Peach." Germans still call it by the common name *Liebesapfel*, love apple.

In this country, the plant ended up in court, the highest court of the land. On May 10, 1893, the United States Supreme Court said the tomato was to be classified as a vegetable on the basis of it being served at dinner with or after soup, fish or meats which constitute the main part of a meal, and its not being served as a fruit, which is generally served as dessert. However, the scientific world still claims it is a fruit. Science defines a fruit as a mature ovary of a plant or tree, with its seed, skin and fleshy pulp all connected as one. A vegetable is defined as the edible part of a plant's seed, leaves or roots.

Through all the fuss, the tomato has remained a very popular food. It is not surprising that it's a hit as a wine, too.

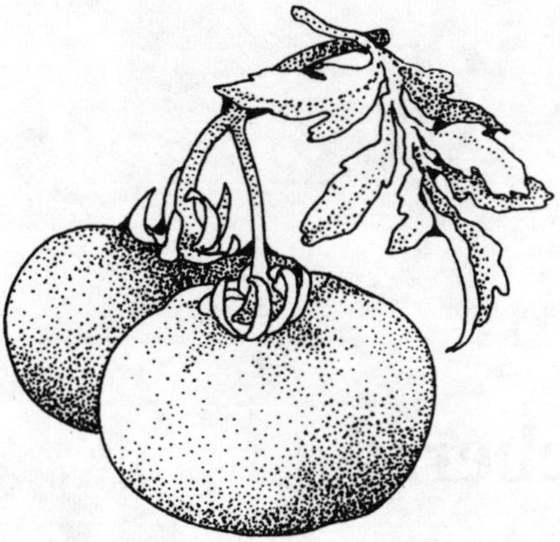

33. Blueberry

Daughter Kandyce and her husband Neil have a farmer neighbor in Indiana who picks his own blueberries and makes a few gallons of wine each year for his family.

When I heard that, I had to taste that wine. Once I had tasted it, I knew I had to try to make it, too. The popular little berries usually go into muffins, cobblers or pancakes, but they are so full of juice, it seemed to me, they were great candidates for the wine barrel, too. I immediately put in my name for some blueberries.

Blueberries aren't available in Iowa. I buy from an Indiana grower. His cultivated fields grow four- to five-foot bushes of *Vaccinium*, the blueberry's botanical name, in long rows in light sandy or peaty, well-drained, yet moist and slightly acid soil. Blueberry bushes need rather severe pruning every year if the bushes are to thrive, be healthy and free of tired and dead branches. Blueberry foliage is so dense you can hardly see the tiny white and pink blooms in the spring.

Birds like blueberries and they go after them as soon as the fruit begins to ripen. Growers tie fabric strips to the bushes, hoping the summer breezes will flutter the strips and scare the birds away.

Blueberry harvest begins in July and lasts a month. The berries ripen irregularly, so pickers cover the field every week, taking only the berries that are ripe. I make blueberry wine the last week of July when I get the ripest, juiciest berries from the very last picking. Of course, that's when the berries are the most perishable, so there can't be any delay. As soon as the berries are picked and boxed, they go on a truck. Six hours later they are at the winery. No matter what time of day the truck arrives, I drop everything and process the blueberries.

I made the first batch of blueberry wine in 1977. Figuring out the formula was simple, but the resistance of the berries to pressing was unexpected.

The blueberry skin is tougher than it looks. I had the idea I would just toss the berries into the press and out would come the juice. It didn't work that way. The rhubarb crusher only crushed about half of the blueberries that I put through it. And once again, I fell back on the old meat grinder. There was lots of snap, crackle and pop going on, but the berries came out a blue mush. That blue mush stews in its own juice for forty-eight hours before it is pressed. Then the juice is formulated and pumped into a fermenting tank.

The formula for blueberry wine is twenty to twenty-five gallons of juice, one hundred to one hundred thirty pounds of sugar and water sufficient to total fifty gallons.

As you would expect, hand-pruning and hand-picking of the blueberries plus freight charges make blueberry one of the most expensive of the Kraus wines. Nevertheless, it has been popular. It is an elegant premium wine with all the color of rich, ripe blueberries, a deep blue with red overtones. It is a semi-sweet wine with a tangy fruit flavor that is a welcome dinner companion for those who are especially fond of its intense flavor.

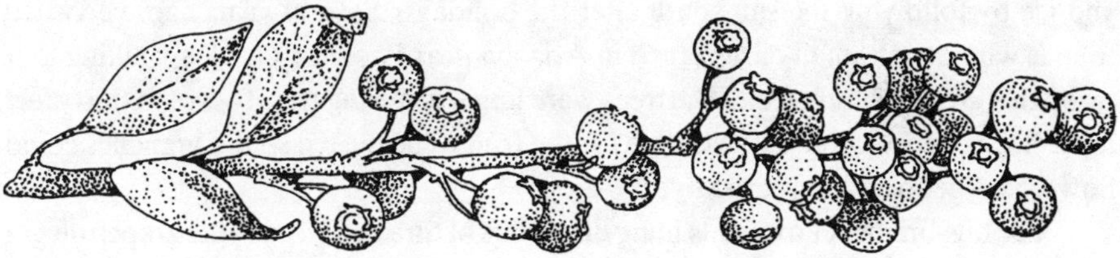

34. Grapefruit and Orange

Helen and I, along with many other Iowans, like to escape some of winter's snow and ice by following the sun south after the holidays. Several years ago we visited friends who own a small citrus ranch in Arizona near Phoenix. I took a walking tour through a grove of grapefruit. The trees were huge, towering twenty-five to thirty feet high. It was February and it was time for the fruit to be picked so the branches could flower and get ready to set next year's crop.

The big, bright yellow fruits hung in clusters of three and four—the grapefruit got its name because the fruit grows in clusters, like grapes. Its name alone tells you it should be made into wine, doesn't it?

Anyway, it looked like a bumper crop to me, but the grower complained that there wasn't a good market for the grapefruit and that he would do well to pay the taxes on the land from the sale of his crop. He was feeling pretty low. I asked how many tons of fruit he would harvest and what that represented in gallons of juice. As we walked the grove, I figured out how many gallons of wine that much juice would make. I always carry a scratch pad and pencil in my shirt pocket. I never know when an idea might hit and I'll need to do some quick figuring.

I showed him my figures which suggested it might be more profitable for him to make wine from the juice rather than to contract the whole fruit to market. He handed the idea right back to me.

"I'll never make wine," he said. "If you want to try, you're sure welcome. Take all the fruit you want."

Together we picked a couple of big bags of grapefruit, put them in the trunk of the car and headed back to Phoenix.

I promised his wife and Helen that I would take them out to dinner if they would help me wash and cut the fruit, then squeeze and strain the juice. They took my deal and when we were through, we had juice squirted and spattered all over ourselves and the kitchen.

I couldn't wait to get that batch of wine set. They had no basement, so we put the five-gallon jug of fermenting wine in the corner of their living room. It was an air-conditioned house, so I knew the wine would be okay.

We waited a whole year to have our first drink of grapefruit wine. Something wonderful had happened to that sour grapefruit juice during that year! We liked it! Our friends liked it! They had not expected to like it, but they did. Some of their neighbors and friends sampled it and nodded their approval, too. So I had another wine on my hands and the source of the juice for that wine was a long distance from the winery.

That was February of 1978. Helen and I flew home. I submitted a formula for government approval and, in March, we drove our van to Arizona just in time to catch the wrap-up of the grapefruit harvest. I had told the grower I would gladly take the last of his fruits, the ones that clung to the tree the longest. Those very last of the ripe "berries"—that's what botanists call citrus fruits—would, I knew, have the most juice and would be the sweetest—well, as sweet as grapefruit can get.

I wanted about twenty-five gallons of juice, which would make about fifty gallons of wine. That was more than could be handled in our friend's kitchen and we used a commercial juicer which has its own short assembly line to sort, wash, cut and squeeze the fruit. It does a fifty-pound box of fruit in minutes. The juice was strained into plastic drums for the van ride back to Iowa where I formulated it and got it set to ferment.

It would be far more efficient and less expensive to make grapefruit wine right at the grove in Arizona. But before growers would invest in equipment, they would have to be convinced that a local market could be developed for the product. Here in Iowa, we quickly had customers. Folks liked what we brought back from the Valley of the Sun.

For all of the Kraus wines, it is crucial to start with fresh, whole produce, not a concentrate, not a frozen or dehydrated form of the original that must be reconstituted. I mention that because grapefruit is so readily available in all of those forms and some people have wondered why I would bother to haul juice back to the winery when I could have made grapefruit wine so much easier if I had used juice in one of the other forms. But that's not how I make wine. I begin with the juice from a fresh, whole product.

Grapefruit is the simplest of all Kraus wines to make. It is a one-day operation, once the juice is at the winery. When you've got the juice, the hard work is done, you go right to formulating. There's no pressing.

The formula for a fifty-gallon barrel is twenty to twenty-five gallons of juice, one hundred ten to one hundred thirty pounds of sugar and enough water to make a total of fifty gallons.

We don't suggest grapefruit wine to a beginning wine drinker who might come into the wine shop. They might find it too dry. It is a beautiful white wine that clears the senses with a spicy bouquet and gives an unexpected taste sensation. It's been called impertinent. How's that for a wine word? Anyway, it calls for more.

One taster in the shop claimed she didn't care for grapefruit and she didn't want to try the wine. Her husband tried it and he liked it, so then she tried it.

"This is grapefruit at its best," she said. I liked hearing her say that. Most people think of grapefruit as a breakfast food, but now it has the chance to show off and be enjoyed in a wine glass. It is a delightfully dry wine and it goes great with any meal and it is wonderfully refreshing in the summer. That ought to make it a good seller in hot Arizona.

A year after I made grapefruit wine, I began to make orange wine. The formula and process is the same as for grapefruit. So far orange wine has not built up as strong a following as grapefruit has but I am sticking with it, making it in smaller batches, trying other varieties of oranges, varying the proportions so the orange wine will become as distinctive as I know it is capable of being.

35. Cranberry

Cranberry is a new Kraus wine. It was first made in 1979 but it was an idea that had been in my mind for several years.

I like cranberries. Every fall, I looked forward to cranberry sauce and I would get to thinking, with all their tart flavor and bright, beautiful red color, they should make a good wine. I was also interested in rounding out the fall winemaking schedule. I worked up the formula proposal and sent it in for approval. Then I got on the phone to try to locate a fall supply of fresh cranberries.

Cranberries prefer extremely moist locales. I use cranberries from the cool regions of northern Wisconsin where the berries grow on dense bushes, in man-made bogs of marshy swampland. Even while the last snowfall of the winter is still on the ground, the first deep, copper colored leaves show up. The leaves gradually turn a burgundy-tinged dark green. The flowers are pink and white. Some say the fruit gets its name from the crane-like shape of the flower petals as they rise from the stalk. When cranberry vines are in full bloom, a field looks like one huge, pale pink macrame—all knotted, twisted and coiled. At first, the tiny fruits are green, then white, then a mottled ivory with red streaks until finally, they are a shiny ruby red.

The growing bogs are divided into ten-acre sections which are then plotted off into one-acre sections. A levee surrounds each one of the smaller sections. It's a levee to control irrigation water in the event additional moisture is needed during the growing season, but mainly, the levee facilitates the harvest of the berries.

By late September or early October, the slender branches are so heavy with ripe berries, they droop to the ground. The one-acre sections of the bogs are flooded with water so the berries, still attached to their viny branches, float on top of the water where they can be picked by a specially built machine that is driven right into the watery swamp. The combine pulls on the vines in what appears to be a gentle rocking motion. Berries drop into the water and the harvester vacuums them out of the water and into a hopper floating along beside the machine. When the barge-like hopper is full, it is dumped into a waiting truck.

At the packing shed an ingenious yet simple trick grades and sorts sound, healthy berries from the over-ripe, too soft or damaged berries. A conveyor belt merely drops the berries onto a slanting board that has a four-inch barrier at the lower edge. Plump, firm and lively berries easily clear the four-inch hurdle on the first bounce as the berries roll and bound down the slant board. The berries that can't make the jump and clear the hurdle are past their peak and they are dropped into a discard bin. It's a cranberry track meet and only the agile, fit berries make it through the competition.

After a light spray washing, cranberries are weighed into large plastic bags for the truck ride to the winery and then it's my turn to go to work.

And work it was, at first. I never knew those pretty little cranberries were going to give me such a hard time. Their firm, taut skins make them a very durable berry and that's good for harvest and for transporting, but it sure makes them a tough fruit to juice. Those hard, round berries rolled around like a bunch of marbles trying to avoid getting smashed. Those that did get crushed were so sugary and sticky, they stuck to the uncrushed berries, protecting them so they weren't crushed. They balled up together in the crusher tray and stuck to the rollers until I knew there was only one way to get them uniformly crushed—put them through the old sausage grinder. It worked. In a crackling, the berries were split open and came out as red juicy pulp. They creaked and squeaked as they went through the grinder, but it really got the job done. And because the berries were so resilient and tough to break open, I knew for sure I had the freshest, sharpest berries of the crop. When cranberries are ground, they give off a very pleasing scent. The aroma is so pungent, you just know it's going to be a great wine.

I expected to be able to press the ground cranberry pulp but I soon found out that even after they are ground up, cranberries still do not release their juice, not even in the press. I scratched the pressing step from the cranberry wine work schedule and I now formulate the pulp and pump it directly into a fermenting tank. Fermentation lasts eight to twelve months. Then the wine is racked and filtered into a fresh aging tank where it will need to rest another few months before it is filtered again. It usually needs one or two more filterings before it can be polished and bottled.

Because formulation does not begin with juice, the formula for fifty gallons of cranberry wine is based on two hundred pounds of ground cranberry pulp, which would be equal to twenty to twenty-five gallons of juice, plus one hundred twenty-five pounds of sugar and water to total fifty gallons.

Crisp, tart, bright red cranberry juice or pulp becomes a mellow and smooth wine with an intense, fruity flavor just shy of being spicy. The color is a deep, pearly red. It is very beautiful and it is a very versatile wine. It can be a refreshing cocktail or it can accompany lunch or dinner and be right at home.

I expected the wine to be popular. It is so popular, I can't keep a stock of it in the shop. I hadn't even told anyone I was making it. When I had the first batch bottled, I just put it out on the counter and it sold right out. Every year I make more and every year it sells out. I wasn't prepared for it to be such a hit.

At Thanksgiving, many people have thoughts of Pilgrims and Indians eating turkey and cranberries. But if the first Turkey Day feast had cranberries on the menu, the berries were gathered from the rare wild bush, which is a cousin to today's cultivated varieties. Agriculture records show cranberries were not grown and eaten until 1816 in Massachusetts, nearly two hundred years after the first Thanksgiving Day was celebrated.

36. Combination Wines

There's another kind of wine that I like to make—combination wines. Wine drinkers probably already know about blending two wines right at the time they are served to create a new wine. But I am talking about blending the juices and then letting the juices ferment together to make what is really and truly a brand new wine. Blending wines from the bottle is one thing but it is nothing at all like the wine you get from the joint fermentation of two or more juices.

When juices ferment together, they make a wine that is unlike either of the wines they would make alone. I encourage anyone who is already making homemade wines to try making combination wines. They are always a delight.

Winery rules and regulations allow joint fermentation of two fruit juices or two vegetables. They do not allow mixed fermentations, the fermenting of a fruit juice and a vegetable juice together. I obtained approval of formulas for several combination wines—dandelion and rhubarb, cranberry and rhubarb, red clover and rhubarb.

The formula for fifty gallons of dandelion-rhubarb wine is ten gallons of rhubarb juice, ten gallons of dandelion extract, one hundred to one hundred ten pounds of sugar and water to total fifty gallons.

When dandelion and rhubarb are paired, you get a wine with an excellent flavor. Crossing the rhubarb with sweetness and making the dandelion slightly drier, you get the best qualities of each wine. Its color is lighter than the dandelion wine but darker than the rhubarb wine.

The formula for fifty gallons of cranberry-rhubarb wine is ten to twelve gallons of rhubarb juice, three to five gallons of cranberry juice, one hundred pounds of sugar and water to total fifty gallons. This has been one of the most popular wines in the shop. It is a light rosy pink, semi-dry wine with its own refreshing aroma and a distinctive, lively flavor.

The formula for fifty gallons of red clover-rhubarb wine is ten gallons of rhubarb juice, ten gallons of red clover extract, one hundred ten pounds of sugar and water to total fifty gallons. This wine won't be mistaken for either rhubarb wine or red clover wine although it is also white. Its flavor is a subtle mix of the clean and sweet qualities of the red clover with the dry zestiness of the rhubarb. Nature does all the work of blending during fermentation and the results are fantastic.

Combination wines could open up the wine market. They have the potential to top any wine made when it comes to smoothness, flavor, aroma and color.

37. The Wine Shop

We are listed in the Amana Colonies brochure and the Amana phone book. Both listings include this information:

"Old Style Colony Winery, Inc., Middle Amana, Iowa 52307. Phone: 622-3451. Wine shop hours are 10-6 daily. Closed on Sundays."

A map in the brochure directs travelers to the cluster of seven villages in east central Iowa, a few miles off Interstate 80, twenty minutes from Cedar Rapids and eighteen miles from Iowa City. Once they get off the main highways, if they follow the map and take the road that curves along the north and west sides of the lily pond, they will see a small low sign pointing up the hill to our winery. The sign is at the first right-hand intersection where the road comes into Middle. If they should miss that sign and arrow, another one catches them about five seconds later at the west edge of Middle—that's about how long it takes to drive from one end of Middle to the other.

Once they are on our street, they can't miss our big barrel sign out front with its bright red letters, "KRAUS WINES."

The slogan "Aristocrat of Wines Since 1949" is painted on the sign arched over the spindle-trimmed, double-swinging wooden gates at the wine shop entrance. Then it's down three brick steps to the canopied boardwalk into Old Style Colony Winery's shop. The sweet smell of wine is an unspoken *Herzlich Wilkommen*, heart's welcome, for them to taste, maybe to buy our homemade, old-fashioned wines.

When the wine shop is crowded on Saturdays, holidays and most summer days, the covered walkway is an open air waiting room. Visitors may sit on a wooden park bench in one corner of the walk, relax among the flowers—jonquils in spring, begonias and ageratum in summer, chrysanthemums in fall. Cardinals and wrens put on a little sideshow in the bubbling fountain, so it's a good place to sit down and forget your troubles.

Inside the shop, shoppers are greeted "Good morning!" or "Good afternoon!" by one of our friendly clerks or it might be Helen or it might be me. I take my turns at the cash register, too, late on weekday afternoons or Saturdays. The wine business is like any other kind of business. You have to get out and hear what the customer has to say. Having the winery right here in our home gives me a chance to do that often.

We welcome people in the shop just as if they were guests in our home, because in a way, they really are in our home. The shutters between the shop and our family room are kept open so we can see into the shop from the house, and the shop seems larger and more inviting if the visitors can look on through and see a fire in the fireplace or a view out the family room windows.

Some years ago, we offered an ornamental wine bottle for sale. A Chicago artist prepared a model of an Amana woman in the garb of the early days. Named *Die Schwester,* "The Sister," it is a highly glazed ceramic bottle, twelve inches tall. She wears a long, dark gray dress, a long black apron, a black shawl and a striped, gray and white sunbonnet. The next year, *Die Schwester* was joined by *Der Bruder*, "The Brother." Like The Sister, he is twelve inches tall and is dressed in black. His hat, suit, shoes and even the book in the crook of his left arm are all black. Head units of each bottle conceal corks. Each bottle holds twenty-five ounces of wine. When the bottles were purchased at the winery, we filled them with either rhubarb or grape wine, compliments of the winery. Bottles ordered by mail were shipped empty in compliance with Iowa law.

Sikston Ceramics of Kentucky cast and finished the bottles. Only 2,500 were made from each mold. I made a trip to the pottery factory to swing the mallet smashing the molds in a special ceremony guaranteeing no more bottles would be made in those designs. We intended them to be a tribute to Amana's past and they quickly became a popular item in the shop. They are scarce now and that has made them a real collector's item.

The success of the first bottles led us to contract with a Montana pottery firm for another pair of bottles, another sister and brother which were sold as a set. Working from old photographs and sketches, an artist devised seven-inch miniature bottles which hold only four and one-quarter ounces of wine. By agreement, the firm turned out only a limited number of the pair before destroying the molds. The second models are in some ways more authentic replicas of the clothing styles of Old Amana. They feature more subtle color variations and are hand-painted to illustrate finer facial features and clothing details. Tiny corks are concealed in the removable head units.

Sister wears a long, dark blue-gray dress, dark gray apron and shawl and a white bonnet flecked with touches of rust. Depicting the work assignments women had in Old Amana, she carries a hoe. Brother is, again, all in dark clothing—solid black hat and coat, dark gray trousers and a lighter gray vest. He has a green book tucked under his left arm.

When the first bottles were introduced, some Amana folks weren't sure what attitude to take toward seeing colony ancestors as ceramic dolls that were also wine bottles. Their uncertainty is understandable if it is remembered that the original community rules were opposed to displaying artistic creations. We have been pleased at the warm reception and acceptance the two sets of bottles have enjoyed as keepsakes and collectors' items.

It has been estimated that 250,000 or more people are in and out of the Colonies in a year. Over 50,000 people stop in at our winery each year. Wine drinking doubled between 1970 and 1980 in the United States and that also increased our business.

Many reasons are given for the interest in drinking wine. Health is a common one. Wines are extremely interesting. They are subtle and they are exciting. There are many different kinds of wines and no two wines are alike. A wine drinker has endless choices. Each wine has its own distinct characteristics and every wine drinker has different taste buds. No single wine tastes exactly the same to any two people. Certainly, Kraus wines are very special and unique in what they offer and they can't be bought anyplace but here.

Wine sales go in streaks, not just here, but everywhere wines are sold. Price, general appeal, personal tastes and current fads affect what sells. I watch the trends and I aim to not be caught short or overstocked.

I jumped from making four hundred gallons of wine in that first batch of rhubarb wine in 1949 to where I now make several thousand gallons of wine every year and I make more than a dozen different kinds of wine.

Eventually our front hall couldn't handle all the people who stopped in to sample and buy wine. The clothes closet couldn't hold even one day's stock of wine. The basement was stacked and packed with so much equipment, barrels and bottled wine, it was almost impossible for me to work down there. We had to relieve the congested situations both upstairs and downstairs.

In 1971, we had the area between the two existing first floor wings of the building excavated, making a much larger basement, but it is only a basement, there is no building over the new part of the basement. It is covered with a ground level roof, or what would be ground level if it were seen from the front of the house. The winery was expanded from the original four hundred twenty-five square feet in just a corner of the basement to over three thousand square feet.

At the time we enlarged the basement, we added on the wine shop, the entrance gate and the walkway. We also got a cash register and hired one fulltime clerk and one part-time clerk.

The prices of Kraus wines vary according to what it costs to buy the produce and get it to the winery. Rhubarb is the least expensive. It grows practically at the winery door. The amount of hand labor involved in growing, harvesting and handling some of

Breaking the mold of the limited edition ceramic bottle Die Schwester.

the more fragile produce and the distance the produce has to be shipped determines the retail price. Now and then someone will quiz me about why there are all different prices on the bottles and jugs of wine. I explain what all I consider when I set the price.

"Why don't you grow all of your own produce?" they ask, thinking home-grown produce would naturally make the homemade wines less expensive.

"Hey," I tell them, "I don't want to be a farmer. I want to be a winemaker."

And as great as Iowa is for most crops, it's not right for many of the crops I buy. Each crop needs an expert farmer, almost a specialist, to raise top quality produce. I would have to be an expert in too many crops, not to mention the investment I would have in land, machinery, labor and processing.

This is a very small winery compared to some of the really large, commercial domestic wineries in this country, but it is large enough now that I can justify buying up-to-date equipment. With a winery this size, I have to sell a certain amount of wine every month in order to have room to make more wine. I must keep a flow going. Thanks to our good customers, I have been able to maintain a nice comfortable pace.

When Old Style Colony Winery was started, there was only one other commercial winery in Amana. Later, other wineries were opened. All of them make the old standbys, rhubarb and grape. That's why I went a little further back and brought out some of the other old favorites and have introduced some new wines. The total production is still what I can personally take care of and watch over. I want to always be on hand to take every wine all the way through its steps.

A winemaker in a small winery, I am convinced, can let go and really get into his winemaking. He can let his enthusiasm and passion for the job have full rein and he can have the supreme pleasure of turning out superior wines.

Liking what you do, that's good in any line of work, but when a winemaker really loves his work, that all comes out in his wines. A good winemaker has just one thing in mind—to make the tops in wine every single time he sets a new batch of wine.

After working outside of Amana, I soon found that I liked to sell, that I liked the dollars and cents part of a business. I like that part of the winery business, too. But there's something else. There's more to it than just making money. I found out the winery got to me in another way, a way I hadn't even thought about and that was how excited I got when I was devising a new formula. I got excited all over again when the new wine from that new formula was in the bottle, ready to be brought out to the customer. I found out it was a lot of fun to introduce new wines.

When a customer comes into the shop, samples the new wine and then that customer likes my new wine, boy, that's some kind of feeling! It's just about as good as hitting three home runs in one baseball game!

By the time I have bottled a new wine and the public samples it, I am already satisfied that I like it. I just hope the public will like it, too. When they do, then I know I got it just right!

38. Customers

We haven't kept a guest book in the wine shop. Now we wish we had. We never in the world dreamed this community of our childhood and its old-world products would have such universal appeal.

We can remember having in the shop people from Germany, France, Holland, England, Japan, Australia, Canada, Mexico, Saudi Arabia, Taiwan, South Africa, Dominican Republic and every state in the United States. When a German-speaking visitor comes in, I love to get into a two-way German conversation. But no matter where people are from, it is always possible to find something to talk about. Iowa weather is a regular subject. When it is just right, it can be beautiful, just about perfect, and that's really something to remark about. Usually, though, it's too cold, too rainy, too hot, too humid, and when it's hot and humid, travelers are just glad to get into our air-conditioning.

When visitors come in, some head straight for the counter and the wines. Others may browse, take in the backyard view or strike up a conversation with us. With a dozen opened wine bottles and a couple dozen two-ounce plastic glasses on the counter, it's obviously a sampling bar. The glasses are really small "cups" ordinarily used to dispense medicines and pills to hospital patients. But they are just the right size for us to offer a few sips of wine. We let the customer take the lead. We don't hover around or push wines on anyone. No one is ever rushed. When they are ready to sample, we are happy to pour for them. When they are ready to buy, fine, but we don't push there, either.

"Are you a wine drinker?" That's the first question we ask someone who is ready to taste. If the answer is "yes," then we want to know whether the customer prefers a sweet or a dry wine.

About half of our visitors say they don't drink wine but they want to sample. For those folks, red clover is the wine we offer them first because it is smooth, mellow, mild and very pleasant, with no aftertaste.

After that, Niagara or Ontario grape or dandelion might be suggested. Most samplers will taste several wines before they decide which ones to buy.

Sometimes, when they can't decide, they will ask me. I'm no help at all, because I like all the wines.

"They're all good," I answer. "If one of my wines can hit your taste buds, then that's the wine for you."

Some taste and taste and then end up buying the first wine they tasted. And then we get two people, usually a husband and wife, who sample and sample, trying to find one wine they both like. No two people taste the same things in a wine.

"Why not get what each one wants? Take one bottle of each wine," I tell them.

Sometimes people ask for a wine we don't make. For example, apricot wine. I tell them apricots that are shipped in can't be tree-ripened and therefore they wouldn't make very good wine.

Then they come back with "Use apricot concentrate."

Possibly there is an apricot concentrate, but I tell them I don't make any wines from concentrates, only fresh fruits. People don't understand the use of concentrates in winemaking. It is a great debate. Winemakers all have their opinions on the subject. Here's a tip: If a winery is making wine in the dead of winter, you can be sure that winery is making wine from frozen or dehydrated concentrates. Concentrates are seen as a way to avoid tedious, troublesome winery work. I don't see it that way.

As long as I make these old-fashioned, homemade wines and put my name on them, they are going to be made just the way I say I make them—from fresh, whole products.

Often, our visitors will try to compare the wines they know with the Kraus wines. Comparing wines made from formulas and wines made only from grape juice is difficult.

Our regular customers never bother to sample, they come to buy. They will sample if I have a new wine, but usually when they arrive at the shop they know exactly which wines they came here to buy.

When someone busts in the door asking "Is this the place for red clover wine?" we like it. Nothing beats word of mouth advertising. It's good to know our exclusive wines have established their own reputations.

Or the customers will stick their head in the door and ask, "You got the *Piestengel* here?"

"We got the *Piestengel* and more," we say.

Tasting wine here is informal and easy. It's not a wine-tasting party, after all. We try to keep the wine talk factual, not fancy. The taster should make a personal reaction to the wine and find his or her own words to identify what is enjoyed about it. Finding words for the wine helps the wine stay in your memory.

I think it's fine to compare smells and flavors of wine to other familiar, pleasant things—like a fruit, a cherry, peach, apple or berry. Or to say a wine is smooth as silk or satin. Those words help connect similarities so someone else will know what you are saying, too.

I do my best to get tasters to trust their own taste and not to worry about the words of the experts. We winemakers tend to be more frank than folks might expect. We know which of our wines are sweet, which ones have edges of tartness and which are dry. Visitors should tell us what they like so we can help them find our wine that will best suit their taste.

There are four steps to remember when you sample wine—see, swirl, sniff, and sip. The total impression from those four steps will tell you if you like the wine or not.

The first thing I do when I sample is to look at the wine, see its color, clarity, viscosity and body. I look at it against the light. The color should be pleasing and right for that particular wine. White wines are never totally colorless. They may go from a faint pale, straw yellow through medium yellow to light gold. Pink wines go from delicate and barely tinged tints to bright, rosy shades. Reds may be tinged with blue and be almost a ruby red or a garnet color or they may be so dark, they seem almost black. Whatever the color, it should be a clear color, with no traces of dullness, cloudiness or haziness and there should be no suspended particles visible.

Second, I swirl the glass gently to see viscosity and body. In the swirling, the wine climbs the sides of the glass and leaves a film. As that film slides down the glass, I watch how it moves—fast, thin streaks or thick, heavy, slow-moving drops. The slower the wine slides down the glass, the thicker the viscosity, the more alcohol and the more body the wine has.

Third, I sniff the aroma and bouquet. It may be light or heavy but it should be pleasant and typical for that particular wine.

And then I sip—a long, slow sip, not a big gulp. The wine's body may be light or it may be robust but it should always be smooth and refreshing. As you roll the wine cheek to cheek, over the tongue so it is in touch with all the taste buds, you should get a flavor that is mellow and balanced. To me, balance in a wine is what keeps it from being too anything—too sweet, too harsh, too tart, too flowery.

And then I swallow. After I swallow I determine the wine's aftertaste. It may disappear quickly or it may linger on the palate, but it should always be pleasant.

For a wine to show its best traits, it should be tasted at the temperature which permits the wine's qualities to be detected. By experimenting, we have found we like the sweeter wines—tomato, beet, dandelion and red clover—at 58 degrees Fahrenheit. Rhubarb, red grape and cherry we like at 63 to 65 degrees Fahrenheit. The dry wines—rhubarb, cherry and white grape—are excellent at 50 degrees Fahrenheit.

Once wine drinkers get caught up in the search for wine, they are always on the lookout for new wines. There is a fascination in finding those wines in a small, hidden away winery. It is a game of hide-and-seek and the wine drinker enjoys the search as much as the find.

The Kraus winery is not the first winery in Amana that a wine hunter will see. It is not on one of the main roads. It is not even in one of the more widely publicized villages. We don't get the first or the last crack at travelers passing through and we aren't next door to one of the major drawing cards in the Colonies. I used to feel our out-of-the-way spot was a drawback. I now think folks enjoy the game of hunting us up.

They sometimes wonder about finding a winery among the Iowa cornfields. But after they get started tasting, then they are amazed.

"This wine was a beet?"

". . .a flower?"

". . .a tomato? You gotta be kidding!"

They shake their heads as if they can't or don't believe it.

But then they taste some more.

"It's delicious."

". . . refreshing."

". . .unusual."

". . .truly different."

". . .super good."

". . .beautiful color."

". . .surprisingly delightful."

"I don't believe it but I like it, I really like it." That's a remark we often hear. Many are never quite convinced the wines are made the way we say they are made, especially the blossom wines. To many, it is unreal that a flower can become a wine.

One May, some San Diego folks were here on dandelion picking day. They watched the children picking, and saw them bring their pails of blossoms to the winery and get paid for the blossoms. They were told the blossoms were used to make dandelion wine. But once they were inside the shop, the man sidled up to Helen.

"Now level with me," he said very confidentially. "You don't really make wine out of flowers from those weeds, do you?" Even when they see it, they still don't believe it.

One California couple now stops here every year. Others tell us they wouldn't dare go back home without a few bottles of *Piestengel.*

"I've promised my coffee club Kraus cherry wine," one woman said as she paid for the bottles she had selected.

Some of our longtime customers are those who first complimented me on my wines and encouraged me after the winery was started. Sure they all talk nice to me. I get it. They want to make sure I will keep making their favorite wines for them. They know it helps to talk nice to the winemaker. That keeps him going.

The regulars have a hard time weaning themselves away from their old favorites.

"Now this time," one man told his wife as they came in the shop door, "stay away from the *Piestengel* and the grape wines and try something different."

Then there was the Texan and his wife. They bought sixteen half-gallon jugs.

"These wines are going to Texas!" the man announced in his Texas-size voice. The way he said it, he made it sound like it was an honor for Kraus wines to be selected to go to Texas.

We have noticed some who once bought only a bottle or two of wine as a novelty or as a conversation piece or a remembrance of their trip to Amana, come back again and again. They now want the wines in their permanent stock, for holidays, for entertaining and for gifts.

Regulars often arrive at the shop with a newcomer in tow. They do more than *tell* newcomers about Kraus wines. They deliver prospective buyers right to the shop.

"Taste this one. Try this one. Here's one you'll like. These are the best wines," they'll tell the new shopper.

You can't beat personal endorsements. I just bag up the bottles they buy and ring up the sale with a big "Thank you."

"Danke schoen und auf wiedersehn," "Thank you, till we meet again," some folks say. But we don't use the German unless it is said to us first.

"Where are the wines made?" is a question we get quite often. When they learn they are made downstairs in the basement, some then ask to see the winery. Visitors who are genuinely interested in seeing the winery in operation are asked to leave their name, address or phone number so I can get back to them. If they can make it, they arrange to return and watch a winemaking procedure.

"Come in your working clothes," I always tell them, "because it gets pretty hectic down there and if I am short of time or short-handed, you might end up having to help me."

On a working day, when I am pressing, formulating, filtering or bottling, equipment is pulled out into the rooms, machines are whirring and buzzing and the basement is a crowded place. But a great deal of the time in a winery, there is absolutely nothing going on, there is nothing for a visitor to see. The winery is all quiet; only the wine is working.

Some people get the idea that all wines sold in Amana are made in one gigantic, common winery located someplace in the Colonies. Iowa law would not allow that. Wine must be sold on the premises where it is made. Even if that weren't the case, I would never ever sell wine that I hadn't personally made.

Sometimes we hide a smile when shoppers tell us shyly and softly they are buying the wine for medicinal purposes. We think nothing of it because we know many folks right here in Amana who swear that wine makes them feel better.

A Georgia couple spent a long time sampling and visiting with each other about the wines. They said their son belonged to a wine club back home and they were thinking of taking him some of our wines to add to his collection. Finally, they left without buying any wines, but they told us they would be back. We dismissed it and thought they wouldn't be back, but the next day they came back and bought a bottle of nearly every kind of wine we have. It was more than one case.

The mail often brings requests for wines, but Iowa law prohibits mail-order sales of wine. Each letter is answered with that explanation and with an invitation for the letter writer to stop in and see us.

We did get a letter recently with a surprise in it—a check.

"While I was at the winery," the woman wrote, "I bought some wine, wrote the check, closed up the check book but forgot to tear out the check and give it to you."

Helen's favorite story from the wine shop is about the two women she noticed standing for a long time on the back walkway. When they finally came into the shop, one woman was sniffing and blowing her nose.

"It's a terrible time of the year to have a cold," Helen said very sympathetically.

"Oh, she doesn't have a cold," the friend of the sniffer said. "All the thick, dark green trees in your shady backyard reminded her of home. She's homesick for the Black Forest of Germany. That's where we are from."

Our old-fashioned German wines soon cheered them up and made them feel right at home.

39. Storing Wine at Home

When we are asked how wine should be stored when the customer gets it home, we say, put it in a spot that duplicates what the wine has had here at the winery. Some folks like wine racks to display their wine. Racks may be nice to look at, but I'm not much in favor of them. Wines are for drinking, not for showing. They should be provided an environment with the right temperature, minimum light, good air movement and a spot that's nice, steady and quiet. The longer wine is stored before it is poured and enjoyed, the more important the storage conditions are.

I recommend Kraus wines be kept at fifty-five to fifty-eight degrees Fahrenheit. A few degrees of variance between summer and winter is acceptable if the change is gradual. Sudden and recurring temperature changes are disturbing to wine. Most basements meet wine's temperature needs but if a basement isn't available, look for a cool spot in a closet or cupboard next to an outside north wall.

Avoid storing wine in the kitchen. There are too many heat-generating appliances—stove, oven, counter-top skillets and other appliances—in the kitchen. That same thing applies to a utility room where a washer and dryer heat things up. If you want to know if a spot will be the right temperature for storing wines, stick a thermometer there and take a reading two or three times a day on a summer day and again on a winter day.

Wine wants as little light as possible. Total darkness suits it just fine. It should be kept away from direct sunlight and fluorescent bulbs. Both affect color and eventually deteriorate flavor. These requirements again make a basement a good spot for home wine storage but many other locations can be effectively blacked out enough to satisfactorily shield the wine.

The best air for wine is dry and well-circulated. Some basements might not score well on these two points if they are habitually damp or have stagnant air. In my opinion, exterior air does not adversely affect the wine in properly sealed bottles. I do agree polluted air can and does collect on the bottle's neck and can then contaminate the wine when the bottle is handled at serving time.

Why run the risk of ruining the wine? Don't store wine in musty, dank surroundings. Keep wine away from strong smelly things, like rubber tires, paint, oil, gasoline and so on.

Wine needs a steady foundation, one that does not shake, rattle and roll if a train passes or someone slams a door or charges up and down a nearby stairway. Wine resents continual vibrations and jiggling. It does not like to be stirred and riled up. If any sediments should rise, they will resettle. But too many jostlings and resettlings and the wine gets tired out and does not clear up completely.

Most winekeepers will begin by stashing a few bottles in the corner of a cupboard. That's fine for starters. But if you get serious about wine, you will soon find you need to give the wines a place of their own. It's surprising how a bottle or two of wine will make itself right at home somewhere in your house and before you know it, you are making room for more and more bottles of wine.

Kraus wine bottles are closed with screwtop caps with an over-wrap of foil paper. They should be stored in an upright position. Custom-built and commercially manufactured racks, bins and cabinets can be purchased for home wine storage. They may be inexpensive or costly, simple or elaborate. Whatever suits the winekeeper's home, but they should have doors—doors which keep out light while still allowing air to move freely around the bottles.

The simplest way to store Kraus wine at home is to leave the bottles in the partitioned, heavy cardboard boxes we pack them in at the winery. The boxes are strong, made to support the filled bottles and they have another advantage—you can keep track of the wines you have on hand just by writing the names of the wines on the outside of the box. By flipping the lids of the box down, you keep the bottles in the dark and keep them clean at the same time.

Kraus wines are ready to drink the day they are bottled. They will have been properly aged so they are bottled at their peak. They will maintain that peak as long as their paper seal and cap are unopened and undamaged if they have been stored in a stable spot that meets wine's light, air and temperature requirements.

After a screwtop bottle has been opened, if the wine has not been used up, the cap can be screwed back on tightly and that will keep out air and prevent the wine's alcohol from evaporating. If air can't get in and alcohol can't get out, the wine won't spoil.

The only way anyone gets to know a wine, any wine, is to drink it. It's an education to learn about wine and one should take the time and take the pleasure to learn those lessons. Studying wine shouldn't be a cram course. Remember, no one ever knows everything there is to know about wines.

Finding a new wine, tasting it and enjoying it so you can share it with others is what makes the wine world go around.

40. To Your Health

Health was a factor in the use of wine in the early days of the Colonies just as it was elsewhere at that time.

The villagers did not have home medicine chests full of pill bottles. The wine was a home pharmacy of sorts. No matter what ailed them, they reached for their homemade wine.

By word of mouth, they passed along remedies for a long list of common complaints. They had no data or scientific statistics to back up the treatments. They were based on experience. There was a saying that if you were sick and you drank some wine, the worst thing that could happen was that you would feel better. So what if it wasn't a sure fix, it gave you a little cheer.

Those old ways haven't died out. Plenty of folks still take a glass of wine which they believe will prevent them from getting sick and will ease the discomforts and ailments they already have.

Swigs of wine were a tonic, sedative or stimulant, and spelled relief for diarrhea, constipation, colitis, upset stomachs, poor appetites, irregular heart beats, nervousness, sore throats, coughs and every ache from a tooth to a sprained ankle. Now we have words galore pouring from research laboratories supporting old wine tales, giving the use of wine some credibility and legitimacy in medical fields. Radio and television carry the message and so do books, magazines and newspapers of case studies on the role of wine in good health. Reports explain how and why wine can improve digestion, promote the flow of enzymes and hydrochloric acid to facilitate the breakdown of fats and the assimilation of vitamins and minerals, dilate blood vessels for better circulation, lower blood pressure, act as a diuretic to throw off excess fluid and salts, lessen angina pectoris pain, reduce tension, induce relaxation, perk up dull, drab low-fat and low-calorie diets and on and on.

In Old Amana there were no chemists sorting out what wine had in it that tranquilized, eased tensions, lessened stress and anxiety, sedated and brought on sleep. They only knew that, for them, it was an everyday thing, a natural. It was handy, it was cheap, it was allowed and it was furnished.

Based on what we now know about wine, the mid-morning and mid-afternoon wine breaks of Old Amana gave the workers a quick energy boost. The lift came from the simple sugars, mainly fructose and sucrose, present in the wine. Of course, they didn't know why the wine made them feel better, they just knew it did. Somehow it made work seem easier.

They knew firsthand that wine helped take away their troubles and shut off the head a little bit so they could get a good night's sleep. Next morning, no problem, there was no hangover. They went off to work, the same as always. I know eighty and eighty-five-year-old men here in Amana who still have their daily glasses of homemade wine and they don't show the physical afflictions much younger men do who drink hard liquors—whiskey, scotch, gin and such. *Opa* said *Piestengel* didn't kill the liver, it didn't make a drunkard out of you and it was easy on the body.

I'm talking about drinking just a FEW ounces of wine each day, not a quart, not a gallon. Too much alcohol, whether in wine or hard liquor, is not good for anyone. And it is an accepted fact, some people cannot and should not drink alcohol, not even wine, just as some people cannot and should not drink milk or eat wheat, strawberries, chocolate, eggs or some other product to which their body may have developed allergic reactions.

Until recent times, there were no such things as care homes or nursing homes for older people in Amana. The elderly lived with their families in the homes where they had always lived, surrounded by children, grandchildren, great-grandchildren. That wasn't always as wonderful as it sounds. Old people then, like now, could be troublesome, cranky, out of sorts. A touch of wine now and then helped them feel better about themselves and their situation. When folks in Amana hear a small glass of wine is passed with the evening meal or at bedtime in some of today's nursing homes, they just nod and smile.

If the ritual encourages patients to talk, laugh, play cards, watch television in groups rather than sitting all alone, isolated in their rooms, what's the harm?

If wine lifts depression, gets rid of fears and that left-out, left-over feeling older people sometimes experience, why not give them some cheer?

Here's a curious thing: Back in the old days, a forty-year-old person was considered old. After forty, it was thought no one really had to work any longer. Why should they continue to work? There were plenty of younger workers coming up to take over the jobs. Older people were taken off the more demanding work assignments. They did less and less. Many of them just plain loafed. Of course, at that time, the life span in this country was much shorter than it is now; still, forty was very young to retire.

From what we hear and read now, retiring from work too soon, being inactive or having nothing that we have to do or like to do or are interested in, can cause people to die much younger than if they had continued to work. Lots of the people in Old Amana died in their forties. They hadn't yet made the connection between not working and the poor health that came too soon after they were no longer working. As they saw it, if they worked hard until they were forty years old, then it was time for them to let down, to lean back and do nothing.

Even without any medical considerations, I am quite certain wine would still have become a fixture in Amana. To the early residents, wine drinking was more than historical, more than romantic, charming, delightful or healthful. It was simply part of their way of life.

Imagine Amana without its wine. I can't and they couldn't. For them, wine made life better, easier, *gemutlich.* Quiet, mellow, peaceful.

41. Which Wine When?

Wine speaks a warm welcome. There's no friendlier expression of hospitality than the offer of a glass of wine.

"But which wine with what food? At what hour?" people ask.

Too much is made of all that. Winemakers themselves seldom follow any rules when they choose wines. They follow their own individual tastes.

Food is sometimes the main consideration when making a wine choice. Other times the wine you choose might depend on the weather. Red wine seems heartier and more warming in the winter. White wine seems lighter, cooler and more refreshing in the summer. Some claim white wine is a thirst quencher. It all depends on your own taste.

Which wine with which food and when wasn't a problem in Old Amana. They didn't cook with wine and wine wasn't a regular part of family meals as it is in Europe. Here, only the men ever had wine at the table and even then, few men chose to have wine right with a meal. The men in my family had their wine before the evening meal and they had it down in the basement.

When Helen is asked what wine to serve with a particular meal, she may suggest that if the meal includes a dish that has been prepared with wine, you can't go wrong if you serve that same wine with the meal.

I say, "Pour the wine, drink it, enjoy it, no questions asked." For the most part, the wine you prefer with a certain food is mostly habit anyway; it depends on what you are used to having together.

Kraus wines can be enjoyed any time—at a cocktail party, before a meal, with a meal, after a meal or for quiet sipping to close out the day.

For cocktails, most people prefer a dry or semi-dry wine, such as rhubarb,

Concord grape or grapefruit. Cranberry, red clover or Niagara grape go good after dinner or as a nightcap.

When it comes to deciding how much wine you need for a party or for serving with a meal, remember to allow one bottle, four-fifths of a quart or one-fifth of a gallon, for every four guests. One bottle makes six four-ounce servings. After a meal or for a nightcap when sweeter wines are served, the portions are usually smaller, maybe as little as two ounces, so a bottle goes farther.

In the language of wine, the opposite of sweet is dry, not sour. Wines with higher acidity are more tart and are identified in that way. They are never called sour. It is a case of using the correct word. You can't call even the driest wine "sour" any more than you can call unsugared coffee "sour coffee." When you say "sour" in regard to wine, you are describing a wine headed toward becoming vinegar. That wine cannot be used as a vinegar, however, without taking the proper steps to make it a vinegar. You can't drink sour wine and you can't cook with it either.

To chill or not to chill? That's another question that we are asked. Homemade, naturally fermented wines are best served at temperatures no lower than fifty to fifty-five degrees Fahrenheit. Exceptionally sweet wines are very pleasant at room temperature, sixty-five to seventy degrees Fahrenheit, but they will release their best flavor and aroma qualities if they are served at sixty degrees Fahrenheit.

Like the choice of wine, the choice of serving temperature is highly personal. Some people always want red wines at room temperature. Others sometimes like them chilled or over ice. There are no set rules, no rights or wrongs.

Those who put wine in the refrigerator to chill should remember that an hour in a refrigerator that has an average interior temperature of thirty-eight to forty degrees Fahrenheit, will bring room temperature wine down ten degrees. The wine only needs an hour in the refrigerator if it is to be served chilled and it should never spend more than three hours in the refrigerator before it is served.

A bottle of wine can be chilled even faster by packing it in ice. It's a practice used by restaurant people who never chill a bottle of wine until the customer has ordered it. In just a few minutes, the chilled wine is ready to open and pour.

Once wine has been chilled and opened, however, then the unused portion should be refrigerated. Once chilled, opened wine loses it freshness quickly unless it is kept cool.

Folks in Amana like wine best right from the cellar. Drinking chilled wine is something we have learned to do and we now find we like some wines a little bit cooler than they are when they come from the cellar. Serving red wine at room temperature was and is the European way, but it should be remembered that rooms over there were and are a good deal cooler than they are in this country where our homes are centrally heated. Perhaps "cellar temperature" is a more accurate description of the temperature of the wine than room temperature. Cellar temperature is about sixty degrees Fahrenheit.

We have also had to learn about proper glasses for serving wine. At first, we didn't know there was such a thing as a "proper" wineglass. Oldtimers accepted wine in a jelly glass, a tin cup or a mug. They took it as it came. The important thing was that it came. Here, like the rest of the world, we now know the six-ounce wine glass is the usual minimum size, eight-ounce is for all-purpose wine drinking and a ten to twelve-ounce glass is the largest you ever use for wine. Furthermore, no matter what size the glass, the glass is never filled clear full, not like the little samplers' mugs were in the old days.

With red wine, the glass is filled only about one-third full. That's not to be skimpy or to hold back on the wine, but it is to give the wine plenty of breathing space so it can let out all of its aroma and expose its bouquet. When you lift the glass and tilt it toward your mouth, the glass acts like a chimney and the bouquet just floats gently right up to the nose so the wine may be smelled before it is tasted.

With white wine, glasses should be only half-full.

Traditionally, before guests are served from a newly opened bottle of wine, the host pours a couple of swallows of wine into his glass. He is supposed to check the clarity of the wine with his eyes, the freshness with his nose and then take a sip to be sure the wine is suitable to serve to his guests, ladies first, of course.

That's another wine convention that came to Amana only in the last decades. Wine drinkers here didn't have time for all that ceremony. They just opened the bottle, rather, they opened the barrel, and got right to the wine. When they heard the host was supposed to look, sniff and taste first, ahead of company, that really set them back on their heels. They thought they were just lucky to get wine in a glass instead of right from the barrel. I'm only kidding, but it has taken quite a while for wine etiquette to reach Amana.

When you understand the reasons behind the host checking the wine first, it makes sense. It's a polite and thoughtful thing to do, particularly for a winemaker who is serving his own wines. If you check the wine, you protect your reputation as a winemaker by making sure you serve only your best wine.

Even before I open a bottle of wine, I hold it up to the light to make sure the wine isn't cloudy or hazy, telltale signs the wine might not be fit to drink. I handle a bottle gently, taking care not to jostle or shake it so the sediments that might be on the bottom of the bottle aren't disturbed.

Sediments are nothing to be concerned about in a bottle of wine. Sediments are natural to some wines and as long as they remain settled, they are not a serious defect. Sediments in bottled wine are only precipitates of sugar crystals and other tasteless and harmless solids. If they are accidentally riled up, just put the bottle in an upright position for a few minutes and they will resettle so the wine can be poured, leaving the sediments in the bottle.

If there should be an accident—horrors—and wine is spilled on the table linens or on someone's clothing, the stains can be prevented from becoming permanent with a little care. Helen has found that the pre-soak or pre-wash laundry products on the market today work very well on wine stains, especially in treating wine stains on the new, man-made fibers.

For pure linen and cotton, she soaks a wine stain first in cold water and then stretches the stained portion of the cloth over a bowl, sprinkles the spot with salt and then pours boiling water from a height of two feet through the spot. Some people sprinkle the wine spot with salt as soon as the spill occurs and then do the rest of the steps later when they are doing the laundry.

42. Cooking with Wine
by Helen Kraus

As a winemaker's wife, you can be sure I cook with his wines. A few glugs from the wine bottle can turn simple, ordinary foods into very special dishes.

Wine is more than a cooking liquid, it is a seasoning. It should not be a stranger to anyone's cupboard.

Its reputation as a mystery ingredient comes from the subtle, hard-to-name flavor and aroma it adds to many dishes. Each wine has its own distinctive spark to give a dish. It's a spark that is difficult if not impossible to identify once the wine has been blended into the food.

The trick of cooking with wine is for the presence of the wine to be elusive, so that you are aware something wonderful has happened without being able to say exactly what it is that you taste. That calls for wine to be added with an easy hand. Don't be tempted to splash in just a little bit more wine than the recipe calls for. Too little wine is better than too much. You can always add more after you have tasted, but taste first. I often add only half the suggested amount of wine, then taste and decide if I want to add more or not.

Wine cooking may seem mysterious but it should also be seen as an adventure because there are no set, hard and fast, rules. The door is wide open for the cook to be creative, innovative and distinctive by giving foods a personal touch with wine.

To some, wine cooking means fancy, gourmet cooking. That's not true. For some good cooks, wine is actually as essential as salt and pepper or garlic or lemon juice. It is lighter, more agreeable, more compatible with foods than bourbon, Scotch or vodka.

There are cooks who will shrug their shoulders at the price of a steak, roast or chop, yet balk at the idea of adding wine to food, calling it a reckless extravagance.

They would be surprised to know that the poorest and thriftiest peasants of the world slosh wine into their cooking pots every day, very matter-of-factly. Wine is as important to their humble cooking as herbs and spices. Peasant food is so delicious, it is continually being "discovered" by food writers and chefs.

If you are just beginning to cook with wine, you may feel more confident of the results if you use recipes which have been tried and tested in someone else's kitchen. Recipes may or may not suggest precisely which wine to use. I cook with the same wines we like to drink. If you like a wine to drink, you will like it in food. I always taste wine before I add it to a dish.

There's no need to buy wine just for cooking. Wines that are labeled "cooking wine" often contain salt and other seasonings, such as herbs, spices or vinegar, all of which affect the balance of other seasonings in a recipe, so proportions would need to be adjusted accordingly. Cooking wines were originally wines which were intentionally salted to make them unpalatable and harmlessly undrinkable so they were not a temptation to the cooks in the kitchens of castles or the galleys of ships centuries ago.

After you have once cooked with wine, it may be hard to hold your enthusiasm for it in check. But moderation and restraint are watchwords when cooking with wine.

Don't put wine in every dish on the menu. Showcase one wine dish. Imagine how tiresome an entire meal might be if it featured, say, lemon—lemon glazed chicken, lemon gelatin salad, lemon meringue pie and lemonade . . . even for someone who loves lemon, that would be *too* much. Wine in every dish for one meal would be too much, too.

When to add wine during the preparation of a dish depends on what the wine is meant to do in that particular dish. Sometimes wine is more than a seasoning, it is a tenderizer. If wine is to tenderize meat or to overcome the "gamey" flavor of venison, pheasant or wild duck, it should go in at the start or be used as a marinade or as a basting liquid.

If wine goes into a cooked dish, the dish should cook 10 minutes before you add the wine. Let it cook another 10 minutes after adding wine before you taste to see if you want to add any more wine. Wine needs time to release its full flavor.

In other cooked dishes where a mellow, almost undetectable wine flavor is desired, wine should be added at the beginning or early in the cooking. For a bolder, more pronounced wine flavor, the amount of wine to be added may be reduced to one-half by simmering it first and then adding it at the end of cooking, just before the dish is served.

A word of caution: Wine reduces rapidly. One cup of wine reduces to 1/4 cup in only 10 minutes. Further caution: Once wine has been stirred into a cooked dish, the cooking from that point on should never exceed a very low, slow simmer. It is also a good idea to warm wine before it is added to already-cooked foods.

Wine cooking is not "for adults only." Children can enjoy wine-flavored cooked foods, because the alcoholic content evaporates with heat in much the same way alcohol present in lemon, vanilla or other extracts is dissipated during cooking or baking, leaving behind only the flavor, aroma and essence. Alcohol passes off as a vapor at 172 degrees Fahrenheit, well below the boiling point. Wine in a casserole dish loses its alcohol after 10 minutes in a 300 degree Fahrenheit oven. Unheated or uncooked foods containing wine do not, however, lose their alcohol and should be "off limits" to children.

Care must be taken in preparing warm wine punches to make sure the punch is not over-heated after the wine has been added, causing the alcohol to be lost.

Wine calories are primarily in the alcohol, so when alcohol vanishes, so does 85 percent of the wine calories. That is why wine is sometimes used in weight reduction diets or in low-sodium diets to relieve them of their dull, boring and monotonous tastes.

If you want to add wine to your favorite recipes that do not already include wine, here are some tips:

Soups

Replace part of liquid with wine, 1 tablespoon per serving, in preparing soup from scratch, from a can, from the freezer or from a dry mix. To a creamed soup, add rhubarb wine; to meat stock soups, Concord grape; to chicken and turkey stock soups, rhubarb.

Sauces

To cream sauces without eggs, add 1 tablespoon of rhubarb wine per cup of sauce. The wine must be added before the sauce has thickened. In cooked cream and cheese sauces containing eggs, milk, cream and/or butter, wine must be added ahead of other ingredients to avoid curdling or separating. Additions must be made gradually and off the heat. Add 1½ tablespoons rhubarb wine per cup of sauce. Add 1 or 2 tablespoons of cherry or tomato wine for each cup of tomato sauce.

Marinades

Wine marinades were originally used by sailors in the days before modern refrigeration. Overworked deck hands didn't have time to catch fish for the crew to eat and it was impossible to keep meat fresh for an entire voyage. They put meat down in wine in stone crocks. When the wine-preserved meats were later cooked, the wine's acid had softened the connecting meat fibers and made it exceptionally tender. It was also delightfully seasoned. Marinades are popular today for those same reasons—to give flavor and to make the meat easier to cut and chew.

Use enamel, porcelain, glass or stainless steel containers when marinating meats. Do not use aluminum. It is perfectly safe, however, to cook with wine in aluminum pans without affecting the flavor of the finished dish.

Only a small amount of marinade is needed. The entire cut of meat or the whole fowl need not be submerged. Regular stirring and turning of the meat or fowl in the marinade so it is well-coated with the marinade does very well. Most marinades contain equal parts of wine and oil or melted butter to give the marinade clinging power.

Other marinade seasonings are the cook's choice—it might be onion, garlic, herbs, spices, soy sauce—in whatever proportion suits your taste. Foods can be marinated in the refrigerator for a few hours or a few days, some as long as 2 weeks.

When meat is removed from the marinade, blot it dry with paper towels before sautéing, braising, broiling, grilling or roasting. The marinating liquid may be used as part of the cooking, stewing or basting liquid.

Roasts

Baste roasts with 1/4 cup of wine per pound of meat. Concord or Niagara grape complement beef or lamb. Niagara grape or red clover complement ham or pork. And it's rhubarb wine for turkey and chicken. A pinch of rosemary, tarragon, oregano, thyme or sage or other herbs and spices plus a tablespoon or two of lemon juice for zest can be added to taste.

Pot Roasts and Stews

Replace part of liquid with no more than 2 tablespoons of wine per pound of meat, using the same wines that were suggested for roasts.

Gravy

After sautéing or roasting meat or poultry, add 1 or 2 tablespoons of wine per cup of gravy to the pan or skillet drippings and bring to a gentle boil. Stir in thickening agent—flour, cornstarch or arrowroot dissolved in water. Bring to a boil, stirring constantly until gravy reaches desired consistency. Concord or Niagara grape, rhubarb, cherry or red clover may be used according to the meat or fowl dish being prepared!

Some gravy calories can be eliminated while retaining all the flavors from the roaster or skillet drippings simply by deglazing the pan with a few tablespoons of wine. Then over direct heat, gently boil to thoroughly mix browned meat particles with the wine. Pour the pan juices over the meat at serving time. Concord or Niagara grape, rhubarb, cherry or red clover can be used. Red clover wine is especially nice for deglazing a skillet after fish has been fried.

Salads

In gelatin-based salads, replace one-fourth of the liquid in the recipe with wine. Add the wine after the gelatin has been completely dissolved in water. Choose a wine that is compatible with the gelatin's color and flavor.

Salad Dressings

Replace a portion of the vinegar or lemon juice in an oil-based dressing with wine, allowing at least 1 tablespoon of vinegar or lemon juice to remain in the dressing. Marinate fresh or leftover cooked vegetables in wine salad dressings.

Desserts

Replace one-fourth to one-half of the liquid with light, delicately flavored wines in gelatin-based desserts, cakes, cookie doughs, puddings, pie fillings or other batters, such as cobbler toppings, waffles and pancakes. (Special note: Kraus wines do not have a high enough alcoholic content to be used in flaming desserts.)

Fruits

Douse fresh, frozen or canned fruits with a complementary wine. Add appropriate wine to a cream sauce to serve over fruit, using 1 tablespoon wine for each cup of sauce. Niagara grape and red clover are versatile "go withs" for any fruits.

Combination Dishes

Enhance casseroles, spaghetti and other combination recipes by replacing one-fourth to one-half of their liquid with wine. Dress up leftovers with wine to make a fresh, newly prepared dish.

Cereals

Plump raisins in a few tablespoons of wine before adding to cooked oatmeal or cream of wheat and serve with brown sugar, cream or milk.

Prepared Mixes

Transform canned, frozen, dried or any other convenience foods with wine. The kind and the amount of wine is up to the cook.

Wine and food combinations are limitless. There are no rules. There is nothing absolute, nothing sacred, and there should be no big mystery about cooking with wine.

I am happy to share some of our family's favorite recipes, made with Kraus wines, of course. The seasonings or the kind of wine used can be varied in many of the recipes. That is just one of the joys of cooking with wine—making your own variations to present your own new recipe.

Wine catches on quickly. Once you have made a dish with wine, that dish will never again taste quite the same without that touch.

Appetizer

Pork Liver Pâté

Slice and serve with crackers.

1½ pounds pork liver, minced
1½ cups finely ground pork
⅔ cup chopped salt pork
strong dashes of nutmeg and oregano
dash of black pepper
¼ teaspoon crushed bay leaf
3 garlic cloves, crushed
2 tablespoons brandy
½ cup dry rhubarb wine
uncooked bacon slices

Mix liver, pork and salt pork. Add nutmeg, oregano, pepper, bay leaf, garlic, brandy and wine and mix thoroughly. Line a terrine with bacon slices and fill with liver mixture. Press down firmly and top with more bacon slices. Cover with aluminum foil and bake at 350 degrees Fahrenheit for 1½ hours. Cool and refrigerate at least 8 hours before serving.

Variation: In place of a terrine, use a 1-quart oven-proof casserole of any shape—square, round or oval.

Breads

Cheese Loaf

A wine-laced show stealer with airy texture, tantalizing aroma and a crunch in every bite.

1½ cups sifted all-purpose flour
2¼ teaspoons baking powder
1 teaspoon salt
¼ teaspoon soda
½ cup whole wheat flour
⅓ cup shortening
⅔ cup sugar
2 eggs
⅓ cup cherry wine
⅓ cup milk
⅔ cup coarsely chopped walnuts
¾ cup shredded sharp cheddar cheese
½ cup crumbled blue cheese
2 teaspoons poppy seeds
2 teaspoons sesame seeds

Resift flour with baking powder, salt and soda. Stir in whole wheat flour and set aside. Cream shortening with sugar. Beat in eggs one at a time. Add wine, milk and flour mixture, stirring just until well-blended. Add nuts. Divide dough in half. To one portion, add cheddar cheese and mix lightly. Add blue cheese to other portion. Spoon dough into a greased 8-inch tube pan, placing cheddar cheese dough on one side of pan and blue cheese on the other. Sprinkle poppy seeds over cheddar dough, sesame seeds over blue cheese dough. Bake at 350 degrees for 1 hour until bread is browned and tests done. Low rack position in the oven is recommended. Let bread stand 10 minutes in the pan, then turn out on a wire rack to cool. Serve plain, with butter or with whipped cream cheese. Makes 1 loaf.

Kirschpfannkuchen

Wine Cherry Pancakes—a delightful switch with tart cherries in soft, delicate cakes.

4 medium-sized French bread rolls
water
1 teaspoon ground cinnamon
1/2 cup sugar
2 eggs
1/4 cup sifted all-purpose flour
2 teaspoons sugar
1/2 teaspoon salt
1/2 cup milk
1/2 cup cherry wine
1 one-pound can tart pitted red cherries, drained
5 tablespoons butter, softened and whipped
1/2 cup sugar
1 teaspoon ground cinnamon

Soak rolls in water to cover. Stir cinnamon and 1/2 cup sugar together and set aside. In a mixing bowl, beat eggs until light. Add flour, 2 teaspoons sugar, salt, milk and wine and beat until smooth. Squeeze rolls dry and crumble into batter. Fold in drained cherries. Drop batter onto medium-hot griddle in mounds 1 1/2 inches in diameter and bake until crisp and brown on one side; carefully turn and brown other side. Serve hot with a dollop of whipped butter, and sprinkle with cinnamon and sugar mixture. Makes 30 to 36 little cakes.

Meats, Marinades, Sauces

Steak in Wine

Makes its own gravy.

1 pound round steak, well-pounded
1/2 cup flour
1 teaspoon salt
1/4 teaspoon pepper
1 medium onion, sliced
1 cup rhubarb wine

Cut steak into four portions. Combine flour, salt and pepper and pound into steak. In a well-greased casserole, layer steak with onion slices and pour wine over all. Bake 1 hour at 350 degrees. Serves 4.

Rindfleisch Ragout

German Peasant Stew—hearty, robust country fixings.

2 tablespoons oil
1 cup sliced onion
1 clove garlic, crushed
3 pounds stewing beef, cut in 1-inch cubes
8½ cups beef broth
½ cup Concord grape wine
1 tablespoon sugar
1 teaspoon salt
1 bay leaf
1½ pounds potatoes, peeled and cubed (4 cups)
2 cups sliced carrots
1 teaspoon dill weed
1 tablespoon flour
½ cup Concord grape wine (optional)

In a large stewing pot or large electric skillet, heat oil and add onion and garlic. Sauté just until tender, not browned. Remove and set aside. Add half of beef, brown on all sides and remove. Brown remaining beef. Return beef and onions to pot. Stir in broth, wine, sugar, salt and bay leaf. Reduce heat, cover and simmer until meat is tender, 1½ to 2 hours. Add potatoes, carrots and dill. Simmer until vegetables are tender, 20 to 30 minutes. Mix flour with a little water and stir into broth. Cook and stir until thickened. Remaining wine may be added at this time for stronger wine flavor in the gravy. Serves 6.

Quick Sauerbraten

Skips marinating, finished with "snaps".

1 4- to 5-pound round or rump roast
¼ cup oil
½ cup chopped onion
2 teaspoons salt
2 tablespoons mixed pickling spices
1 cup red wine vinegar
3 cups water
½ cup packed brown sugar
12 gingersnap cookies, crushed

Brown roast in oil in heavy skillet. Pour off oil and add onion, salt, spices, vinegar, water and sugar. Simmer 3 to 4 hours, until meat is tender. Remove meat and keep it warm. Strain liquid and measure 4 cups of the broth into the skillet. Add gingersnaps and cook and stir until smooth and slightly thickened. Serves 8.

Sauerbraten "Mit Cakes"

Marinated before roasting and served with Kartoffelpuffer, *potato pancakes.*

1 5- to 6-pound round or rump roast
4 slices bacon, halved
1½ cups red wine vinegar
2 teaspoons salt
10 whole peppercorns
2 bay leaves
3 cloves
2 onions, chopped
2 carrots, sliced
3 tablespoons butter
½ cup boiling water
1 cup Concord grape wine
1 cup sour cream

Cut 8 gashes in meat and tuck a piece of bacon in each gash. In a saucepan, combine vinegar, salt, peppercorns, bay leaves, cloves, onions and carrots. Bring to a boil. Remove from heat and let cool for ½ hour. Place meat in a glass or porcelain bowl and pour the vinegar mixture over it. Marinate 3 to 5 days in refrigerator, turning and basting several times.

When ready to cook, drain meat, save marinade. Pat roast dry with paper towels. Melt butter in heavy Dutch oven and brown meat on all sides. Add marinade and boiling water. Simmer 2½ hours. Add wine and continue simmering another 30 minutes or until meat is tender. Add sour cream, stirring constantly and keeping heat just below simmer for next 15 minutes. Slice and serve with gravy and *kartoffelpuffer*, potato pancakes. Serves 8.

Kartoffelpuffer

Potato pancakes.

6 medium potatoes, peeled, grated
½ onion, grated
2 tablespoons flour
2 eggs, beaten
¼ teaspoon white pepper
dash of nutmeg
2 tablespoons parsley, minced
1½ teaspoon salt

Drain grated vegetables and combine with remaining ingredients, mixing well. Drop by spoon onto hot lightly buttered griddle. Fry until brown and crisp on both sides, turning only once. Serve hot.

Marinated Beef Roast

Be sure to thicken the drippings and serve as gravy.

1 2-pound beef roast
3/4 cup soy sauce
1 cup tomato wine
1/2 cup honey
1/4 teaspoon oregano
2 garlic cloves, crushed
1 teaspoon basil
1 teaspoon seasoned salt
1/2 teaspoon pepper
2 slices ginger root

Combine all liquids and seasonings and pour half of it over roast. Marinate 3 to 4 hours. Add remaining liquid when roast goes into oven. Bake 1 hour at 375 degrees. Serves 4.

Beef Shortribs

Fork-tender ribs cooked with vegetables.

3 pounds beef shortribs
1 medium onion, sliced
1 teaspoon salt
1/4 teaspoon pepper
1/2 teaspoon marjoram
2 beef bouillon cubes
1 cup water
3/4 cup Concord grape wine
1 bay leaf
12 small potatoes
4 carrots, cut in 2 1/2-inch lengths
1 tablespoon flour
1/4 cup water

Trim excess fat from ribs and use trimmings to oil hot skillet. Brown ribs on all sides. Add onion and cook just until limp and tender, not browned. Sprinkle in salt, pepper and marjoram. Dissolve bouillon in water and add to meat along with wine and bay leaf. Cover and simmer 2 to 2 1/2 hours, until meat is tender. Add potatoes and carrots and continue simmering 30 minutes. Stir flour into water and then into pan drippings. Cook until slightly thickened and serve as gravy over ribs and vegetables. Serves 4.

Perfect Steak Marinade

A thick steak, thinly sliced crosswise. Will feed four hungry people.

1 cup olive oil
1 cup Concord grape wine
1/2 onion, grated
2 cloves garlic, minced
1 tablespoon salt
1 teaspoon freshly ground pepper
1/2 teaspoon paprika

Combine all ingredients in a glass baking dish. Thoroughly coat a 2½- to 3-pound sirloin steak, cut into 3-inch wide strips, with the marinade. Refrigerate for several hours or overnight, turning several times. Remove from refrigerator 2 hours before time to grill or broil. Pat dry with paper towels before cooking.

Steak Marinade I

A thick, rich marinade with many wonderful seasonings.

1 cup Concord grape wine
¾ cup chili sauce
½ cup salad oil
¼ cup catsup
2 cloves garlic, minced
2 tablespoons honey
1 tablespoon brown sugar
1 teaspoon dry mustard

Combine ingredients in a glass baking dish. Coat a 4-pound sirloin steak, cut into 3-inch wide strips, with marinade and allow to stand at least 4 hours or overnight. Turn several times during marinating. Pat steak dry with paper towels before grilling. Serve by slicing in thin diagonal slices, cutting across the grain. For a delicious gravy to pour over the sliced steak, heat remaining marinade with 1 cup beef broth. Serves 6 to 8.

Steak Marinade II

Skip chopping onion and mincing garlic, and instead reach for bottled seasonings.

½ cup salad oil
½ cup Concord grape wine
2 tablespoons lemon juice
1 teaspoon onion salt
1 teaspoon Worcestershire sauce
⅛ teaspoon freshly ground pepper
⅛ teaspoon garlic powder
½ teaspoon seasoned salt

Combine all ingredients. Thoroughly coat a 2- to 2½-pound sirloin steak with marinade and let rest for several hours or overnight in refrigerator. Turn several times during marinating. Pat steak dry with paper towels before grilling.

Pork Loin Roast

Stuffed with fruit and sauced with a zippy gravy.

1 4-pound pork loin roast
8 prunes, pitted and chopped
1 tart apple, cored and diced
1 teaspoon seasoning salt
¼ teaspoon ginger
¼ teaspoon pepper
⅛ teaspoon garlic powder
½ cup rhubarb wine

1 tablespoon flour
1/4 cup water
1 small jar currant jelly
1/8 teaspoon garlic powder
salt and pepper

Make a hole in center of loin (better yet, ask the butcher to do it) and stuff with prunes and apple. Combine seasoning salt, ginger, pepper and 1/8 teaspoon garlic powder; press to coat the roast. Dust roast with flour and place in roaster. Pour wine into bottom of pan and roast 2 hours at 400 degrees. Pour off drippings and thicken with flour stirred into water. Stir in jelly and remaining garlic powder. Salt and pepper the gravy to taste. Serves 4.

Denny's Pork Steak

Simple seasonings make a quick supper.

2 pounds pork steak, 1 inch thick
shortening
4 tablespoons shoyu (soy sauce)
3 tablespoons sugar
2 tablespoons vinegar
1 tablespoon dry rhubarb or dry Concord grape wine

Cut steak into strips and brown on all sides in shortening. Add remaining ingredients, cover and simmer 30 to 40 minutes until pork is tender. Serves 4.

Braised Pork Chops and Cabbage

A country casserole fit for company.

3 pounds cabbage, coarsely chopped
3 tablespoons butter, divided
1/2 cup finely chopped onion
1/2 teaspoon minced garlic
salt to taste
freshly ground pepper
8 pork chops, 1 1/2 inches thick
1/2 cup dry rhubarb wine
1 cup whipping cream
1 bay leaf
4 teaspoons Parmesan cheese
2 teaspoons bread crumbs

Boil cabbage in salted water 5 minutes. Drain well. Melt 2 tablespoons butter in skillet and cook onion and garlic until soft, not browned. Stir in cabbage, salt and pepper. Cook 5 minutes until almost all liquid has evaporated. Transfer to a bowl and set aside.

Season chops and brown in 1 tablespoon butter. Remove chops and almost all oil from skillet. Add wine and boil rapidly to reduce wine to 1/4 cup. Mix wine with cabbage.

In a lightly buttered casserole, layer cabbage and chops, ending with cabbage. Scald cream until tiny bubbles appear at edges of pan; pour over cabbage. Place bay leaf on top. Cover and bake 1½-2 hours at 350 degrees. Combine cheese and bread crumbs and sprinkle on top of casserole. Return to oven for another 30 minutes. Serves 8.

Wine Braised Pork Chops

Chops in a colorful vegetable sauce.

4 large loin pork chops, 1 inch thick
3 tablespoons shortening
1 green pepper, sliced crosswise into rings
1 clove garlic, crushed
½ pound fresh mushrooms, sliced, or 1 6-ounce can of sliced mushrooms, drained
2 teaspoons salt
¼ teaspoon pepper
2 cups quartered fresh tomatoes or 1 2½-cup can of whole peeled tomatoes
½ cup rhubarb wine

In a heavy skillet, melt shortening and brown chops on both sides. Remove chops and all but 2 tablespoons of shortening from skillet. Add green pepper, garlic and mushrooms and sauté 5 minutes, stirring continuously. Return chops to skillet; add salt, pepper, tomatoes and wine. Cover and simmer 1¼ hours or until chops are tender. Serves 4.

Wine Sauce for Ham

A beauty of a sauce with a cheery flavor.

1 can cherry pie filling
1 cup currant or apple jelly
½ cup raisins
⅓ cup brown sugar
⅓ cup cherry wine
1 teaspoon prepared mustard

Combine all ingredients in a saucepan and heat thoroughly. Spoon over ham every 20 minutes during baking time. Serve remainder with ham.

Chicken Almondzini

With a touch of rhubarb and a bit of a crunch.

7 ounces spaghetti, cooked and drained
3/4 cup mayonnaise (not salad dressing)
1/3 cup flour
2 tablespoons instant minced onion
1 teaspoon garlic salt
2 1/4 cups milk
1 cup shredded natural Swiss cheese (4 ounces)
1/3 cup rhubarb wine
2 cups chopped cooked chicken (or turkey)
1 10-ounce package frozen chopped broccoli, thawed and drained
1 1/4 cups sliced almonds, divided
1 4-ounce can sliced mushrooms, drained
1/4 cup chopped pimento

Cook spaghetti according to package directions. In a medium saucepan combine mayonnaise, flour and seasonings. Gradually add milk and cook over low heat, stirring constantly until thickened. Add cheese and wine. Stir until cheese has melted.

In a large bowl, combine spaghetti, mayonnaise mixture, chicken, broccoli, 3/4 cup almonds, mushrooms and pimento. Toss lightly. Pour mixture into a 12x8-inch baking dish. Top with remaining 1/2 cup almonds. Bake 40-45 minutes at 350 degrees. Makes 6-8 servings. Pass grated Parmesan cheese at serving time.

Chicken Delight

A short cut to perfectly seasoned grilled chicken every time. Quantities depend on how many you plan to serve; allow at least 1/2 pound of chicken per person.

2 1/2-pound frying chicken, cut up, or 1 1/2- to 2-pound broiler, halved
lemon pepper
Concord grape wine
Italian salad dressing

If using broiler halves, remove wingtip and break joints of drumstick, hip and wing so halves stay flat on grill. Sprinkle chicken with lemon pepper. Shake together equal parts of wine and dressing. Place chicken on grill, 5 inches from heat, bone sides down. When well-browned, turn and brush with basting mixture. Continue turning and basting several times until chicken is done. Total cooking time is about 45 minutes. Test for doneness by cutting into thickest part of thigh. If it cuts easily and no pink is visible, chicken is done.

Chicken Sauté

With a sprightly ending.

1 frying chicken, quartered
all-purpose flour
4 to 6 tablespoons butter
salt and pepper to taste
1 cup dry rhubarb wine
chopped parsley or chives

Dip chicken pieces in flour and brown in butter in large, heavy skillet. Turn each piece so it browns evenly on all sides. Add salt, pepper and wine. Lower heat to simmer; cover and cook 1½ hours or until chicken is tender. Turn chicken 2 or 3 times during cooking time so flavor of liquid will be absorbed. Remove chicken and keep warm. Add additional wine if necessary and simmer pan drippings over increased heat for a few minutes. Pour juices over chicken to serve. Garnish with parsley or chives. Serves 4.

Oven-fried Chicken

Pack this in a basket and head for a picnic—it's good hot or cold.

12 pieces of frying chicken
1/3 cup cornflake crumbs
2 teaspoons salt
2 teaspoons paprika
3/4 teaspoon dill
1/4 teaspoon crumbled thyme
2 tablespoons butter
2 tablespoons shortening
3/4 cup cherry or Concord grape wine

Toss chicken pieces with crumbs and seasonings. Melt butter and shortening in shallow baking dish. Arrange seasoned chicken, skin side down, in a single layer in the dish. Bake uncovered at 400 degrees for 30 minutes. Then turn chicken, add wine to dish and continue baking another 25 to 30 minutes or until chicken is tender. Serves 6.

Orange-Pineapple Chicken

Guests at the Kraus table often ask for this recipe.

1 broiler chicken, cut up
1/4 cup biscuit baking mix
1 teaspoon Accent (MSG)
1/2 teaspoon salt
1/4 teaspoon sage
1/4 teaspoon basil
1/4 cup corn oil
1/2 cup frozen orange juice concentrate
1/4 cup pineapple juice
3 tablespoons brown sugar
2 tablespoons dry rhubarb wine
1 teaspoon prepared mustard
1/3 tsp. ground ginger

pineapple slices
orange wedges
parsley

Combine biscuit mix, Accent, salt, sage and basil. Coat chicken pieces with mixture. Heat oil in frying pan over medium heat. Brown chicken on all sides in oil. Place chicken in foil-lined baking dish. Combine orange and pineapple juices, brown sugar, wine, mustard and ginger, and brush chicken. Bake at 325 degrees, uncovered, about one hour or until chicken is tender. Baste chicken with the sauce every 15 minutes throughout baking time. Garnish with pineapple slices, orange wedges and parsley. Serves 4.

French Herbed Chicken

Chicken sparked with Piestengel.

1 3-pound broiler, cut up
1 tablespoon shortening
salt and pepper
1 8-ounce can small whole onions, drained (1 cup)
½ cup coarsely chopped carrot
1 clove garlic, crushed
2 tablespoons snipped parsley
¼ teaspoon crushed dried thyme
1 2-ounce can sliced mushrooms, drained
1 cup dry rhubarb wine
2 or 3 stalks celery, sliced
1 medium bay leaf

Brown chicken in shortening in hot skillet. Season with salt and pepper and place into 2-quart casserole. Drain excess fat from skillet. Place remaining ingredients, except celery and bay leaf, into skillet and heat, scraping loose all browned particles. Pour over chicken. Tuck in celery and bay leaf. Cover and bake 1¼ hours at 350 degrees. Remove bay leaf and celery before serving with remaining juice and vegetables. Serves 4.

Roast Turkey Baste

Brown to a wine finish.

1 cup dry rhubarb wine

Baste turkey with wine every 15 minutes during last hour of roasting. Wine tenderizes the meat and gives the skin an even rich brown color. Thicken turkey juices and wine to make gravy.

Wild Duck

Wild birds are tamed in grape wine marinade and finished with a touch of rhubarb wine.

4 wild ducks
dry Concord grape wine
bouquet garni (½ teaspoon thyme, 2 bay leaves and fresh parsley sprigs tied in cheesecloth)
vegetable oil or shortening
salt and pepper
16 small white onions
6 tablespoons butter
½ cup dry rhubarb wine
2 cups sliced mushrooms

Singe end feathers of well-cleaned ducks over a flame. Then place the birds in a glass, porcelain or stainless steel bowl and add bouquet garni. Cover birds with Concord grape wine. Allow to marinate in a cool place or the refrigerator at least 24 hours or up to 3 days.

When ready to cook, drain ducks well and pat exteriors dry with paper towels. Sauté ducks in hot oil or shortening in large flameproof casserole or roaster, turning to sear on all sides. Pour strained marinade over and allow to come to a gentle boil. Sprinkle with salt and pepper. Cover and lower heat to maintain a slow simmer for 1 to 1½ hours. Cooking time will depend on size and age of ducks.

Sauté small onions in butter, turning to soften, but do not allow to brown. Add rhubarb wine and gently poach onions until tender. Do not overcook. Sauté mushrooms in butter for 5 minutes. Add onions and mushrooms to ducks just before serving.

Optional: Thicken drippings with 1½ tablespoons arrowroot or cornstarch blended with ¼ cup cold water for gravy to serve over the ducks and over small boiled potatoes tossed in butter.

Rabbit with Tarragon

A delightful way to prepare rabbit: top-of-the-stove Hasenpfeffer.

1 young rabbit
¼ cup flour
1 teaspoon salt
¼ teaspoon pepper
4 to 6 tablespoons butter
1 cup dry rhubarb wine, divided
¼ cup fresh tarragon or 1 teaspoon dried tarragon

Skin and clean rabbit, reserving liver. Cut into serving pieces. Combine flour with salt and pepper. Dredge rabbit pieces in seasoned flour. Melt butter in large skillet and brown rabbit quickly on all sides, being careful that butter does not burn. Lower heat and add ¾ cup dry rhubarb wine. Cover and simmer gently about 45 minutes, or until rabbit is tender. Soak tarragon in 1/4 cup dry rhubarb wine for 30 minutes and add to skillet. Increase heat and turn pieces of rabbit. Cook 5 minutes. Remove rabbit to heated platter. Pour sauce over to serve. Liver may be sautéed in butter 5 minutes, minced and added to the sauce just at serving time. Serves 4.

Baked Fish

A delicious diet recipe.

1/2 cup chopped celery
1 1/2 pounds catfish fillets (or any other fish fillets), fresh or frozen
3/4 teaspoon salt
1/4 teaspoon crushed rosemary
1/4 teaspoon pepper
1/4 teaspoon paprika
1 medium-sized tomato, sliced
1/2 cup chopped green onion
1/4 cup dry rhubarb wine

Layer celery into shallow baking pan. Arrange fish over celery, slightly overlapping fillets. Sprinkle with seasonings, top with tomato and onion. Add wine. Bake at 350 degrees for 25 minutes or until fish is flaky. Serves 4.

Vegetables

Oma's Beets

Nice way to dress up an often neglected and overlooked vegetable.

1 8 1/4-ounce can small whole beets
1 teaspoon cornstarch
1/4 cup red beet or sweet Concord grape wine
1/2 tablespoon butter
salt and pepper

Drain beets, reserving 1/4 cup of liquid. Thinly slice beets and set aside. In a saucepan, gradually stir reserved liquid into cornstarch until smooth, then add the wine. Cook over medium heat, stirring constantly, until sauce is clear and thick. Stir in butter and beets and reheat. Add salt and pepper to taste. Serves 2 or 3.

Red Cabbage in Wine

Longtime favorite in Amana.

½ cup butter or margarine
4 pounds red cabbage, shredded
1 cup Concord grape wine
2 cups sliced apples
pinch of cloves
1 tablespoon sugar
grated peel of 1 lemon

Melt butter or margarine in a large, heavy skillet over low heat. Add cabbage and stir while cooking until cabbage is softened and limp. Add wine and apples and stir to mix well. Cover tightly and cook until cabbage and apples are tender. Add cloves, sugar and lemon peel and cook three minutes more. Serves 6.

Salads

Molded Cherry Salad

Luxuriously rich with color and flavor

1 cup cherry juice (add water if necessary to make 1 cup)
1 3-ounce package cherry gelatin
1 cup sweet Concord grape wine or cherry wine
1 1-pound can pitted black cherries, drained
1 cup chopped walnuts

Heat cherry juice to boiling. Add gelatin, stirring until dissolved. Cool. Add wine and chill until slightly thickened. Fold in cherries and nuts. Turn into rinsed large mold or 8 individual molds. Chill until firm. Serves 8.

Blushing Fruit Elegant

Versatile—can be salad, or add a dollop of whipped cream and call it dessert.

1 1-pound can pear halves
1 1-pound can peach halves
1 9-ounce can pineapple slices
1 package strawberry gelatin
1 stick cinnamon
4 or 5 whole cloves
1 teaspoon lemon juice
few drops red food coloring
½ cup sweet cranberry wine

Drain fruits, reserving liquids. Arrange fruit in a deep bowl. Measure juice from fruits and add water to make 2½ cups. Add gelatin, spices, lemon juice and coloring.

Bring to a gentle boil, stirring until gelatin is dissolved. Simmer 5 minutes. Remove from heat and add wine. Cool. Pour over fruit. Refrigerate 1 to 1½ hours. Baste occasionally. (Note: This does not "set" completely but is beautifully congealed and shimmery.)

Old-fashioned Hot Potato Salad

An old-time German specialty.

6 medium-sized waxy-fleshed potatoes (about 2 pounds)
4 slices bacon
¼ cup chopped green onions, tops included
1 teaspoon salt
freshly ground pepper
3 tablespoons vinegar
2 tablespoons rhubarb wine
2 teaspoons sugar
2 hard-cooked eggs, chopped

Boil well-scrubbed potatoes in skins until tender. Peel and dice and keep hot while preparing bacon and dressing. Fry bacon until crisp. Drain and crumble. Measure ¼ cup of bacon fat and return to skillet. Sauté onions slightly in fat. Add salt, pepper, vinegar, wine and sugar. Heat to a full boil and quickly pour over potatoes. Add chopped eggs and toss lightly to blend dressing with potatoes and eggs. Serve immediately while hot. Serves 4.

Zigorrie Salat

Dandelion Salad—a delicate springtime treat in Amana.

1 quart dandelion greens
2 chopped hard boiled eggs
2 tablespoons bacon drippings
1 tablespoon flour
1 cup water
2 tablespoons vinegar
salt and pepper
½ cup sour cream or buttermilk
minced onion

Harvest young dandelion greens in early spring. Cut the plant an inch or two under the soil, so part of the root keeps the plant intact. It will be easier to clean. Thoroughly wash roots and leaves under running cold water. Then in deep water, rinse by lifting plant up and down, in and out of the water. Be sure no soil or sand remains. Cut off roots, separate and sort leaves, using only young, tender leaves for the salad. Chop the tender leaves as finely as possible. Rinse once more. Drain well and crisp in the refrigerator for an hour or longer.

—*more*

Heat drippings, sauté onions, blend in flour and add water. Boil until slightly thickened. Add vinegar, salt and pepper and remove from heat. Cool slightly. Add sour cream and buttermilk and pour over drained dandelion greens. Toss well with chopped eggs and serve immediately. Serves 4.

Spinach Salad and Dressing

A barbecue special—toss and serve with a last-minute flourish.

2/3 cup salad oil
1/4 cup vinegar
2 tablespoons rhubarb wine
2 teaspoons soy sauce
1 teaspoon sugar
1 teaspoon dry mustard
1/4 to 1 teaspoon curry powder
1 teaspoon freshly ground pepper
1/2 teaspoon salt
1/2 teaspoon garlic salt
2 bunches spinach (about four quarts)
1 pound bacon
2 hard-cooked eggs, coarsely chopped

Combine oil, vinegar, wine, soy sauce, sugar and seasonings in a covered jar. Shake well. Chill. Wash spinach thoroughly, remove stems and tear into pieces. Drain and crisp in refrigerator for an hour. Fry bacon until crisp. Crumble drained bacon and toss with eggs into spinach. Shake dressing again and pour over spinach, toss and serve. Serves 8.

Easy Chicken Salad

Slightly exotic version of an old luncheon standard.

4 chicken breasts
1/2 cup rhubarb wine
1/3 cup French or Italian salad dressing
1 cup seedless grapes, halved
2 tablespoons slivered almonds
1/2 cup mayonnaise
salt

Line a pan with foil, add chicken breasts and pour wine over. Cover and bake 1 hour at 350 degrees. Cube chicken, add salad dressing and refrigerate overnight.

Add grapes, almonds and mayonnaise. Season with salt to taste. Serve in lettuce cups. Serves 4.

Desserts

Wein Sosze

Wine Sauce—a simple but very pleasant wine recipe that once was prepared in old Amana communal kitchens and served over squares of sponge or water cake.

1 cup water, divided
2 tablespoons flour or 1½ tablespoons cornstarch
¼ cup sugar
1 cup Concord grape wine

Bring ¾ cup of water to boil. Add flour or cornstarch which has been already blended with ¼ cup water. Cook until clear and thickened. Add sugar and cook a few minutes longer. Remove from heat and add wine. Cool. Pour over cake and serve immediately.

Water Cake

To go with wine sauce.

2 cups sugar
4 eggs
1 cup hot water
2 cups all-purpose flour
2 teaspoons baking powder

Beat sugar and eggs together until well blended and fluffy. Add hot water. Sift together flour and baking powder; add gradually to sugar, egg and water mixture, blending well. Bake in a greased and floured 13x9-inch pan at 350 degrees for 30-35 minutes.

Wine Drops

A soft, dainty, sweet treat.

½ cup margarine
1¼ cups sugar
2 eggs
2½ cups sifted flour
¼ teaspoon salt
½ teaspoon baking soda
½ teaspoon baking powder
½ cup sweet Concord grape wine
1 cup chopped raisins or dates
1 cup chopped walnuts

Cream margarine and sugar. Beat in eggs. Sift dry ingredients together and add alternately with wine, mixing well after each addition. Add raisins or dates and walnuts. Drop by teaspoonfuls onto greased cookie sheet and bake 12 minutes at 350 degrees. Makes 6 dozen.

Wine Cake

A mellow cake with an invisible spirit.

1 package yellow cake mix
1 package instant vanilla pudding
4 eggs
3/4 cup Concord grape wine
3/4 cup oil
3/4 teaspoon nutmeg

Combine all ingredients in large electric mixer bowl. Beat according to directions on cake mix package. Bake in an ungreased tube pan 40 minutes, or until done, at 350 degrees. Cool 10 minutes before removing from pan. Sprinkle with powdered sugar. Serves 16.

1, 2, 3, 4 Marble Cake

The bride and groom's own special cake at an Amana wedding party.

3 cups sifted cake flour
3 teaspoons baking powder
1/2 teaspoon salt
1 cup butter
2 cups sugar
1 teaspoon vanilla
4 large eggs
1 cup milk
1 4-ounce package sweet baking chocolate

In a medium mixing bowl, sift together flour, baking powder and salt. In a large mixing bowl, cream butter, sugar and vanilla 10 minutes with an electric mixer at medium speed or longer if by hand. Add eggs, one at a time, beating well after each addition. Gently beat in flour mixture in four additions, alternating with milk, beating until smooth after each addition. Turn half the batter into prepared deep fluted Bundt cake pan. In a small saucepan over low heat, melt chocolate. Fold it into remaining batter and spoon gently over plain batter, being careful to spread it over the first layer thoroughly. During baking, the chocolate batter, being heavier than the plain batter, will sink into the plain batter and create a marbling effect. Bake for 1 hour and 10 minutes at 350 degrees or until a cake tester inserted in center of cake comes out clean. Remove carefully from the pan with a spatula and store in a tightly covered cake tin. Serve with wine.

Cranberry Splash

Makes the last bite of dinner fresh and bright.

lemon sherbet
seasonal fresh fruits (melon, grapes, pears, berries, cherries, plums, bananas, etc.)
fresh mint
cranberry wine

Heap firmly frozen sherbet into sherbet dishes or individual crystal serving bowls. Surround with bite-size chunks of fruit. Garnish with mint. At serving time, pour cranberry wine over all and serve immediately. Niagara grape wine would also go nicely with fruits.

Or simply ladle sweet wines, such as cherry, blueberry, cranberry, red clover, beet, Niagara grape or Concord grape over ice cream or sherbet.

Or skip dessert and offer in its place a glass of sweet wine. That's a nice and light, yet sweet way to end any dinner.

Jellies

Dandelion Jelly

What could be more pleasant than picking the bright yellow blossoms on a sunny, summer morning to make jelly to sweeten breakfast on frosty winter mornings? Even if only a few dandelions can be found, a few is enough to make jelly. Directions are simple and easy:

1 quart dandelion blossoms
1 quart water
1 package pectin
1 teaspoon lemon or orange extract
4½ cups sugar
paraffin

In the morning, while the sun is shining to open the blossoms fully, pick 1 quart of blossoms—no stems, just blossoms. Boil blossoms in water for 3 minutes. Strain 3 cups of liquid; discard blossoms. To the strained liquid, add pectin, lemon or orange extract and sugar. Boil 3 more minutes. Pour into sterilized jars. When jelly is firm, seal with paraffin cooking wax.

It is so lovely and light, it resembles the taste of honey.

Wine Jelly

Any and all Kraus wines can become jelly for hot breads.

3 cups sugar
2 cups wine
½ of a 6-ounce bottle of liquid fruit pectin
paraffin

Measure sugar and wine into the top of a double boiler and mix well. Place over but not touching boiling water. Stir until sugar is dissolved, 3 to 4 minutes. Remove from heat and quickly stir in fruit pectin, mixing well. Quickly pour hot jelly into sterilized jars. When jelly is firm, cover with melted paraffin cooking wax.

Beverages

Wine is the ultimate party-goer, any kind of party. It is versatile and can be enjoyed chilled, unchilled, in a punch, as a cocktail, with a meal, after dinner or heated in a mug. Whatever the mood of the moment, wine can fit the mood. Wine is companionable. It is for sharing with old friends and new acquaintances. Where wine is, there are sure to be toasts raised, for wine inspires.

White Wine Cup

A zippy, icy punch with sparkle.

5 cups rhubarb wine
3 cups orange juice
2½ cups cold water
1¼ cups pineapple juice
½ cup sugar
¼ cup grated lemon peel, absolutely no pith
2 tablespoons honey
6 cloves
½ teaspoon cinnamon
½ teaspoon nutmeg
scant 2 quarts ginger ale
crushed ice

Mix all ingredients, except ginger ale and ice. Refrigerate 3 hours. At serving time, strain, add ginger ale and pour over ice. Serves 20.

Mulled Wine

Perfect when the snow flies.

2½ cups Concord grape wine
juice of ½ lemon
¼ cup sugar
1 stick cinnamon
3 whole cloves

Measure all ingredients into a saucepan and bring to a boil. Simmer 2 to 3 minutes, stirring constantly. Place a silver spoon in a tumbler so when hot mixture is strained into the glass, the glass does not break or crack. Serves 4.

Glüh Wein

Hot Wine—a hot drink for slow sipping on a cold and rainy or snowy night.

2 cups Concord grape wine
1⅛ cups sugar
6 whole cloves
½ stick cinnamon

Mix ingredients in a saucepan and heat just to boiling point; serve immediately. Serves 4.

Hot Cranberry Punch

A zippy holiday drink.

1 bottle (⅘ quart) cranberry wine
1½ cups orange juice
2 tablespoons lemon juice
1 teaspoon whole cloves

Mix all ingredients and serve hot or cold. To serve hot, bring mixture to a low simmer; *do not boil.*

Can be kept refrigerated for several days, ready to be served chilled or to be heated and served.

Eier Punch

Egg Punch—for a German-touched holiday.

1½ quarts Concord grape wine
1 quart water
1⅛ cups sugar
juice of one lemon
nutmeg and whole cloves to taste
8 eggs, beaten

Combine all ingredients except eggs, and heat. Add beaten eggs and continue beating until frothy on top. Do not boil or mixture will curdle. Serve at once. Serves 10.

Cranberry Hot Drink

A fruited version.

1 quart cranberry wine
2 cups sugar
2 cups orange juice
2 cups pineapple juice
2 1/2 teaspoons lemon juice
1 teaspoon whole cloves
1 cinnamon stick

Combine all ingredients and heat slowly to boiling point; serve.

Summer Party Punch

Nippy and refreshing.

1 bottle (4/5 quart) Catawba wine
1 bottle (4/5 quart) grapefruit wine
1 quart ginger ale

Mix and refrigerate 1 hour. Pour over an ice ring in a punch bowl. Makes 20 1/2-cup servings.

Concord Grape Wine Punch

Ladle or pour from a pitcher.

1 bottle (4/5 quart) medium-dry Concord grape wine, chilled
1 quart ginger ale, chilled
1 quart sparkling water, chilled

Combine at serving time and serve over ice with a twist of orange or lemon. Makes 20 1/2-cup servings.

Rhubarb Punch Wine

For the punch bowl.

2 bottles (4/5 quart each) dry rhubarb wine, chilled
1 quart 7-Up, chilled

Combine at serving time and serve over ice with a twist of lemon. Makes 20 ½-cup servings.

The Amana Cocktail

The Amana Cocktail was discovered in the early days of winemaking, when only rhubarb and Concord grape wines were made. The rhubarb is normally a dry wine, and the Red Concord is a sweeter wine. A third wine was created by mixing the two in equal parts to have a medium taste wine. It was immediately called "The Amana Cocktail" and remains popular today.

Rhubarb Martini

For a Rhubarb Martini on the rocks or up with a twist, mix a very dry rhubarb wine with gin. The portion may vary for each taste, one part rhubarb wine to three or four parts gin. A recommended method is to fill a glass pitcher with ice, add the rhubarb wine first and then add the desired quantity of gin. Another recommendation is that after two or three drinks you put a steel ball and chain on your leg and do not leave the house.

Kraus Sangria

Mix equal parts of sweet Concord grape wine and grapefruit wine. Serve chilled.

Amana Sangria

Mix equal parts Concord grape wine and club soda. Or, mix one part Concord grape wine with ½ part 7-Up and ½ part club soda. After combining, garnish sangria with orange slices, whole white grapes, plum wedges or other fresh, seasonal fruits. Serve over ice from a pitcher or punch bowl.

It is true, wine came into being in another country, in another world and in another time in history, but the splashy, icy, fizzy drinks called "Coolers" and "Spritzers" are American inventions. Such unconventional treatment might be considered wine abuse by purists of other countries. Here, they are sparkling refreshments that are especially kind to dieters.

Wine is much lower in calories than other liquors so when you make a mixed drink with wine and club soda or a non-cola, carbonated, diet drink, you are cutting the calories even more. Even those who are watching their weight can still be a part of the party.

Wine Cooler

Pile ice cubes in a chilled large wine goblet or tall glass and add equal parts wine and club soda.

Wine Spritzer

Pile ice cubes in a chilled large wine goblet or tall glass and add equal parts wine and a carbonated non-cola diet drink. Serve with a lemon twist or a lime wedge.

For either a cooler or a spritzer, use rhubarb wine, either sweet or semi-sweet. Rhubarb is high in acidity and low in sugar so it is a good mixer with soda or other carbonated drinks. The number of possible combinations is limited only by the number of wines or mixers you have on hand and, of course, your own personal taste.

It's also possible to make a brand new drink just by mixing equal parts of two wines, such as rhubarb and orange wines, and then mixing that with club soda or 7-Up. Or mix club soda and 7-Up for one part and use rhubarb wine for the other part of a drink. The proportions and combinations could go on and on, according to whatever your favorites might be in the wines or the mixes. When the ice is clinking in the glass and you smell the wine, it's like a summer breeze. It's no wonder these cooler and spritzer type drinks are such refreshing summer drinks.

Blending Wines

We also like to blend two wines at serving time. Pour and blend the wines right in the glass. The two wines become partners in the glass to get a new and different wine taste.

It's usually best to blend a dry wine with a sweet wine to take away some of the dryness in one and to cut the sweetness in the other. Combinations blended half-and-half that we enjoy are: rhubarb and dandelion, rhubarb and Concord grape, cherry and rhubarb, cranberry and rhubarb, rhubarb and grapefruit and cranberry and Niagara grape.

Further variations are possible when the amount of each wine is changed, such as blending four parts rhubarb with one part grapefruit or two parts rhubarb with one part red clover. Again, the possible combinations could go on and on. Some wine drinkers in Amana blend sweet red grape half-and-half with rhubarb and call it the Amana cocktail. Others substitute a very dry rhubarb wine for vermouth in a martini recipe, mix it with gin, shake it with ice and pour the Amana version of the martini.

Wine on the rocks is a hard subject for us. We really do not like to drink wine on the rocks but many people do, so we try to give some suggestions as to which of the Kraus wines can handle that icy treatment.

When wine is poured over ice cubes or crushed ice, the ice melts and dilutes the wine. Then, as the ice melts, the alcohol of the wine is cut nearly in half. Anyone who enjoys drinking wine probably does not like having the wine diluted. But if someone insists on having wine over ice, he or she should choose a full bodied, flavorful wine. Sweeter wines usually fare better over ice than dry wines. Dry, light wines over ice seem watery.

Wine over ice is compared to serving beer in a glass—the glass must be very cold and dry. Beer drinkers want to get the full flavor, the full gusto, as they say, of the beer. It's the same with wine. If you want all the flavor, all the aroma, the very best the wine has to offer, serve it chilled, poured into a dry, cold glass rather than over ice.

The Kraus wines that can take a little ice are Concord and Niagara grape, red clover, cherry, cranberry and blueberry.

43. The Old and The New

Everything is up-to-date in the Colonies now. Kerosene lamps, outhouses, open sewer ditches, horses and wagons are out. Street lights, automobiles, stop signs, telephone lines, television antennas and credit cards are in. Even so, much of yesterday remains to hold this community as though it were caught in a nostalgic timelessness.

The boxy, square, plain, simple brick, sandstone and frame buildings appear unchanged standing on freshly trimmed lawns, framed behind neat fence rows, beside weedless gardens under the towering old trees—trees under which commune workers took wine breaks on warm, sunny days one hundred thirty years ago.

The old village-to-village trails are now surfaced roads rounding the rolling wooded hills past flatland fields neatly laid out in precise rows and furrows, a trademark of Amana farmers. Neatness was very important to everyone in Amana, neatness and hard work.

As a child, I saw Mama and Papa, *Oma* and *Opa* and everyone else work hard at their jobs and I also saw that they took great pains to do the job just right, to take care of the equipment they used and always to make it clean and neat. Neatness gets to be a habit and a darned good habit, I think. It's still a habit Amana folks live and work by—and it shows.

"What's the secret to keeping all the yards and homes so beautiful, so well-groomed?" a woman in the wine shop asked.

"It's no secret," I told her. "It's just a lot of hard work." And it is. When you consider the thousands of tourists who come to the Amana Colonies every year, you know we need every man, woman and child here to do their part in keeping the villages spic and span.

The combined population of all seven villages has been right around eighteen hundred for several decades. Middle's census has stayed at about three hundred fifty.

Many who live here work elsewhere, but many make their living catering to the tourist trade. The Amana Colonies are one of Iowa's most popular tourist attractions. In 1965, the villages were registered as a National Historic Landmark by the United States Department of Interior, National Park Service.

The tourist business here relies on preserving the past. Most of us in Amana are interested in keeping the best of the past for ourselves and for our children and grandchildren, so why not let the public come to see it and enjoy it, too? We want the tourists to come, to have a good time, to get some bargains and to take away many good memories. We hope they will come back and see us again. One thing is for sure, they can drive this country from coast to coast, border to border, and they won't ever find anything like Amana.

Amana isn't a wonder of nature, a spectacular sight or a monument put up in the memory of a person or an event and it isn't a spot built especially to attract and accommodate tourists. Yet it's funny how tourists nowadays have come to expect something like a Disneyland, a make-believe place or a place which has been recreated and restored to be what it once was—like Williamsburg in Virginia or a Colorado ghost town.

That's not what Amana is, not at all. We all live here in these villages and in these buildings; some of us even live in the very same buildings where our families have always lived, where we were born, where we grew up.

Now it's true, we don't live exactly like our ancestors did. We can't. But our lives are a mix of the old and the new.

Our homes may look over a hundred years old on the outside, but inside the mix of yesterday and today can be seen. Amana-made rag rugs scatter over man-made no-scrub no-wax vinyl floors. The very latest in chrome, baked enamel, stainless steel and black glass appliances nest side by side in harmony with old Amana-made walnut and cherry cupboards. We may eat our meals from a cherry table crafted by an Amana furniture maker a hundred and thirty years ago but the food we eat was probably cooked in the newest model of an Amana Radarange microwave oven.

Visitors act surprised when they see that our homes are modern, that we have indoor bathrooms, wall-to-wall carpeting and air-conditioning.

"But from the outside, your house looks so old," they will say.

"That's good," we say. "We want it to look that way." And we do. With each remodeling our home has gone through, we have been careful to maintain its appearance so it fits the Amana picture. Our home has a special connection to Amana and to Middle and that makes it an historical place and maybe that makes it a landmark, too. But it is still our home, not a museum.

There are several designated museums in the Colonies. There's the Museum of Amana History at Amana, Amana Heim (home) Museum at Homestead, The Barn Museum at South Amana, and the Community Kitchen, Cooper Shop and Hearth

Oven Museum in Middle Amana. Those are all displays of what *was.* The rest of Amana is a *now* place. The rest of the village businesses are going concerns. Maybe the Amana Colonies could be called a living museum.

Visitors touring the woolen mill actually see raw wool being carded, spun, dyed and woven into patterns designed by Amana artists. Visitors are welcome at the furniture and clock factories where they can watch the talented and skilled craftsmen close-up. Every piece of furniture is hand-made from start to finish. Each worker hand-picks the lumber he himself will cut, sand, fit, including lock-jointing corners and dovetailing drawers and hand-setting hinges and handles. Amana furniture is made to last.

We have many pieces which we will one day pass along to our children. One, a small walnut table, has great sentimental value. Some would call it an heirloom, but that suggests it is expensive or is priceless, which it isn't. Helen says it is a keepsake.

"We're keeping it for our children and grandchildren," she says, "for the sake of helping them to remember the story that goes with it.

"The table was made of lumber that came from a tree cut down in the woods near West. *Opa* Miller had it made as his engagement gift for *Oma* Miller in 1894. Back then, it was considered a thoughtful and very romantic thing for a man to give his bride-to-be something new for their new home even though their new home was to be only one room in the parents' home."

There are shops throughout all the villages selling locally hand-crafted items. Rag rugs, brooms, baskets and other homemade, hand-made items once considered necessities are now considered folk art that should be preserved.

Baskets of all shapes and sizes once used to carry laundry, gather fruits, vegetables and eggs are now being bought, not so much for their utilitarian purposes as for their decorative value—to hold flowers, magazines, plants or to hang on the wall as conversation pieces. *Omas* have had to teach classes so the younger generation can learn to cut, soak, peel and strip willow switches and weave them into baskets.

Scraps from the woolen mill are sewn and braided into rugs. Cotton scraps are woven into rag rugs. Hand-made brooms, big ones and small ones, all sell well in the shops. Even tinsmithing and wood carving have been revived.

Amana women have never stopped sewing and they now have a market for their fine handwork—embroidery, crocheting, knitting and quilting. Quilts are particularly popular.

Bed covers were made by two different methods in Old Amana. Helen has done both, and even now quilting is one of her pet projects and subjects to talk about.

Because clothes used to be made at home, every family had boxes and boxes of cotton and woolen remnants. The remnants were cut into four-inch squares and then were hand-sewn together to make patchwork block quilts. The wool batting between the top and bottom of a patchwork quilt was held in place by tying a knot of heavy cotton thread in the center of each block.

But it is the fancier quilts, the ones with the fine, tiny hand stitches in fancy designs that Helen tells about.

"The fancy quilts might be for a bride's hope chest," she says, "and those quilts were always made of brand new fabrics—never remnants. One side could be a solid color and the other a printed calico with a wool batting in between.

"A fancy design was outlined on the plain side of the quilt and then stitched in by hand with a thread of harmonizing color. One of the most popular patterns was *'Schlange Kranz'* ('Serpentine Wreath'). They also did 'The Scroll,' 'Wild Rose,' 'Clematis,' 'Sunflower,' 'Water Lily,' and 'Flower Basket.'

"The patterns were on heavy cardboard sheets twenty-four to thirty inches square. The pattern was drawn on the cardboard, then it was cut out with a sharp knife so the design could be traced onto the quilt with a pointed chalk. Seldom was a pattern used in its entirety. They selected a pattern that they liked—and some would add extra flowers, leaves, butterflies or even initials. In that way, few quilts were ever alike, and that made each quilt very special and very personal for the bridal couple's first bed.

"After The Change, Amana women discovered American quilting patterns and soon they were piecing and appliquéing 'Double Wedding Ring,' 'Sunbonnet Girl,' 'Log Cabin,' and many other old familiar block designs."

Middle's points of interest in addition to the three museums are the General Store, Amana Refrigeration, Inc., Hahn's Hearth Oven Bakery, Hahn Brothers Furniture and Clock Shop and, of course, Old Style Colony Winery.

Having Hahn's Bakery as our neighbor across the street is good. Bread and wine go together well.

Fifty years after the Great Change, the original wood-fired open-hearth oven is the only one of its kind operating in the Colonies. The bakery is part of Hahn's home just as the winery is part of our home. They keep a six-month supply of wood for the oven piled in neat stacks along their driveway. They use two kinds of wood—cottonwood, which burns fast and gets the fire off to a fast start, and maple, which burns long and hot. The wood is cut and split into thin strips, three inches thick and three feet long so it fits into the oven which is recessed in a brick wall.

It takes several hours for the stone in the oven to heat up. The wood is jam-packed into the oven and a fire is started at three o'clock in the morning. After the fire has burned itself out, the coals are raked and shoveled out of the oven and the hand-shaped loaves of bread dough are shoved deep into the oven on long-handled, wooden peels. When the dough hits the hot stone, the bottom of each loaf is baked instantly, making a thick crust. Is that crust good! To me, it's the best part of the bread! It has an almost sweet, caramelized flavor that can't be duplicated in dough baked in pans. And there's nothing like that wonderful aroma of baking bread. You just can't resist it!

The smell of the bread attracts the tourists, too. Tourists are always ready to eat, and in Amana we have lots of good food. All restaurants serve family style meals of *wiener schnitzel* (veal cutlet), *sauerbraten* (marinated beef sirloin roast), brats, sauerkraut, hot German potato salad, rhubarb pie and *obst kuchen* (fruit cake). Amana-made breads, cheeses, bacon, ham and sausages—liverwurst, bockwurst, cervelat, bologna, schwartenmagen and old-fashioned summer sausage—all prepared, smoked and slowly cured the way Amana ancestors made them in Germany, are sold at the meat markets in Amana and Homestead and in other shops in the Colonies, too.

"When's the best time to see Amana?" folks ask.

"Anytime," we answer, "Amana is great anytime!"

In the springtime, apple, cherry and crabapple trees bloom, the fields are freshly plowed and planted and everything is breaking out, sprouting and ready to grow.

In the summertime, the countryside goes green. There's every imaginable shade of green in the trees and shrubs and the fields of soybeans, corn, wheat, barley, oats, alfalfa and clover. In the villages, the yards are full of flowers—cannas, marigolds, dahlias, petunias, geraniums, zinnias. There are flowers everywhere you look.

October—that's a great time to be here. There's no prettier place to be than in Amana the first weekend in October. The leaves of the oak, maple, walnut, elm and linden trees will have turned rust, red, yellow, brown and orange by then and under the brightest, clearest, bluest sky, it's a beautiful sight. Iowa's weather is just about perfect then. It is sunny, warm in the sun but cool in the shade, with only a light breeze to stir and rustle the leaves. Folks looking for just one more outing before winter like to come here in the fall.

Tourist traffic cuts back with the first snowfall. But even in the wintertime, visitors tell us they like to come to Amana then, when it is quiet. They say they find a snug and cozy serenity here that is peaceful and relaxing.

44. And Now?

A man is shaped by his past. My past is one I am proud of; it is one I respect and cherish.

No one who comes to Amana from the outside can ever know and understand all there is to know and understand about Amana. There is more to Amana than is seen and heard. Part of what was and still is here in this community will always be known only to those who have lived here.

I'm not one to dwell on the past or to be buried by my past. I appreciate it and I have kept many things from my past. They are part of my life today. And sure, it's fun to look back, to talk about how it once was, and to listen to those who lived here long before I was born, but I'm more interested in today and tomorrow.

Helen and I were looking ahead when, on that Saturday night in January 1949, we decided to have our own winery. We are still looking ahead. I saw a future then for the old-fashioned, homemade wines of Amana, and I still see a future for them.

These wines won't die out. No way will they disappear, not as long as they are liked by so many folks. Right here in Amana, homemade wines are "in" again. They are somewhat of a delicacy. I can't help noticing how many young Amana people are now buying our wines and enjoying them like their parents and grandparents did and do. Young people drink and serve the wines but they are not making them to any great extent, nor in the variety or quantity they did in the old days.

The founding fathers and mothers of this community didn't know what a popular and profitable commodity they had in the wines they made and divvied up among the people. Amana wines turned out to be a hidden asset.

With a cellar full of equipment and all my years of experience in winemaking, not to mention my genuine pleasure in making wines and especially in developing new wines, and now with more time than ever to spend down in the cellar, I intend to stay on course.

The winery will never be bigger than what I can handle myself or can closely supervise myself on a daily basis. I don't want to expand and lose the feeling of control that I now have or to lose the personal touch with my wines. I have to make a quality wine—that's first. Then I think about quantity both in the volume of wine I make and in the numbers of wines I make.

In talking with winemakers who operate other small wineries, I find they, too, aim to stay small. Low volume wines sometimes have a sounder market in the long run. If I stay small, then I can let myself go on creating new wines.

Experimenting keeps the winery from getting dull and boring for me. Keeping the winery small lets me adjust to the public's responses and to their tastes. And the public has been great. I can count on them to be full of suggestions.

"Why don't you make wine from muskmelon. . .or peach. . .apple. . .raisin. . .sorghum. . .molasses. . .wheat. . .potato?" they ask.

The suggestion I hear a lot, probably the most, is strawberry. Strawberries aren't available locally in large enough quantities to make it worthwhile. Shipping them from California or Florida would be very expensive. They are so perishable normally and having them ripened on the vine as I would have to have them, the strawberries would be mushed beyond use even before they reached the winery.

"Well, fly 'em in!" That's always the follow-up suggestion. Now that's talking big bucks and the wine I would get would have to be priced so high, I'm afraid the wine wouldn't sell.

"Corn," that's another suggestion I get a lot. Iowa is called "The Corn State." Well, now, maybe that's not so far-fetched, after all. Take the potato. Russians make vodka with it, why not a wine from corn?

Or the carrot? Carrots would involve some of the same problems I had with beets, but look what I got out of the beets.

One summer, a woman shopper remarked that she just wished I would make zucchini wine. She went on to say she had planted a few hills in her garden and it took over the garden. Zucchini will do that. No one ever raised just a little bit of zucchini—if you get any at all, you get a wagon load. I told her I would give it a try if she would promise to come back next year to see if it was any good. Zucchini wine, that would be something! It would probably turn out to be a real pale green wine and that could be an interesting addition to our list of wines.

When Helen and I travel, we are always on the lookout for other small wineries. We have toured them in Germany, Austria, France, Hungary, Spain, South Africa, South America and Mexico and also in this country. Small private wineries with their exclusive wines not only survive, they thrive. Even a small town will have two or three such wineries. The tiny private wineries remind me of our winery and the other Amana wineries. They are down in the basement, in the cellars of the homes. They raise the grapes they put into the wines in their own little vineyards. The family members pick the grapes and do all of the winery work.

Of course, that's not the case in Hungary. The wineries in Hungary are under an entirely different set-up. For as far as the eye could see, it was grape vines, grape vines—vineyards covered field after field, over the hills and up and down again. Their vineyard equipment and the equipment in the wineries was all the very latest and the very best.

What struck me was how much the set-up in Hungary now is like the set-up in Amana in the old days, before 1932.

Hungary is a communistic nation and in that kind of a society, the government owns and operates everything, including the wine industry. The government owns the land the grapes grow on, and the wineries the wine is made in. The workers all work for the government. That's how it was here once, only it wasn't a whole nation. It was just this one small community, but the community was owned and operated pretty much like the whole country of Hungary is. I couldn't help but wonder if any of the people of Hungary are making their own family wines in the basements of their homes. If they are, I'm sure they are going to be in bigger trouble if they are caught than the people of Old Amana were when they made a few gallons of family wine on the sly in their cellars.

And I must say, for all their big vineyards and their modern wineries, the wines passed out for us to taste when we were in Hungary weren't one bit better than wines we have sampled in little, tiny, local, private wineries nearby in West Germany. Small wineries can and do turn out wines that are superior in every way—in flavor, aroma and color. Wines from a small winery will have a special individual appeal that a large winery just can't match.

"When George Kraus is no longer the winemaker at Old Style Colony Winery, what will become of the winery?"

That's a good question. I'm not sure just what the answer is. How can I predict what can or may or might happen to this winery? I couldn't even have predicted that I myself would end up as a winemaker. And if someone had ever predicted for me that I would be a winemaker one day, I would have laughed at them and refused to believe it.

At this time, I have to say, it does not look as though any of our children will take over. But then, too, I didn't take up winemaking from Papa, I took it up from *Opa.* So, who can say? Now wouldn't that be something, if one day there might be another. . . . well, who's to say what will be?

The winery as it looks today in Middle Amana.

45. Back of This Wine

A verse on our business card says:

Back of this Wine is the Vintner.
And back through the years his skill.
And back of all are the vines in the Sun,
And the rain and the Master's Will.